# A Year in Motion

Road Dog Publications was formed in 2010 as an imprint of Lost Classics Book Company and is dedicated to publishing the best in books on motorcycling, motorsports, and adventure travel. Visit us at www.roaddogpub.com.

*A Year in Motion*
Copyright © 2023 Michael Alan Fitterling
All rights reserved.
All illustrations and maps by the author.
*Graphite pencil with conté crayon and white chalk pencil highlights on Strathmore toned gray sketch paper.*
ISBN 978-1-890623-91-3
Library of Congress Control Number: 2023935055

An Imprint of Lost Classics Book Company
This book also available in eBook format at online booksellers. ISBN 978-1-890623-92-0

# A Year in Motion

## On the Road after Recovery

*by*

## Michael Fitterling

Publisher
Lake Wales, Florida

## Dedication

*To all the riders who are quietly roaming the planet expecting no reward beyond the journey itself. To those without YouTube channels, vlogs, blogs, or books. To those who have stickers on their bikes of the places they've visited, instead of logos of the brands of gear they use. To the hundreds, perhaps thousands, whose stories may never be heard outside their own circle of friends but who find a way around work schedules, financial barricades, and perhaps even physical limitations to climb on their bikes just for the love of the ride and to push their limits.*

# ABOUT THE AUTHOR

Michael Fitterling was born in northern Indiana in 1957 in Mishawaka and was raised nearby in southern Michigan. He attended Anderson College (now University) in Indiana from 1976 through 1978. In 1979, he took a break from his studies to travel to Central America, which was followed by other journeys around the US, Central America, and Caribbean. He returned to school in 1989, attending the University of South Florida in Tampa, where he graduated with honors from the school of the arts in 1992.

After art school, he began work as a graphic designer. In 1997, he was working as cover designer and illustrator for Lost Classics Book Company and later became Managing Editor. He acquired the company in 2010. Finding himself the owner of a publishing company, his natural inclination was to turn to publishing books about what he loved, so in 2011, he started Road Dog Publications, an imprint dedicated to books on motorcycling and adventure travel. In 2013, he became Editor of *Vintage Japanese Motorcycle Magazine*, the official publication of the Vintage Japanese Motorcycle Club of North America, where he also currently serves on the Board of Directors.

Trips around the US with his family when he was young sparked his interest in travel, and he has continued traveling by one means or another ever since. In the 1980s he became interested in sailing and bought a small sailboat in which he lived and traveled along the coast of the US and eventually through the Bahamas and parts of the Caribbean, while working stints doing boat deliveries. He served as a professional captain aboard a large sailing catamaran in the Cayman Islands during summers while he finished his art degree in Florida during the winter months.

After returning from the Cayman Islands to the States, an old interest in motorcycles resurfaced when he found a forgotten and non-running 1968 Honda CB350 in storage. He finished its restoration in 2009, learning about motorcycles as he worked on the project. He traveled much of the eastern US on that first motorcycle. Over the years, he has owned several motorcycles, both vintage and new, including a Suzuki Savage 650, a Honda CL250, a Honda CB500 Twin, a 2011 Triumph Bonneville T100, and his current bikes: a Suzuki GS550e and a 2018 Triumph Tiger 800 XCa. He has travelled over 150,000 miles by motorcycle since 2009 in both the United States and Canada.

Michael is also the author of *Thoughts on the Road: Riding, Wrenching, and Reflecting* and *Northeast by Northwest: Two Restorative Journeys*. He lives in the small town of Lake Wales in central Florida.

# Table of Contents

### This Time Northwest

### A Ride around the Block

## A Complication

# Preamble to a Book I Haven't Written Yet

*[Written before any of the following journeys had begun.]*

It was the day after Thanksgiving in 2017. I was only sixty and had only started to notice that I was quite a bit closer to the end of life than the beginning. I was strong and had plenty of time. It had not been long since I'd returned from an extended motorcycle ride on my trusty Triumph Bonneville to Colorado and up into British Columbia, a trip that eventually taught me the therapeutic value of being alone on a motorcycle for an extended time. As a result, when I returned, I felt better, not just physically, but mentally as well.

We were all idling along as we usually do after a big holiday, with time on our hands and no real plan for the day. My son wanted to go across our street to the baseball fields where I could toss some easy pitches to him while he practiced his hitting. We walked onto the red clay, taking our respective places, he at the mound and me fifteen feet or so away, in line with the pitcher's mound, behind a protective net. I tossed an easy one toward home. Then it happened. Somehow, I'd failed to duck behind the netting between him and me, and instantly, a powerful line-drive ball was in my right eye. It happened so fast I couldn't even blink before the missile found my eye and watched as the ball hit, only feeling my lashes encounter it a microsecond later as my lids tried to close and protect me.

Before I knew what had happened, I was on the red clay ground. I staggered, trying to get up with my hand cupping my eye, while bright red blood poured through my fingers. When I removed my hand from the damaged eye, there was nothing; I had been blinded.

What followed was three years of hospitals, surgeries, and so many ophthalmologist appointments that I lost count. Slowly, very slowly, my vision in that eye came back to a point where meetings with the doctor usually ended up with me rhetorically asking, "It probably won't get much better than that?" and the doctor just nodding his head in agreement. I could see, but not clearly and if it had been my only eye, my driving and riding days would have been over. Luckily, I still had use of another eye, which had been developing a cataract but had been taken care of and corrected, leaving me with clear vision in my left eye. Eventually, finances would not allow me to continue going in for checkups, especially with knowing nothing more could be done, so I settled into the idea that I'd have to manage with just the one good eye for my primary vision.

Life went on, and I got used to my new mono-vision and was able to function again, and most importantly, to ride motorcycles. The checkups and surgeries had taken years out of my life.

Then, when I was approaching my middle-sixties, the Covid-19 pandemic hit. During that time, travel was difficult, with each state having different rules about masks and distancing, and some in denial there even was a pandemic. Events with the VJMC were screeching to a halt, and so was my riding.

A fluke of an event, a last hurrah before Covid set upon us in earnest, got me out to Iowa, where I would cover an event for the Vintage Japanese Motorcycle Magazine, of which I was editor. It was my small opportunity to strike out from there (after all, I was halfway across the country from my home in Florida by that point) and take a quick ride of a few extra days to see some of the things I had missed previously in the American West, before the country would come to a standstill. I rode to the Black Hills, the Badlands, then Devil's Tower in Wyoming, before turning back toward Florida by way of a southerly route though Colorado, a corner of New Mexico and from there east across Texas, Louisiana, Mississippi, and Alabama—a good, but short, break from daily life.

And then the country closed down. It would be months before the country's gears would start turning and opening the gates again to travel. However, I did manage to sneak in another little escape to eastern Tennessee and a campground in Tellico Plains, meeting up with a band of adventure riding friends and giving the National Forest Roads a not so brilliant go on my Triumph Bonneville T100, resulting in a ride home with a cobbled together repair of my shifter after a slow-speed fall.

Another New Year passed. The pandemic seemed to be in remission as more and more Americans were getting vaccinated. In the spring, a chance came again to get a ride in, and I was able to return to Tellico with my friends, knowing I had some level of protection.

Leaving Tellico on a Sunday, I decided I would, again, extend my ride, this time east to Virginia Beach to see my brother before returning home. I calculated it would be an easy day to get to a campsite in Meadows of Dan, Virginia, just off the Blue Ridge Parkway, where I would meet up with another friend, before heading on to my brother's place the following day.

The distance seemed easily manageable, so I left in no particular hurry, but as I approached the Virginia state line, the sun was already settling behind the western mountain ridges. In the little light still provided by the darkening sky,

I could see deer loping along near the trees, feet from the road. After my eye injury, I tried to make a habit of not riding after dark. My right iris would not dilate, making oncoming headlights overpower what was left of my vision; but now the appearance of deer added to the urgency of getting off the road. My destination blinked at the edge of my GPS screen, but darkness had finally fallen. Just four or five more minutes more and I'd be off the road and safe.

Then, BLAM!

There was no avoiding it. Instantly, the brown, broad side of a leaping deer was in my windscreen. I woke up on the ground. I was on the edge of the road with my feet in the grass, the GPS softly glowing from the bent handlebars of my prostrate bike, yards down the road. I tried to get up and instantly crumpled back to the ground. I lay still, checking myself, thinking I might have broken something, but no bones were sticking out anywhere, and no limbs were pointing in unnatural directions. I tried again to rise and, this time, was able to get to my knees, then my feet. I wobbled my way to the bike to make sure it was off and clicked the GPS off as well. I was alone in the dark. I'd not seen a car for miles and would not for the remainder of my time on the Parkway. Even so, I doubted my wisdom in turning off the only light emanating from the wrecked Bonneville in the darkness of the roadway.

I'd done something to my ankle and wrist. There was no doubt that I could not pick up the bike and get it off the road alone. I knew I'd need help. I got out my phone and dialed 911. Nothing; no signal. Then I remembered how close I was to the campground where my friend, Dustin, was waiting. I tried a text message to him, and it went through immediately. In four or five minutes he was there, with his bike pointed toward the oncoming lane, with its light on as a warning to any approaching vehicles.

Dustin got the Bonnie standing back up, then we did a more thorough check of my body. My left ankle was painful, and I was not able to put much weight on it. The sleeves of my riding jacket had ridden up a bit, and I had some blood oozing from lacerations on my wrists and arms, but it was nothing serious. My right wrist, which had taken the brunt impact when the deer struck my right handlebar grip, was useless.

Dustin made a call, and in another five minutes, Will, the owner of the campground, was there with a trailer. He and Dustin got the battered bike loaded, Dustin got on his bike to ride back, and I climbed onto the truck's passenger seat. Soon, we were all back at the campground. Dustin and new helpers appearing from the campground got my wounds cleaned up and bandaged and a compression bandage around my ankle to keep it relatively in place. There was not much we could do about my wrist. We discussed going to a hospital, but the closest one was far away, and I seemed to be in one piece and not in critical condition. I called my brother and filled him in. He would come the next day with a motorcycle trailer to gather my bike and me and haul us to his house. On the way there I could decide if a hospital visit was prudent. The rest of the evening was passed by the campfire taking copious swigs from a whiskey bottle that was set down beside me.

The next morning, after a five-hour drive, my brother pulled in. I said my thanks to everyone who had so generously helped me, and Tim and I headed east toward the coast with the bike in tow. I was worried about what this all would cost, especially any medical care. Maybe I could get by on my own without going in to be checked. On the ride east, searching on my phone, I found out that all motor vehicles in Florida must have at least $10,000 in PIP (personal injury protection), so I decided that should at least cover some X-rays, just in case. My brother pulled into the hospital closest to his home, and I walked into the emergency entrance, being met there by a nurse and a wheelchair. I was quickly processed, it now being mid-evening and things being slow in the ER.

A CT head-scan was ordered, because I had been knocked out for an indeterminant length of time. The CT scan operator assured me that I had been very fortunate and should have been dead coming off the bike at forty-five and landing on the pavement. Luckily, the scan showed nothing wrong. X-rays were done, along with more thorough cleaning and bandaging of my rash. My ankle, apparently, just had a bad sprain, or at worst, a torn ligament, as the X-rays showed no broken bones. That was a relief. Then I got the results of my wrist X-rays: broken, in two places. A splint was made, and I was sent on my way after being instructed to find a surgeon as soon as I got back to Florida. I only later found out that in Florida motorcycles are not considered "motor vehicles" and that I had no coverage for the care I had just received, other than what Medicaid would provide.

After a week of dealing with the bike, a wildly inaccurate insurance adjuster, a Triumph dealer who knew their stuff, and of popping pain pills like there was no tomorrow, I flew home. Retrieving the bike and my stuff would have to wait. I spent another week trying to get in to see an orthopedic surgeon who would take Medicaid, the only choice I had as an uninsured American, and finally, I was in surgery.

When I woke up, I asked what had gone wrong; my pain was so intense I could only think that there had been trouble. A half-dozen post-op nurses and the anesthesiologist were looking at each other with quizzical, and as I perceived them, worried looks on their faces. But they insisted nothing went wrong and I was in the recovery room. They looked strangely at each other again, and someone ordered more pain killers, then again more at a higher dose. They numbed my right arm with a blocker for a second time, and finally, I was in a level of pain I could tolerate. I was released and sent home with more pain medication.

The next day, I awoke to excruciating pain. The painkillers were not making any impact. By afternoon, I was desperate, and a family member took me to the ER at the same hospital where I'd had the surgery. The ER was busy, so I spent most of the evening desperately waiting for some relief. Finally, I was put on a bed in the ER, and the doctor injected something into my IV. I could feel the relief flowing through me as my neck grew warm and my mind relaxed. By eleven o'clock, I was sent home again. I got through the rest of the night, and that same intense level of pain did not return, so I tried to get used to the idea of pieces of metal permanently living in my arm and the idea of a long recovery.

Meanwhile, my thoughts turned to replacing my bike, which in the end, was totaled by the insurance company, after 108,000 miles of trusty service. With assurances I would eventually be able to ride again, I started looking at bikes. I had been riding off-pavement more often, even though I felt challenged by it, and tried to take gravel roads when they appeared enroute to wherever I was going in hopes of getting used to that kind of riding and to improve my ability. I had ridden gravel Route 67 in Colorado, Sage Creek Road on the north rim of the Badlands, and explored the unpaved roads stretching from Sundance to Devil's Tower in Wyoming in the Black Hills just the past summer to test my skills. I had "scramblerized" my Bonnie about as far as I could take it, but no matter what I did, it would never have the suspension travel of a made-to purpose offroad bike. An adventure bike was the obvious next step, and my Triumph had been so dependable that another Triumph, the Tiger, would be on my short-list of possible new bikes.

I'd ridden that year's new 900 model of the Tiger before the accident, and I knew it had the edge on features—lighter and lower weight, tubeless spoked wheels, better lower throttle response—over the previous 800 model, but it also came with a price tag well over seventeen thousand dollars. I could not justify that amount of money, and by all counts, notwithstanding the superiority of the 900, the 800 still had a solid reputation for ability, comfort, reliability, and modern safety features, so it became my target. I scoured the Internet and found some good options, all thousands of miles from home, from California to Maryland. I found a used Tiger 800 in Annapolis that had barely been broken in by its first owner and had not even arrived at its first regular oil change interval. Besides that, it was an XCa model, top of the line for 2018, and the price was barely over ten thousand, thousands less than the Tiger 900 equivalent model, the Rally Pro. The XCa had features I would appreciate having, including cruise control, which I thought would be a boon while riding with a damaged right wrist.

Three days after my visit to the ER, I was driving my late father's old S10 pickup to Annapolis, towing a small flatbed trailer behind, to pick up the new Tiger. My brother's place was, more or less, on the way, and I would be able to grab all the stuff I'd left behind before and bring it back in the truck. The problem with this plan, though, was the S10's air conditioning had stopped working and it was a hot and rainy May.

The drive up was an ordeal of driving with the windows open, closing them to a crack as I passed through numerous thunderstorms, and straining to see through a fogged-up windshield. Besides all that, I was driving with my arm in a cast-like apparatus and unable to take any pain medications for fear of going to sleep at the wheel. To say the trip was uncomfortable is a huge understatement, but I persevered and arrived home with a new Tiger, which I parked in the garage, leaving it there lonely and waiting for me to recover enough to ride again.

I continued my physical therapy and follow-ups for my wrist, and by the end of July, the cast/splint was off, and I was able to ride again. I took a couple very short neighborhood rides on the Tiger to get a feel for it, then got ready for a long ride out to Iowa to cover the same Midwestern rally for the magazine that I had previously used as my jumping off spot on my last ride west on the Bonnie. From Iowa, I planned to extend my ride and head northeast until reaching Michigan's upper peninsula for a ride along the south shore of Lake Superior, with an open-ended return date and route. I'd been waiting a long time for a chance to get away and reset my brain, and finally, by the 28th, the Tiger was all packed and waiting in the garage for an early morning departure on the 29th.

On the 28th, a couple friends had ridden over to visit. Tim and Marisa had been delayed on an around the world motorcycle adventure by the pandemic while they'd been in Africa and so had returned to the States to explore more of North America and to bide their time until the crisis was over, when they could continue their travels. They had ridden down to Florida to visit Tim's mother, who lived only a hundred miles from our place. They'd ridden over for the day, and I'd led them on a short ride to a quaint diner I thought they'd enjoy in Frostproof, just fifteen miles south of Lake Wales, to have lunch. After lunch, back at the house, we were saying our goodbyes as they were about to leave to return to Sarasota when I noticed a dark spot in the lower left field of my vision. It was small at first, but by the next morning, it was larger and scary enough I thought I'd better postpone my departure until I could get it checked out. Hopefully, it would be nothing, and I would just have to leave a day late.

We called the doctor who had handled my previous right eye damage and arranged to see a specialist that same morning. By that afternoon, I was in surgery. I had tears in my retina, which had detached, possibly a delayed result of head trauma from the crash, but really, it could have been from anything. The one sure thing, I was told, was that if I had not had it taken care of right away, I would have gone completely blind with no chance of restoring my sight in that eye, my one "good" eye. Surgery involved laser suturing the tears and injecting gasses into the eye to force the retina into place.

The next question was recovery time and my chances of getting back full vision. I would not be going to Iowa, that was sure. I was burning through the summer . . . again . . . and the much-needed relief of a long ride would be delayed . . . again. Recovery time was an unanswered question—"Wait and see." At least I had a small chance of seeing clearly again, and hopefully, I would not have another detachment, the chances of which were anywhere between ten and sixty percent.

The first week and a half was hell. I had to lie flat on my face, keeping the bubble of gases floating at the back of my eye to hold the damaged retina in place so it could reattach. I could only leave that position for a few minutes each hour to use the restroom or to eat. Staying still was an ordeal for me, having just regained some freedom of movement after my wrist had healed, it was now hard to go back to being inactive. I killed time listening virtually all day to Adventure Rider Radio podcasts, which I'd usually had difficulty finding time to do.

Finally, I was told I could sit up normally, as long as I slept with my face down and, at all costs, not sleep on my back. Weeks went by, and I stuck to doctor's orders, frightened to cause any disruption in the recovery, meanwhile continuing my daily wrist therapy as well.

Eventually, I had my last visit with the surgeon who had repaired my wrist. I would not need to go back. Still, I kept up the exercises for a few weeks while I concentrated on getting through the ordeal with my eye. Weekly, then bi-weekly appointments came and went, and by October, I was told I was free to ride a motorcycle again. I had 20/20 vision in my left eye. I'd been lucky I was told. "Only three percent of those who have been treated for the same condition recovered full sight again." Still, the doctors told me it was common that the retina would detach again, but I hoped for the best and tried to return to normal life, with only sporadic returns to the doctor from time to time.

So, now here I am. It's the tail-end of November 2021, and now I am almost sixty-five. Not old many would say. But I look toward to a future with mild, constant pain in my wrist and what had been mild arthritis in my hand was now worse, which I was told was exacerbated and accelerated by the impact from the crash. I also live with the distinct possibility of another bout with retinal issues that would either mean another couple months of recovery or blindness. I now find picking up a dropped bike much more difficult, if possible at all. My grip has weakened dramatically. Just getting a motorcycle on a centerstand is a challenge. The total recovery from this last accident (the first of my life) took almost twenty-four weeks. That's half a year. A year is a much bigger of slice of your life in your sixties than it was when you were in your thirties. And hell, I have a hard time just getting my socks on these days. All that makes me wonder how many good riding years do I have left, even if nothing else goes wrong? In six years, I'll be seventy. In sixteen, eighty. What will realistically be possible for me? How many more rides? How many places I've wanted to see will I never get to experience?

When you're young, you think you have forever; when you're in your mid-sixties you realize the river of time is flowing . . . fast . . . in the not-too-distant future the final bell will toll for you. I began to realize that while I was paying attention to other things, mayhem had moved in next door, and the Grim Reaper now lived just two doors down. So, the thing to do is to make those years count, to cram in as much riding and living as I am able, before either my body gives out or catastrophe strikes. I am going to try to do as much as I can with that time left. Make any time I still have count.

Let's see what happens.

△ camping
**F** stayed with friend
**H** stayed in hotel

# PREFACE

What follows is the story of several rides, much-needed rides, I took between October 2021, following the six months of recovery from my encounter with the deer, through the next October in 2022.

For me, there was no year-long time off to ride, as my family, finances, and my multiple jobs kept me too busy to leave for very long periods of time. The magazine that I edited came out every other month, and between issues from their final approval from me to go to press and the time I had to start work on the next issue gave me about a month of clear time, which I could sometimes fudge out by a few more days. Whenever and wherever I traveled on the motorcycle had to be possible within that one-month window.

I wrote this book by typing up my journal entries when I got home and later adding stuff I'd remembered or learned about the places I'd stayed or seen and filling in gaps where journal entries were missing. My travels were insignificant compared to those of so many world travelers, or "overlanders," who'd written much more exciting and descriptive books about much more exotic and far-flung locations. I found myself thinking that I must be arrogant to think anyone would want to ride along with me in these pages. I don't think you'll find much profound here. These are just my simple thoughts as they occurred to me. Sometimes they are about the ride, sometimes about the people I met, and sometimes they are about, well, almost anything. There's nothing like being alone inside your helmet to have time to just think.

Human society often baffles me. It seems largely based on vacuous consumerism, group think, and superstition without logic applied from outside that worldview. That often leaves me feeling alone, as if looking in from the outside, out of step with the rest of the world. While, broadly, society seems strange and illogical to me, I like most people individually. I can enjoy one-on-one or small group interactions, although discovering a way to participate can be awkward. However, finding a place in a crowd is largely uncomfortable, and usually I find myself retreating into myself, a natural loner, only interacting with the crowd superficially, while inwardly donning a stoic attitude. That often results in my being seen as cold and unfeeling. At times, when society requires a particular emotional response, I back away from emotion altogether. I'm sure that has taken its toll on my family. My usual response to the inevitable emotional conflict or crisis is to back away from it, silently pretending it doesn't bother me. I disengage, turning off emotion. During times of heartbreaking loss we have endured, my daughter has commented that I never showed my feelings. When my father died, she remarked, "You never cry!" She's right, but it's not true that I have no feelings.

On occasion, attempting to confront my own deficiencies, I'll push myself to initiate conversation with others. It's a struggle to maintain a connection. I can hide behind a veil of meaningless chit-chat, seemingly at ease, but the deeper me usually stays hidden and quiet. Occasionally, though, when I've been bold enough to make contact or someone has made that effort toward me, I'll meet people with whom I share values, interests, and perspectives and with whom I am comfortable, as you'll see in these stories. Of course, there are no friendships like those that are forged by youth, and while I may not have many close friends, the ones I do have come with deep and strong roots. Some of my efforts to push myself beyond my natural inclination have also yielded friendships that I value deeply, such as with my companions in the Super Happy Fun Group. Working for the magazine has often forced me to be more outgoing, enabling me to forge friendships in the VJMC as well.

Despite my shortcomings in the art of human interaction and my desire to overcome them, I still find great value in solitude, relief from what often seems like an overwhelming and unmanageable world. I treasure the complex simplicity of the natural world. The logic that is missing from society in nature rules supreme, and I find comfort and beauty in that. Perhaps that is why in these journeys the natural places I visited were the root of the adventure, more so than the people I interacted with along the way.

However, from time to time I did meet up with kindred spirits who, for one serendipitous reason or another, I happened to mesh with. None of the times with new friends lasted long; that's the way it is for those traveling by motorcycle. Ships passing in the night. Maybe we'd meet up again later, maybe not.

Some readers of this year's-worth of riding may think I visited some amazing places for all too short a time and didn't dive substantially into them, hiking deep into their interiors or studying their history, geology, and social significance. There are a couple reasons for that. First, financial considerations kept me from paying for tours or entry fees to some natural wonders that some others may have found a trivial expense. That might, I hope, change over time, but for this trip I had to be frugal. Another reason was time, which was almost as precious as money to me. I kept my eyes on the biggest prize, seeing the Pacific Ocean and southern Utah, but there were some places I simply had to bypass. There is so much to see in North America that, unless you have unlimited time and resources, you must choose for yourself which are the most important to visit and let others go, hopefully to be visited another time. Perhaps the biggest reason I didn't linger too long at any one place was my insatiable desire to be on the move, to just keep going. The journey is also the destination for me. I'm not sure what I relish most, being in the saddle motoring down a road I've never been on before or stopping to gaze at natural wonders.

Perhaps all I needed was to always be in a different place than I had been the day before. I've been that way since I was young, seldom able to satisfy it, but always wanting to be moving. Maybe I was running from something: my religion-instilled guilt, my feelings of inadequacy, my inability to connect with others. Even in high school, when I was an avid bicyclist, I always wanted ride further and see what was over the next hill, and the next, always wanting to push a little further. Over the years since, I was able to give myself over to that urge for short periods. In the seventies, I took a five-week journey into Mexico and Guatemala and then a sojourn in the Midwest, working on the prairie, trying to live a completely different kind of life than I'd lived before. The longest extended time that I was able to satisfy that itch to move was when I sailed little boats on the East Coast, Gulf, and in the Caribbean. I got away with that for several years before planting myself back on dry ground.

Additionally, depression and stress haunted me constantly, especially when off the bike. Living with depression is not something you do, get through, and then are done. It accompanies you through life, and you, if you are to succeed at having some happiness, must devise strategies for dealing with it. Accompanying my depression, and perhaps an integral part of it, was a feeling of low self-worth. My being deeply involved with the church and in a large part being raised by it, with its constant message of my being undeserving of God's grace, largely fed my feelings of inadequacy. I'd heard never-ending sermons of how unworthy I was of God's love, how only His blood sacrifice could save me from my wickedness. I'd had the lyrics of hymns constantly driven into my head such as "Weak and unworthy tho' I be, Yet Christ, the Savior, died for me;" with the added threat of "Shadows are gathering, deathbeds are coming, Coming for you and for me." After all, we are "born into sin," as I was told so many times, and "For all have sinned and fallen short of the glory of God." A child constantly bombarded with messages that tell them that what and who they are is not sufficient, but that only by yielding to a higher power can they be worthy can do nothing but negate feelings of self-worth. No matter what you do, it is never enough to compensate for your human shortcomings. Even now, when I hear the old hymns, which I'd heard so many times as a child performed in four-part harmony around my grandparents' piano or from behind a pulpit or a choir loft, instead of feelings of comfort or even nostalgia, I experience a sense of deep sadness.

Riding a motorcycle calms my mind and helps put aside my depression and those feelings of low self-worth, shoving them into the background, so I can rearrange myself into, hopefully, something better. So, this ride was not only a satisfaction of my wandering urges but a way of combating a state of mind into which I had often fallen deeply back into. It was also a way of doing something personally meaningful with part of the time I still had on this planet. There is nothing like a close call to make one appreciate one's remaining time.

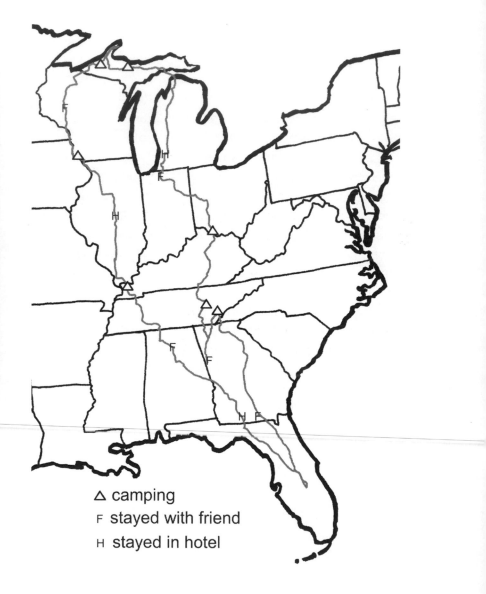

△ camping
F stayed with friend
H stayed in hotel

# Northbound in
# October

## Preparation

The day had finally arrived. The doctor gave me the green light to ride again, and it coincided with a big event I go to every year while working for the magazine. Barber Vintage Festival is in Birmingham, so north by northwest from central Florida. It was a one-day ride if you started at dawn and didn't dawdle. You could do it quite more leisurely if you left the midnight before, but I no longer rode at night if I could help it. The event also fell in that magic window between issues, after finishing one issue and before I'd need to begin work on the next.

I'd had my Triumph 800 XCa since May but had only ridden it a few miles between recovery of my wrist and the start of my eye problems. I had not had a chance to really get to know it and to get comfortable riding the much taller and more off-pavement-oriented adventure bike. This would be my opportunity to do just that. From Birmingham, I could head off after the festival and have some time to get acquainted with my new traveling companion. I still had things to do other than magazine work, but I could manage a week or so to get my legs back under me and my feet on the pegs once again. With an idea to continue north from the festival, I worked ahead as much as possible to make a clear path of time for me to allow at least two weeks of travel.

## BARBER VINTAGE FESTIVAL

Sixty miles out from my home in Lake Wales, Florida, I stopped in Mascotte, at the Rainbow Family Restaurant, which had become a favorite of mine for its cheap and honest breakfast. As I was backing the Tiger into a spot in front, the bike seemed hard to move. I thought it was just my imagination and my still-sore wrist being too weak to pull on the bars to force it in reverse into the spot.

Breakfast was its usual goodness, made up of scrambled eggs with cheese mixed in, grits, and a couple cups of hot black coffee. When finished, I went out to discover the real reason why the bike had been hard to move. The rear tire was completely flat, the culprit, a screw dead center in the tread.

I filled the tire with a small compressor I carried with me, and it seemed to be holding, at least enough to get to a Harley shop in Groveland I had been told about in the restaurant, which was just a mile or so back in the direction from which I'd come. It was about eight-thirty, and the shop didn't open until nine. I rode down and parked up in the gravel in front of the shop to wait.

As soon as the owner showed up, the first thing he said as he exited his pickup was, "I don't work on those—only Harleys." Not surprisingly, he had a "Fuck Biden and Fuck You for Voting for Him" sign plastered across his building, along with a Trump flag flying from a pole near the door. He walked inside without saying more, although he conceded to letting me park my non-Harley-Davidson in his gravel, while I walked across the highway to a McDonalds to get in the air conditioning, get some coffee, and to the make a call for a tow.

My home until the tow truck arrived

Three hours later, back across the road at the bike shop, I was still sitting in front of the shop, sitting on the ground in the thin sliver of shade cast by the building, waiting for the tow vehicle, while conservative talk radio blasted from inside the shop. I could fix the tube myself, as I had packed all the tools, but the one thing I didn't have was the special patch for the inside of the tire, and I did not want to start such a long ride with only fixing the tube and not addressing the tire as well. But I did have towing from the American Motorcyclist Association, having luckily just re-upped my membership a week or so before, which I had let lag for a couple years because of our financial situation. I made the call, and a little after noon the truck arrived. Of course, the tire was flat again, and I started to get my little compressor out to pump it up enough for us to easily roll the bike to the truck when the shop owner, who knew the tow driver, finally became helpful and offered us the use of his compressor. He even wished me luck.

With the Tiger mounted securely on the truck bed, I jumped into the shotgun position, and we were off to a shop in Oakland, south of Lake Apopka and northwest of Orlando, about fifteen miles away. The driver also rode motorcycles, proving it by showing me his scar, saying he'd had the same injury as me. We talked bikes and broken bones all the way to the dealership.

It being a weekday, traffic was dense, and it took at least a half-hour to reach the shop, after which they went to work on the tire while I strolled around the showroom and lot outside looking at all the different models they had in stock. Surprisingly, they had two Honda CRF300Ls, a bike that my friends in north Georgia were finding hard to find and had to order, waiting weeks for them to arrive. The 300 Rally had been made famous by Noraly, a YouTube traveler also known as Itchy Boots, who was traveling the length of South and Central America on one, which might have explained the scarcity of the model.

After checking out the bikes and sitting in a deserted corner of the showroom fiddling with my phone, by about two o'clock the bike was ready. I went out to check it and was met by two employees drooling over the Tiger. We had a little chat about the bike and what I had found I liked about it so far, after just seventy-five miles or so of riding it. While the tow was free, I had to go back inside to pay a whopping $135 for the repair, which would cut significantly into my already meagre budget.

The tire delay meant I would not make it to Birmingham that same day, or at least before dark. With a damaged right eye that had never fully recovered, along with my run-in on the Bonneville with a deer after dark, I'd sworn to stop riding after nightfall. I'd have to stop somewhere. Where that somewhere would be and how much more it would affect my budget, I'd have to see. I'd ride until late afternoon before starting to look for a cheap motel. I wasn't going to camp and spend the time tearing down and packing up the gear in the morning. I needed to get to the Vintage Festival as early as possible, already being a day late and missing events that I should have already been at, getting photos for the magazine.

For those missed events, I'd need to track down members who'd been there and get promises that they'd send me some images to use.

It was late afternoon when I got to the Georgia state line, north of Monticello, Florida. I had already spotted a deer roaming around the fields on the side of the road at about three-thirty, so I wanted to find a place as quickly as possible, well before total darkness set in. By Thomasville, I spied the names of a couple chains of usually economical motels side-by-side and pulled in. For eighty-five dollars a night, I had a room in some sort of merged double motel in a bit of a scruffy part of town. The clientele wandering around the parking lots looked a little unsavory, but the room was clean and had a bed, which was all I needed. I had been told continental breakfast was also included, so I expected to save time and money in the morning, not having to stop somewhere for breakfast. I emptied my panniers and detached all the easily removeable stuff from the Tiger and hoped for the best with it parked outside my room, where I could keep an eye on it from time to time. To top off the evening, there was also a Waffle House within walking distance, so I took a stroll there for a quick bite before retiring to my room for the rest for the night.

In the morning, I was pleased to see the empty soft panniers still on the bike. As I went out to begin repacking the Tiger, two doors down was a pair of police officers having a talk with a man about what I thought I heard as "domestic violence." I packed quickly as voices were raised, got on, and rolled to the front of the lobby to drop off the key and grab breakfast.

Pickings were slim, but they did have a self-serve waffle maker for a hot item. I poured the mix in, closed the lid, rotated the iron, and went to get coffee while I waited for my waffle. Hearing the ding, I retrieved my meal, buttered it up, poured on the syrup, and scarfed it down, while out of the corner of my eye I could see a police officer in the adjacent lobby talking to the apparent victim, or perpetrator, of this morning's conflict.

While the police were still there, I made my escape and headed north. The temperature was pleasant most of the way, after a short run through the trailing edge of a front with accompanying rain. The sun came out on the other side and stayed out all the way to Birmingham. Along the way, I experimented with all the bells and whistles of the new Tiger and found the cruise control to be very useful for someone with a barely-healed broken wrist.

After blasting up a major highway toward Birmingham until about thirty miles out of the city, I turned right and took a little shortcut I knew of up to Leeds. It was a run through a couple mountains, with enough twists to make it a fun ride, and it allowed me to approach Birmingham from the east, and less busy, side of town, with Barber Motorsports Park literally straddling the eastern city limits of the big city. Because part of the journey was intended to let me have some time to get to know the Tiger better, this stretch was also perfect to see what Sport Mode would do. Turning onto Highway 21, I switched modes and let it rip and was delighted with the performance increase.

From Leeds, on the other side of the mountains, it was a quick ride west to Barber, where I checked in, ran down some photos from earlier events, caught up on the schedule, and started the photography work.

I'd been chatting with a fellow about his book about an overland ride he'd taken with his wife and an infant daughter in a sidecar. He and his wife were camping at the festival, near the trials and off-road racing areas, and had invited me to stop by. It had rained torrents the day before, and most of the park was still soaked and muddy. The route to their campsite, being soft wet grass torn up by dirt bikes, with muddy ruts everywhere, had me expecting it would result in my first drop of the Tiger, especially considering the primarily street tires that were original equipment on the bike that I had to work with. But, surprisingly, I made it in, and later out, muddy but still upright.

Dinner was about ready when I arrived at the campsite, and we shared spring rolls, pork, and rice, while discussing the book and meeting friends camping with them, with others dropping by.

My friends lived in Georgia, as did their camp mate, who it turned out, had been at Anderson College while I had attended. We learned we had many mutual friends and common stories to share. Other people came and went. A young couple on a muddy dirt bike, two-up with a baby in a chest harness dropped by, and an interesting young woman joined us who had come from Miami to ride her first trials and, surprisingly, ended up coming in third.

After dinner, I risked the two miles in the darkness to my friend Ken's place, just outside the motorsports park, and arrived unscathed after a very cautious and slow approach on the final road to his place in hopes of avoiding deer, which I'd seen in his neighborhood before at just that time of night and in the area that I was riding through. We listened to music and caught up with each other until midnight, after which I made my bed on the couch and was soon fast asleep.

After breakfast buffet at Laney's, a local favorite, with Ken, Saturday was another workday at the festival, where the Vintage Japanese Motorcycle Club was having a contest for the loudest bike in a few categories, a couple of technical presentations, a huge bike show, and an awards presentation, with awards given by a well-known past Motocross champion and AMA Hall of Famer, Mary McGee. The sun had been blazing all day. I was hot and worn out and happy to see the afternoon fading as the club's annual barbecue dinner got underway on the, by then, slightly drier lawn, which was so wet earlier in the day that it had to be abandoned for the bike show in favor of the paved street-side.

I got back to Ken's just after dark and spent another night listening to music and kicking back with some drinks. It felt good to know my work was done and there would be no need to get up to an alarm the next morning. Sunday would be the real start of my journey, making decisions each day on the fly on when to leave and when and where to stop.

## North to Corn and Tornado Country

Ken and I shared breakfast at a Waffle House at the exit that I would take leaving town, so we said our goodbyes there, with Ken heading back to the last day of the festival to help friends tear down their booth in the swapmeet area, while I would be striking out north and a little west, aiming roughly for western Kentucky.

I only took the Interstate north to get out of the Birmingham area, then once clear of the city, I headed northwest on smaller highways. The rain that had made a mess at the Barber Vintage Festival the week before was long gone. I had sun and benign, fluffy white clouds and temperatures a few degrees lower than the inferno that had been the Barber Vintage Festival. At a stop, I looked in my top box for something, only to discover I had left all my food and cooking tools in Ken's kitchen. Gone were my stove, my pots and cup, all my breakfast bars, and a bag of cacao, which I had switched to drinking instead of coffee a few months before the trip. I'd have to pay for cooked meals for the rest of the trip. I was too far out to make a return to Birmingham worth the journey to retrieve it all. I called Ken and asked him to box it all up and to mail it home for me, then got back on the road. Very soon, about 130 miles out from Ken's, I crossed into Tennessee, then slipped along minor highways between Memphis and Nashville toward western Kentucky.

As I rolled up and down the green hills, I watched for any signs of fall, some change of color, but everything was still cloaked in mid-summer green. Autumn had not yet arrived in Tennessee or Kentucky.

As the day progressed into the afternoon, I noticed that the sun was going to be setting earlier than I had expected, but then I recalled the latitude I was at and remembered how short the days were when I had lived in the North. I stopped and bought water and a sub and threw both in the top box. Checking the area on my phone, I found a campground west of Paducah that would be close to an easy crossing into Illinois over the Ohio River the next morning. I failed to look at any details of the place while stopped, and as I rode, I hoped it would not be an RV-only kind of "campground." What passed for campgrounds these days often were not exactly the quiet, pristine, wooded paradise for tents that I had in my mind. I hoped for the best. I'd just plugged its address into the GPS and hoped I would make it there before dark. I couldn't be picky that late in the afternoon, so if I had to pay for an RV spot for pitching my tent, that's what I'd have to do.

The ride from that moment was a race against a setting sun, guessing, based on the GPS's arrival time, how dark it would be when I would arrive. As I sped along, I was constantly glancing at the dropping sun and estimating how long until it would disappear behind the trees in the west. Every speed zone slowing me down worried me as I watched it sink ever lower. Finally, the sun was below the horizon, but still the landscape was illuminated by the lingering light of the sky overhead, and I still had that light to see by as I pulled into the campground, pleasantly surprised that they did have tent space and the price was a reasonable fifteen dollars—sold.

I'd made it in before twilight had ended, but by the time I was setting up camp, it had to be done in the dark. Usually, that was a fast process, but this time it was a struggle in the night, made more difficult when the tent pole segments refused to go together. Right after my crash with the deer, I had checked the camping gear stored on the pillion. Despite a hole ground through the bag holding the poles, the poles themselves looked alright, although some of the metal ends were a bit scraped up. But as I began putting the poles together at the campground that evening, I found that a few of the metal ferrules at the end of the fiberglass poles, into which the pole segments inserted, had been bent slightly out of round, making it impossible to assemble the poles. I fumbled around in the bottom of my pannier for my tool roll and found some pliers, which I used to reshape the ferrules until the poles would slip in and assembly could continue. The poles, the darkness, and the long time since I had gone through this setup routine made that night's pitch a challenge, but eventually, all was set up and I was sound asleep on top of my sleeping bag in a still and warm night.

A fierce wind arrived out of the south the following morning. After a shower, I returned from the bath house to find the tent blown onto its side, despite the weight of all my gear being stowed inside it. The wind complicated breaking camp, with anything loose threatening to fly away toward the Ohio River, but I managed it without losing anything to the zephyrs' whims. The bike finally packed, I left. Only a quarter mile away, I stopped for a hearty breakfast before getting on the adjacent Interstate to cross the Ohio into extreme southern Illinois.

The wind strongly blew all day, and often, as I rode downwind, directly north, I watched the instant mileage indicator, blinking at me from the instruments, go up from 58 mpg to over 80, and even over 90 occasionally. When I fueled up, apparently, the top range that the gauge could show was 240 miles, but it would stay at that number for thirty miles or more after filling up, before slowly registering less than a full tank. It looked like one fill up per day would be all that would be needed for most of the trip, with ranges around 260 miles possible.

The day before, while cooler than it had been in Birmingham, had still been quite hot, but today, Monday, the temperature stayed in the low-70s Fahrenheit, only dipping into the upper-60s as showers passed. A man at the diner that morning had told me that it was supposed to rain, but that it would pass quickly. Rain was not a worry for me. My gear, which was new, replacing my damaged set from the crash, was truly waterproof, so when rain appeared, I'd just zip up the neck and wrists and keep on riding, with confidence that I'd stay dry. The rain that morning, indeed, came and went quickly, leaving a bright sun shining through scattered, small, fluffy white clouds.

Corn is King in Illinois

It was obvious that corn was king in Illinois. While there were still some fields standing uncut, as I rode further north through central Illinois, more fields had been harvested, and they revealed what they would usually hide: oil pumps pecking Mother Earth to draw out the liquid resins left eons ago by dinosaurs and other ancient life. I was surprised. I'd never known Illinois was an "oil state."

The wind was unrelenting the entire day, but the temperature was perfect and the skies brilliant . . . until about five o'clock, when my mind turned to picking up some portable food and finding a place to camp. The skies ahead and on my right stayed beautiful, but to the west a bank of darkness had appeared and was closing—quickly. I tried to calculate how much time I had to find food and a campground and still get camp set up before the approaching downpour. It wasn't much.

Time went by with no sign of a place to pick up a sandwich as the wall of black clouds moved closer. I looked hopefully ahead at the clear weather in the east when the road veered that way, then would despair as the road veered back to a little west of north and the darkness was there again and even closer. I thought, though, that if I could just get camp set up before the rain and wind arrived, I'd be alright. I could retreat within the tent and the rain could come down with little harm to me. But as time passed and I had found neither food nor a campground, I knew my time was running out.

With the storm almost overhead, I reluctantly decided to try to find a motel to avoid having to pitch camp in a gale of wind along with that rain that would arrive any minute. Luckily, I found a place with restaurants nearby, so I could at least stay dry and not go to bed hungry.

I went inside to register, and the friendly clerk, knowing what kind of weather was coming, offered to let me keep my bike parked by the lobby door, where I could still see it from my room but where there would be a roof above it. As I returned to the bike from the motel desk to unload the Tiger, the storm was unleashed, and buckets of rain were blowing sideways, driven by the wind, now from the west. The simple task of unloading the bike had me completely soaked, even though it was parked under the entrance drive-through overhang. After transferring everything to my room via an inside corridor, a quick trot down a sidewalk flowing like a creek to McDonalds was all I could manage. Although there were better options for dinner all around, they were all further away and meant a soaking if I was to try to get to one of them.

Back in the room, I was feeling a bit of a coward for bailing on camping just because of some rain, until I turned the television on and saw the local channels pre-empting network feeds with emergency weather warnings, with multiple tornados on the ground and right along the path I would have been in had I not stopped when I had. I'd made a good call, even if it cost me more of my over-stressed budget.

## BOUND FOR THE MISSISSIPPI
## AND THE DRIFTLESS AREA

In the morning the rain had cleared, but threatening winds remained. The storm's passing brought cooler temperatures, and I left under cloudy skies in 56 degrees. All that was required was a long sleeve shirt under my jacket with all its vents closed, and I remained quite comfortable.

By mid-morning, the low overcast had lifted and dissipated into individual spots of cloud with intermittent sunshine returning in defiance. The sun slowly won the battle, and by the afternoon the temperature had risen into the mid-60s.

Taking advantage of the prairie wind

After twenty to thirty miles of Interstate, I turned left onto smaller state roads trending west and then north.

Along the way, the highways ran through thick herds of giant windmills purring away on the prairie. Approaching the Mississippi, the land became more rolling, and pull-offs often provided great views of the countryside. Eventually, I reached the Great River Road and followed the Mississippi River, the route sometimes alongside it and sometimes wandering away, but always winding north.

Passing through the small river town of Savanna, I was surprised enough to turn around and park for a photo when I spotted Frank Fritz Finds in the old downtown. I remember talking to Frank, well-known for his role on the American Pickers television show, at an AIMExpo motorcycle industry show about how he and Mike each had their own antique shops, despite the show portraying only one shop. And there was Frank's; and I just caught it out of the corner of my eye in a chance passing. I wanted to move on to the Driftless Area of Wisconsin and its famed roads, so I didn't peek inside. Instead, I moved back out onto the road after my photo and soon was in Wisconsin.

Frank Fritz Finds

I shot north on a minor country road to avoid Dubuque traffic, and at Cuba City, I took another west to rejoin the Great River Road.

It was time for a gas stop, so I took the opportunity to ask about camping, as it was around five o'clock and I wanted to get a place earlier than I'd been doing and not sweat finding something as the sun went down. Luckily, twenty miles further down the River Road there was camping near Cassville. I first went into the little town to the small grocery store, bought snacks, a sandwich, and a massive single can of beer, then hauled it all back south to Sandy Bottoms Up Campground on the Mississippi, with only a slight delay and backtrack to find the turnoff when I'd realized I'd passed it.

I got everything set up in plenty of time to get my phone calls made, eat my dinner, and even take a short walk to the riverside. With the remaining light in the sky fading after my walk back to camp, I climbed into my tent and sleeping bag as the temperature started to fall and darkness set in.

As the night progressed, I realized I should have taken it as a warning when I crossed the train tracks as I entered Sunny Bottoms Up that afternoon. An hour into trying to sleep, and at least every hour after that, a cacophony erupted, signaled by the bell at the crossing rising to an ear-shattering crescendo of blaring horns, apparently on top of the tent, then the rattling and rumbling of steel cars rocking along the tracks, eventually roaring away into the night. It was hard not to wake in a panic, even knowing after the first time what was happening. I had been assured by the camp host that it would be a quiet night, as the place was virtually empty, but between the crashing symphony of train music, my ears were assailed by the raucous sounds of laughing and cajoling voices somewhere in the campground. The train noise would dissipate, only to be instantly replaced by another racket of laughter. As one dissolved the other increased, making sleep an iffy prospect, although the human noise eventually trailed off into silence, leaving only the train to terrify me for the rest of the night.

Eventually, I would fitfully fall asleep, until the next train came and started the cycle again.

Backwaters of the Mississippi

By midnight, all I was left with was the night train terror. Of course, being sixty-four meant multiple needs to pee in the night. I would grab my wadded-up jeans, just in case, and run into the nearby bath house, hoping no one would be up to see my naked dash. Putting jeans on in the tiny tent, with about thirty-six inches of headroom, in the dark was not something

I wanted to attempt multiple times, so I took my chances. Luckily, I was never caught.

The morning was in the low-50s with rain. I packed all I could while inside the tent into my waterproof bags, deposited them in the bath house, along with my riding clothes, and then went back out to pack up the wet tent. Once each bag was closed and secure, they were packed onto the Tiger, and I took off, bound north in the drizzling downpour.

A rainy day on the Great River Road

I continued up the Great River Road to Prairie du Chien, where I stopped for some corned-beef hash, eggs, and coffee and to clear the water from the inside of my visor, which was making it almost impossible to see. By the time I left, the rain had stopped and the temperature had increased a small amount, although not enough to convince me I didn't need the heated grips on to warm my fingers inside water-soaked, perforated leather gloves. I had hoped to have found a winter replacement for those back at the Barber Vintage Festival, but none of the vendors there had what I needed.

I followed the Mississippi until I was through La Crosse, then peeled away from the river and toward Eau Claire on a scenic ride through the heart of the Driftless Area on Route 93. The fall colors I had been hoping to see still eluded me, and other than some reddish swamp maples, the rest of the forest was still full and verdant.

The Driftless Area is known for its motorcycle riding roads and its beautiful scenery. It is an area of southwestern Wisconsin and parts of Minnesota that was never covered by ice during the last ice age, and because of that, it has no glacial deposits, also known as drift. The land retains its original topography, with rolling hills, elevation changes, forest, and deeply-carved river valleys, not unlike the topography of Vermont or New Hampshire.

By mid-afternoon, I'd arrived at Ron's place. He was the author of Shiny Side Up, which I had published not long before. He had been involved with motorcycles most of his life, especially with BMWs, one of which he had parked in the garage in Eau Claire, so he and I had a lot in common. Ron and his wife graciously served a wonderful meal, then I got a shower and did my laundry, which had been piling up since I'd left Florida. It was about time, as the jeans I'd been wearing were first put on seven days before.

My rough plan was that, while stopping in Eau Claire, I would make my mind up which direction my ride would take me from there. I had hoped to head to the Upper Peninsula of Michigan and the shores of Lake Superior.

Just out of high school, my father and I had taken a road trip to the UP, but had driven the southern shoreline along Lake Michigan, eventually returning to Michigan via a ferry that ran from Milwaukee, on the Wisconsin side, to Muskegon, on the Michigan side. But we had missed the north shore completely, and I had ever since wanted to see that area.

Going to the UP in the middle of October was a counter-intuitive goal, because at that time of year it could be in the

70s or snowing, and there would be little advance knowledge of which would be when. Being close now in Eau Claire gave me the chance to check the weather forecast and determine if that direction was doable. If not, I thought perhaps I'd turn southwest, cross the Mississippi, and head down in the direction of Texas and maybe take a look at Big Bend National Park, another place I had heard great things about, and which would be definitely superior to sleeping in the snow. Besides, I had been missing my favorite breakfast fare that was so easy to find in the West, huevos rancheros, and I was sure I'd be able to have that every morning in Texas. But as luck would have it, the Upper Peninsula had been having a run of warmer than usual weather lately. The weather reports for the UP for the upcoming week looked promising, with sun most days and temperatures predicted to mostly be in the sixties. It would cool a little, but the trend would generally be holding for at least the next week; and at the very least, it would likely not be snowing when I would be passing through.

With laundry sorted, a decision made to strike out for Upper Michigan, and a new route roughly planned, I went to bed without the fear of being run down in the night by a locomotive.

## Mind Made Up, I Head North to the Upper Peninsula

Ron was up before me and had eggs and bacon going and coffee brewing when I walked upstairs, drawn by the aroma. After breakfast, he offered me his heated bib-like vest, which he thought he was done using for the season, and a balaclava that I could mail back to him when I arrived home at the end of the ride. We loaded all the stuff back onto the Tiger, including all my now clean clothes.

It was cold as I rode north from Eau Claire in 46 degrees, with overcast skies but no rain. I made a coffee and warm-up stop after leaving the major highway out of Eau Claire. And, of course, how could I have coffee and not the tempting custard pie that was on offer?

I took some small roads toward Ironwood, Michigan, and the UP. I'd finally found autumn, with a mix of many bare trees and others with yellow and orange leaves still hanging on their branches. The birches were uncertain. Some still wore their golden cloaks, while others boldly had shed their clothes and bared their naked white torsos to the cold wind.

I stopped again at the Michigan border at a small bar to get some lunch. I figured that I could afford the calories from a burger with all the cold I'd be riding through. I'd burn right through them.

The road took me through the Porcupine Mountains, surprisingly tall and cloaked in fall colors. Eventually, I turned toward the Keweenaw Peninsula, aiming to visit Copper Harbor at its tip, sticking into cold Lake Superior like a hitch hiker's thumb. I rolled through the diminutive village of Winter and had to stop for a photo at its sign. Just earlier in the day I had encountered autumn, and now I was already in Winter!

Welcome to Winter!

It was getting late, so I started looking for a camping spot. Copper Harbor would have to wait until the following day. Nothing showed up, and as the day wore on, I decided I didn't need to pick up food to bring to camp. Stopping for it would eat into the daylight I had left for finding a campsite, and I remembered that Ron had put a banana and a pastry in the top case. After my big lunch, I reckoned that would do for dinner.

Finally, I saw a diminutive, brown "Camping" sign and a "Pike Lake Boat Slipway" sign as well, so I turned down a little road running south into the forest. Soon, it became gravel, well-groomed and not too intimidating, so I continued on. After a few more miles in, I still had not seen any sign of a campground. I thought I'd give it a couple more miles, and when I saw another camping sign, I gave it another one or two, but still with no sign of a place I could pitch my tent. Eventually, I saw another road turn off to the left with a Pike Lake sign pointing that direction, so I took that the mile more it said it was to the lake. There, at the end, was an empty boat ramp, a dirt parking area, and a few campsites, completely deserted on the shore of Pike Lake. I picked a spot and unloaded the pillion bag that was still full of wet gear from having put it away in the rain back on the Mississippi River at Bottoms Up. I set the tent up in the brisk breeze coming off the lake, leaving it open to let the wind dry it out, then found appropriate broken branches on various small trees to drape the rest of the wet things on to dry.

I got out the food Ron had thrown into the top case, and wandered down to the parking area, where I gobbled down the food, and where I could dispose of the banana peel, leaving the scent of food well away from the camp, for fear of bears sensing a tasty treat in the night. Back at my spot, I quickly set up the rest of camp as light was fading. Everything had dried quickly thanks to the breeze, and soon all was installed where it was needed, then I readied myself for sleep. I'd put on thermal layers beneath my shirt and jeans, and I wore those and my top layer of clothes to bed. The night was cold, but I stayed warm in my bag. As I lay there and thought about it, I realized that, although I had camped many times before, I had always done it with others, and this was the first time I had probably camped completely alone and truly in the wilds. Thoughts of bears, wolverines, and other creatures crept into my mind, but I tried to ignore them and went to sleep. But nothing disturbed me all night as I lay there in the deep North Woods.

Camping in the North Woods

The morning again was in the mid-40s by the time I got up and packed, unusually late for me, but I'd sworn "no alarms" on this journey.

I'd memorized the turns to the camping spot on the way in, so reversing them, I made my way along the dirt roads again until I found the paved highway where I'd turned off late in the day the previous afternoon.

I rode up the Keweenaw on cruise control, running up the middle of the peninsula until Houghton and then crossed over to Hancock, on the north side of Portage Lake on a beautiful high ridge overlooking Houghton Lake and the tremendous lift bridge connecting the southern Keweenaw to Copper Island, the remainder of the peninsula jutting into Lake Superior, separated from the mainland by Portage Lake and the Keweenaw Waterway cutting across from the northwest to the southeast.

In Hancock, I stopped at the Kalena Café, a fixture in the town since 1918. The place was packed, but I got a seat quickly, and while I sipped on my coffee, I read the history lessons printed on wall-art hanging above my booth telling the story of the bridge and community. I had a much too big breakfast of eggs, corned-beef hash, potatoes, toast, coffee, and two enormous blueberry pancakes. Even with the cold, I couldn't afford that many calories, so I left with half still on my plate and me about to burst.

Keweenaw history lesson for breakfast

But before leaving, I went into the little bathroom protruding from the wall into the middle of the dining room to alleviate some of the pressure I was feeling. Finishing the task at hand I reached down and pressed the lever to flush, and as I did so, I watched in horror as the water and other . . . um . . . material rose toward the bowl's rim and then cascaded over and across the floor like a dirty, toxic, polluted waterfall. I quickly retreated and closed the door behind me, sheepishly notifying a waitress of what was happening in there, and then, red-faced, I left as quickly as I could before the flood could make its way under the door to underneath the nearby diners' chairs. I guessed I would not be stopping back there for lunch on my way back from the tip of the peninsula.

Snowfall records

I was riding up the central route toward Copper Harbor when I passed a very tall, red and white sign, or marker of some sort, which prompted me to turn around to investigate. What I found in the little roadside park was a register of sorts, tall and narrow like a thermometer, denoting snowfall for

Keweenaw County scaled to actual size. At the very tip was the record set in 1978-1979 of 390.4 inches, or over thirty-two feet! About two-thirds down was the fifty-four-year average snowfall at 240.8 inches, and the all-time low, about halfway down, was still 161.1 inches, or fourteen and a half feet. It was certainly a photo-worthy sight.

The highway continued its central path, so I turned off when I got to a road that would take me to Eagle Harbor, on the north shore. The route took me alongside Lake Superior, curving away through little villages and lined close on both sides by evergreens, making me think of the Christmas holiday, with the powerful Christmas tree smell permeating the air as I passed through it.

Finally, I reached Copper Harbor, the last village on the road. I rode a couple more miles further, to the very northern end of US Highway 41, with its southern terminus in Miami, over 3,000 miles away in the direction from which I had come eight days before.

The top of US 41

I retraced my steps to Copper Harbor, after the obligatory photo in front of the "End" sign, then took the

central highway back to Houghton and the only bridge
connecting to the mainland over Portage Lake Canal.

Lake Superior at the Keweenaw Peninsula

Once I had reached the base of the peninsula at L'Anse, I
rode south for a while into the interior, then continued the
trek across the UP, going east through forested land toward
Marquette, where the highway rejoined the shores of Gitchee-
Gumee.

It was getting close to five o'clock, so I started scouting for
a campground. Near the little hamlet of Christmas, I struck
out at Bay Furnace Campground in Chippewa National
Forest. I followed the driveway to the campground, only to
be stopped at a closed barrier at the entrance. The National
Forest campgrounds had already closed for the season; I'd
have to look elsewhere.

Disappointed and watching the sinking sun, I only had to
go a mile or so further east before I spotted Munising Tourist
Park Campground on the shore-side of the highway. No one
was in the office, but it was obviously still open, as evidenced
by the many campers scattered around the site. It looked like
the campground was used primarily by RVs and camping

trailers, but a small map of the grounds posted outside the office showed a "Primitive Tent Camping" area at the west end, with a rather high price tag of twenty-nine dollars. It would have to do. I would take a spot and settle the bill in the morning, as it was too late to look for something else. I rode across the park to the west end and past the car barrier onto the beach sand, being careful to put a kickstand puck under the side stand to keep it from sinking in. I was also careful to not move out of the tree cover to where the sand became softer and might have presented a problem getting the bike out in the morning. The sites were directly on the shore among a clump of pines. I chose the nearest one to set up camp. There were magnificent views across the water to Grand Island, just offshore to the north. It was perfect and made the cost feel insignificant.

## TURNING POINT TO THE LOWER PENINSULA

In the night, it rained for a short while. In the still dark hours before sunrise, I lay hoping the wind would dry the tent again before dawn, but it wasn't to be, and I had to pack the tent, fly, and footprint while it was all still slightly damp. Again, it was in the 40s while I set to repacking. The chill made me think better of a plan to get a shower in the unheated bath house. I could live with dirty hair for one more day.

While settling-up at the office, I learned that campground was closing in just a couple days as well, so my time in the UP was limited, unless I wanted to pay for motels the rest of the time, which was not a practical option for me.

I headed east, away from the coast and through the heart of the Upper Peninsula. After a fuel stop, I turned right on a county road transiting the peninsula south toward Lake Michigan, leaving dark clouds and rain that had been pestering me behind. From there, I'd be aiming more or less south for the rest of the journey and leaving the cold behind me a bit more each day. The heated grips and seat on the Tiger had performed well, and I never felt the need to use the heated vest or the balaclava Ron had loaned me. Five fewer degrees would probably have had me donning both, but the temperatures had stayed just above that threshold, and I had never really felt chilled.

Emerging from the thickly forested interior and arriving at the coast, the sun was out, shining brilliantly and reflecting off blue waters, white caps, and spindrift being blown from the southwest. The highway ran directly beside the big lake sparkling in the sunshine, and it was not long before the Mackinac Bridge came into view in the east.

At Saint Ignace I rode up to the mighty bridge, paid a four-dollar toll, and crossed with a gale of wind blowing from ahead and my right side, making it necessary to make constant steering and leaning adjustments to stay on my solid right lane and not drift onto the grated left lane, which on a motorcycle is a squirrely prospect at best and a bad choice on such a blustery day with two hundred feet below you before the icy waters' surface.

As soon as I made landfall, I took a turn off the Interstate onto a smaller US highway. Glad to be off the busy and characterless Interstate, I rode south amid forests, past lakes, and through little towns. The rich aroma of fallen, decaying deciduous leaves mixed with a mild aroma of pine accompanied me to Boyne Falls, where I'd once spent a memorable evening stopping at my high school Spanish teacher's home, tucked back in the woods on the shores of Thumb Lake. This time, I did not stop to visit but was glad for the warm memories passing that way brought back to me.

With my southern progress, the color show of leaves slowly returned to a solid green, with the exception of the swamp maples, which seemed to turn red at the first blush of cold.

I stopped at a restaurant to reorganize my tank bag maps, which needed refolding to the next section, and to get a bite for lunch, having skipped breakfast altogether. I had seen numerous signs in the UP for the ubiquitous "pasty," a pastry shell filled with meat and vegetables. I had always been too full before from big breakfasts, which is my preferred must-have meal when on the road, so now I hoped to finally give the pasty a try.

As I walked to the entrance, I wondered if it was open, as the parking lot was quiet and empty, but there was a big sign by the door saying, "We Are Open." I entered, only to learn I'd been lied to by the sign. The place was empty, except for a skeleton crew of three, and they were actually closed. It was warm and cozy inside the log walls, so I asked if I could just use one of their booths to reorganize my maps. I was told I was welcome to do that, so I chose a booth and sat down and began removing the maps from my tank bag, which I had carried in with me.

The lady out front apologized for being closed and told me that it was only because they had no wait staff to handle orders, which was a nationwide problem at that time. She turned the lights on for me over the booth, and I asked if there was any place further south where I could get a pasty. She said, "Well, if that's all you want, then we'll make one up for you."

Soon, a hot pasty, much bigger than I had imagined and covered in brown gravy appeared at my table, along with coffee. I tucked in while looking over the maps and telling myself this would be my last meal that day, and really, it was enough for two.

I thought about stopping to see my old high school friend, Jeff, who lived near Benton Harbor, not far off my intended course. I rang him up but found out he was in Niles and would not be home until late that night. "Next time," I said, "Planning too far ahead on this trip is difficult, so this kind of thing is inevitable. We'll catch up another time."

Another customer came in but was told the restaurant was closed. I was hidden away behind a half-wall, and the person who'd served me put her finger to her lips, indicating to me to be quiet, so I obeyed. I waited until he'd left, paid my bill, and thanked them profusely for being so kind, and got back on the Tiger to head out, now a couple pounds heavier than when I had entered.

Near Cadillac, the road turned more southward and grew, eventually morphing into an Interstate in all ways but in name. It became a four-lane, divided highway, with limited access and exits instead of intersections. The speed limit jumped up to seventy-five, a speed I wasn't willing to go, as my mileage dropped substantially at that speed. I set the cruise control at seventy, which in reality, per the GPS, was an actual speed of sixty-five. There was little traffic at that point, and on the wide highway, I would not be holding anyone up rolling at that much under the speed limit.

As I rode south, the highway became busier. It started raining again late in the afternoon and dropped back into the 40s. I decided that I didn't want to set up camp in the rain, so instead I'd try to find an inexpensive motel if it continued to rain, and damn the budget.

Miles flew by. I guessed there would be plenty of options at each exit, but as afternoon turned to dusk, each exit I passed listed gas stations and fast-food restaurants, but no motels. Eventually, I saw an exit with both a "Lodging" and a "Camping" sign, so I pulled off to investigate. I found no motel or hotel anywhere, but did pass a campground that looked deserted, probably closed for the season.

I got back on the highway and continued south, scrutinizing every exit for signs of a motel. More miles rolled under me, with no signs of lodging. The highway was obviously quite new, and it appeared like the first thing to get built on the new exits were gas stations, which were plentiful, followed by fast-food restaurants, but planning and erecting hotels must take longer, and none had been built yet.

It was getting dark, but still no places appeared where I could stop for the night. I gave up completely on looking for camping, despite it having stopped raining, and resigned myself to paying whatever was required at the first motel I saw. Light had almost faded completely, and I would soon be breaking my rule to not be on the road at night, and in Michigan, the land of horse-sized deer!

I was approaching Grand Rapids, a large city, so I hoped my chances would improve the closer I got. Finally, on the north side of Grand Rapids, I spotted a motel that looked fairly pricey, but by then it had fallen completely into darkness, and I was exhausted. I figured, "What could it cost? $100?" So, I'd pay whatever I needed to. After pulling under the porte-cochère, removing my gloves, and helmet, and unzipping my jacket to get to my credit card, I entered the lobby, only to be asked if I had a reservation. I said, "No. Do I need one?" I was told there were no vacancies because there was a mountain bike rally of some sort, along with homecomings and reunions, going on that weekend, and everything was full, including the hotel next door. The clerk called somewhere further south on my route and informed me that they were also filled up. I trudged back to the bike, redonned all my gear, clicked into first gear, and headed back onto the dark highway.

The now truly Interstate-scale highway ran straight through the heart of the city. It was unnerving riding in the heavy traffic in the dark in a city with which I was completely unfamiliar. I managed to get through and emerged on the south side of Grand Rapids, where I stopped at another exit and motel, only to get the same answer: "No vacancy." But that time, at least, I was smart enough to not get out of my riding gear before asking and so got back on the highway quickly.

I made another stop, this time well south of Grand Rapids and north of Kalamazoo, again only to find no vacancies. Luckily, the clerk made a call and found a place in Allegan that had rooms. I thanked her and set out again, this time off the big highway and bound for Allegan to the southwest.

Arriving in Allegan, I took the left at the second light, as I had been instructed to do, and found the motel. I went inside to finally be told they had a room available. I said, "Fine," and pulled out the credit card, thinking that in that little sleepy country town at least I'd probably pay a lot less than I would have back on the highway in the bigger cities, when the person behind the counter said, "$150"! By that time, I was too tired to argue or to ride any further, so I paid the bill as she was telling me to be sure to not smoke in the room. "State law prohibits it."

I found the room on the second floor of the shabby, elevator-less place, a fifty-dollar room at best, and opened the door to the stench of stale cigarettes saturating the room. So much for state laws. I made a second trip to the bike for the rest of my gear and lugged it up the stairs to my "non-smoking" room. At least it was reasonably clean, and I could see the Tiger from my window. After a quick check of the forecast on television, indicating 70s and dry for the upcoming days, I hit the bed like a bag of rocks.

## TIME WITH OLD FRIENDS AND MEANDERING TOWARD THE OHIO RIVER

The motel "breakfast" I had been promised was pretty slim. I had a muffin and coffee before saying au revoir to the place. Before I fired up the bike, I texted my old high school sweetheart, my very first love, who now lived in PawPaw, situated on the same small highway I'd be following from Allegan, and asked if she fancied a cup of coffee. I told her where I was so she'd know I was in the area and not far away, and she texted back a couple places we could meet. I picked one and headed out.

The Copper Café was easy to find, being located where the road I was following crossed an Interstate highway. Her husband, Rick, with whom I'd also gone to high school, was there too. We all enjoyed talking old times and current news over an enormous breakfast. We took a few photos before I climbed back on the Tiger and was off again, heading toward my boyhood home on Redfield Road, which ran a quarter-mile north of and parallel to the Indiana/Michigan state line. On the street in front of the still-familiar house I stopped for a quick photo under the tall, old black walnut trees that still lined the roadside as they had when I was a child.

I knew my way into South Bend without the need for maps, as I had visited there several times over the years and still knew my way around the area relatively well. I was heading to see my best friend from high school, Joe, at his home on the south side of South Bend, so I entered his address in the GPS, only needing it to guide me for the last couple blocks. About noon, after a nostalgic ride on nostalgic backstreets into Indiana and through Mishawaka and South Bend, I pulled into his driveway.

My Boyhood Home on Redfield Road

Joe and I enjoyed some cold beers sitting in the warm sunshine in his backyard as we caught each other up on what had been happening in our lives. Beer followed beer, followed eventually by some Maker's Mark in his basement woodshop. Over the years, we had both become proficient at woodworking, which was a craft we both enjoyed doing and discussing. Back upstairs, we concluded the night together with his wife and some nostalgia TV, watching a series on the year 1971 that was mostly about the music of that special year, when Joe and I had just entered high school.

The following day was a rest day from the road, and Joe and I just hung out talking and mostly doing nothing. It was relaxing to not have miles to cover or a place to have to try to get to before dark. There'd be no camp to set up or break down, just the comfortable feeling of being with people I loved and knew so well.

The next morning, the road was calling again. It had been a mellow, make plans as you go trip, but I had to be back home before the end of the month to wrap up articles and photos for another magazine issue, and I had people to meet and places to go along the way, and it had now, somehow, become the twenty-fifth of October.

I leisurely packed the bike for the ride to the Ohio River, where I had already made a reservation and paid for a campsite in Ripley, Ohio. Joe handed me the Maker's Mark and told me to take it. It was still almost full. He said that he'd bought it for me, and besides, his wife didn't care for him having it around. We tucked it into a safe, padded place among my cold weather clothes in my right pannier as I continued packing. Once everything was ready, we said our goodbyes, and I cajoled another not so convincing commitment from Joe to come to Florida to visit. "The road runs both ways," I said, receiving a "Um hum" reply from my homebody high school friend.

I decided to wing it heading out from South Bend, taking random country roads east and south, with a cursory glance at the tank bag map every so often to identify those that satisfied both desirable directions by trending southeast on average. The route took me through a land of corn and wheat, filled with Amish buggies and horses trotting peacefully along the back roads, With the growing season virtually over, I was spared the usually abundant smell of manure that in the spring was spread liberally over those fields.

By the time I had reached the Ohio line, I realized I had forgotten to take my blood pressure medication that morning, so I pulled into a diner to get a coffee and to take my pill. I also hoped to find fried mush on the farm country menu, a breakfast favorite of mine that my grandmother used to make consisting of yellow corn meal, boiled, refrigerated into a sliceable loaf, then cut into slices and deep fried into a crusty golden cake that would be smothered in butter and syrup. I rarely found it anywhere except in the Midwest, especially in northern Indiana and Ohio, and to my delight, there it was on the menu. My ten-minute stop became forty-five minutes as I devoured the treat.

Satisfied, I set out again, trying to avoid big cities like Dayton, Columbus, and Cincinnati. Morning turned to afternoon, and it became obvious that my nonchalant attitude at navigation was resulting in the possibility of arriving at dusk, or worse yet, dark, so I started following my GPS obediently to make up for lost time. I had gotten about as far east as necessary, and the rest of my route was predominantly south, occasionally on major highways, although the Garmin kept its promise to "Avoid Highways" (highways being its name for what were called in the non-Garmin world Interstate highways).

As I approached the Ohio River, the sun was quickly setting, and my eyes were constantly darting side to side in search of movement possibly indicating deer. By the time I arrived at the river, the sun had set, and my senses were only tuned to the road and signs of deer that might still be visible in the waning light, provided by that time by only the blue dome of the darkening sky. At least along the river I generally had only one side with which to be concerned, the other being the riverbank or, increasingly, riverside homes. Civilization also returned, making leaping, wild creatures less likely. It was not long before I found the final, short road to Logan's Gap Camping Resort veering left off the main highway.

Pulling in, I found the office dark and saw no one around. I rode past the building and down a hill, looking for someone to ask for instructions or to just find a spot to camp and then deal with business in the morning. I passed an open, but deserted, gate and stopped, idling in front of a group of campers, to figure out my next move when I heard a voice coming from the closest camper. I killed the motor and realized it was the proprietor calling to me. He was very cordial and pointed to an empty field where I could pitch my tent. He then opened the camp store, so I could buy a drink and some food, as I'd not eaten anything since the mush early that morning. Some water and a candy bar would have to do, because the season was at its end, and the store was almost empty of everything else. The owner, hearing my plight, said he and his wife had just made a roast and would bring me a plate once I was set up.

I parked in the field and set camp. True to his word, as I finished up, the owner drove up in a golf cart with a hot plate of roast beef, potatoes, and carrots from his own kitchen. He asked nothing in return. Just a few weeks ago, he told me, he had taken over the reins of the campground, and he just wanted visitors to enjoy it. I think he will do a great job of sprucing it up and making it a pleasant place to stop. There certainly were enough amenities, such as the store, miniature golf, bath house, and a pool, and I was told on weekends there were usually activities or a band playing. All the place needed was a fresh coat of paint and some care, and he certainly cared.

Back in the sleeping bag, the only downside I could find, or rather, hear was a continuous hushed roar coming from somewhere over the hill that echoed throughout the little hollow all night. It wasn't loud enough to disturb sleep, but I wondered at the audacity of industry that they would usurp the peace and quiet in that otherwise sleepy little village. The townsfolk lived with the sound hour by hour, day by day, and night by night. I planned to try to find out what was causing it the next day, as it obviously came from the river and the direction I would be riding in the morning. I slept soundly, despite the distant roar, and awoke rested.

## KENTUCKY HILLS AND BREAKING-IN THE TIGER

The following morning, I had a bit of a problem when I was changing my tank bag maps. I discovered I was missing one map and that the map was of Kentucky, where I'd be in a very short while, after crossing the Ohio River. I'd have to give the GPS the honors of guiding me through.

Riding east along the river, I soon found the source of the hushed roar at a powerplant nearby, noisily pumping out electrons for the Ohio River Basin. In just a few miles east, I crossed the Ohio on the William H. Harsha Bridge and found myself in Kentucky. From there, I struck south through the hills toward the Tennessee line.

When I say, " . . through the Kentucky hills," I literally mean through them. A mountain wasn't a barrier to Kentucky dynamite, and most passes were a result of blasting a path through the granite heart of a ridge. Passing through some was like riding through roofless tunnels, with stone walls towering overhead on both sides of the road. However, the further I got from the Ohio River, the more gentle the hills became, and riding over them, instead, became the norm.

Riding *through* Tennessee

Before I arrived at the Tennessee line, I passed through a little town named Snow. It occurred to me that I had traveled all the way to Wisconsin to see autumn, and then in Michigan I'd passed through Winter, but it wasn't until I had traveled all this way back south that I had finally, and ironically, found Snow!

In South Bend, I'd planned in advance and had contacted a fellow "inmate" from the advrider.com forums' Tent Space Map who lived roughly halfway across Tennessee, at a place aptly named Crossville. The Tent Space Map was a map of fellow advrider.com members who had offered a place to stay for fellow motorcycle travelers, be it a space to pitch a tent, a spare guest room, mechanical assistance, what have you. I was a host, as well as a traveler who often took advantage of the list, and I'd found that both experiences had always been a pleasure. On the ride out from South Bend, I had received a reply and an invitation to set up my tent on Andy's farm in Crossville. He had asked me if a quarter-mile of gravel driveway would be a problem for me. I'd replied, "No problem,"—I mean, come on; I was riding an adventure bike! I was heading his way, secure in knowing I had a place for the night.

Tennessee was a roller coaster of green hills dotted with small farms. I rolled along pleasantly, only stopping once for caffeine in the form of some unsweetened iced tea. This time still with plenty of light, I found the gravel driveway and started down the long hill to Andy's place. The gravel was large and loose and not at all the graded and compacted path I had expected. It was also narrow and crowned, with a small trench perhaps a foot or so deep running along each side. I nervously made my way down, the front wheel wandering this way and that at its own volition, until deciding it wanted to go left more than right. I soon found myself riding in the trench on the left side of the track. I was going slowly, looking for a suitable place where I could get back up on the middle of the rounded grade when I felt the heavily-laden bike pitch to the right, and down we went. I pulled my foot out from underneath the Tiger and stood up unharmed, reaching down to hit the kill switch. There was no leaking gas—that was good.

I stepped back to take the obligatory photo to prove that the Tiger had finally been broken-in properly. After all, the Tiger had been designed for off-pavement riding, and in that scenario, a drop is expected from time to time.

Breaking-In the Tiger

I went back to the bike to assess the damage. Luckily, other than a scuffed right-hand engine guard and some chalky residue from the gravel coating the crash bars and soft panniers, all was intact and undamaged. Still, there was the problem of standing it back upright. I tried to lift it, but whether it was due to the weight of the luggage added to the heavy bike or my weakened wrist that was now filled with titanium, I couldn't budge it. I considered removing all the luggage but wasn't convinced that was the problem; rather it was just due to my weakness. I texted Andy, telling him I was in his driveway and could use a hand.

Andy arrived in a side-by-side, and we removed the easily-detached tank bag and pillion bag, packed with all my camping gear, to make lifting the Tiger a little less of a chore.

Together, we managed to get the bike back upright and on its side stand and the gear in the back of his four-by-four.

I still had half of the driveway to go, so I climbed back on the bike, and without starting the engine, I paddle-rolled it with the clutch pulled in down the ditch, which in places got deep and narrow enough to threaten to catch my left foot peg. I avoided another disaster and eventually found a path back onto the road-proper and rolled the rest of the way down in the middle of the camber to my camping spot.

While setting up, Andy and I chatted a bit about bikes and travel. I mentioned that I had intended to pitch camp and then return to the highway to pick up a sandwich and a beer for dinner to bring back to the tent, as I had only had breakfast many hours earlier, but after the recent mishap, I'd skip it and avoid riding back up and down the drive. He said, "No problem; I'll take you in the side-by-side." Thankfully, I hopped in, and we took off on a tour across the edge of his 500 acres to a gas station convenience store nearby.

By the time we got back, the temperature was falling as quickly as the sun was setting. I thanked Andy for the spot to camp, for his help with the bike, and for the ride to the store, then he rode off to his house and wife down the hill, while I climbed into my sleeping bag for the night.

## SOUTH INTO GEORGIA THEN BACK TO TENNESSEE

There was a bakery at the highway on the edge of Andy's land that tempted me with pastries and coffee, but I decided to get out on the road for a while before stopping for breakfast.

I de-camped and reloaded the bike. I considered taking a route back out on the grassy field we had taken the night before with the side-by-side, but I didn't want a little gravel to intimidate me, so I climbed back up the driveway instead, telling myself that riding up a gravel path was much easier than riding down one. I stayed in the middle of the driveway and wobbled my way up, this time making sure to not let the Tiger wander too far to one edge or the other. At the top on the pavement, I stopped to congratulate myself and punched in the next stop on the GPS.

It would not be a long ride that day, so I tapped the "Adventurous Routing" button on the GPS, instead of the normal "Go" button. Very soon, I was weaving along twisting, minor roads through the Tennessee mountains. The roads became so minor that I double-checked to make sure that the "Avoid Unpaved Roads" choice was selected before I was sent not only up and around but also off pavement.

I was heading to the home, or really the complex, of the author I had visited at the Vintage Festival, who I was either going to publish or, at least, help get his book printed. The place doubled as his BMW motorcycle repair shop and his home, set in the rolling western Georgia countryside. The rambling house and outbuildings were all built on top of wooden piers, and unique rooms were added here and there as they were needed.

When I arrived, I immediately took a shower, the first I'd had since South Bend. During and after dinner and wine, we discussed his book, and I looked over the materials he'd collected to get an idea of what it would take to get it in print.

Once finished with book business, we opened more wine and watched old footage that was featured years ago on the BBC with a segment of their travels, then wound up the evening watching footage from One Man Caravan by Robert Edison Fulton, Jr., who had ridden a Douglas motorcycle around the world back in 1932.

Soon, we were all sleepy, and after crawling into a comfortable bed in their guest room, I was serenaded to sleep by a thunderstorm lullaby.

A knock on the door in the morning announced breakfast, and because the day's ride would be just a few hours, after breakfast we leisurely walked from building to building and shop to shop while I was shown the collection of mostly vintage BMWs with a few British bikes mixed in.

I eventually loaded the Tiger again and headed back north the way I had come, all the way to Rome, Georgia, where I caught another highway running northeast past Interstate 75 and into the Blue Ridge Mountains of eastern Tennessee. The day was sunny and pleasant, with the temperature hovering in the mid-60s. I didn't bother with maps and just let the GPS make the route while I did its bidding. The last turn took me east, directly into the mountains from Etowah, out of the valley through which flowed the Little Tennessee River and Chickamauga Lake, and into Tellico Plains, planted at the western end of the Cherohala Skyway that started further east in North Carolina at Robbinsville.

It was a happy coincidence that my return south coincided with a camping weekend organized by my friends I had met through Horizons Unlimited, a worldwide online group of travelers who share information with each other on a variety of topics pertinent to world-travelers. My friends had decided, when the annual Horizons Unlimited Travelers' Meeting in North Carolina had been cancelled a couple years before, to stay in touch with each other through the Covid-19 pandemic and to get together when we could. The group had gathered at Cherohala Mountain Trails Campground, in Tellico Plains, back in April, and this weekend another campout had been planned at the same place. It would be a nice touch to finish up my ride seeing old friends before turning toward home.

I arrived mid-afternoon, with most of the group already there. While many went out on on-road and off-road rides together, I hung back and took the opportunity to take a break from the highway and catch up on my journal before leaving on the two-day final push to home in central Florida.

The sun was warm through the day, but the air held a slight edge of chill as the evening came on. A few sat down around a fire, and as evening dissolved into night, the Maker's Mark was installed atop a large log, where anyone who cared for a sip could partake. As the cold set in, more people joined the ring, until twenty or so were crowded around a roaring, warm fire. Being used to going to sleep when the sun set by that time, I retired early, leaving them to the fire, the night, shared stories, and the whiskey.

I climbed out of the tent early enough for coffee and breakfast in the campground's combination office and dining room the next morning. Having not eaten the day before, other than toast, coffee, and a granola bar, I ordered a large plate of eggs, biscuits and gravy, and bacon to regain some energy. The rest of the morning was spent catching up on writing and enjoying the warming sun, while clumps of riders went out or came back from various group rides.

A little before noon, I caught wind of a group, some riding their motorcycles and some going in cars, heading into Tellico Plains, where the Cherohala Festival was being held. I tagged along in a car, not wanting to put all my gear back on for the short ride to and from town. After exploring the little festival, complete with a town beauty walking around in a huge silk dress and posing for photos, and bluegrass music being played vigorously on an adjacent stage, our group gathered at a Mexican restaurant for lunch and conversation.

After our repast, back at the campground, there were a few hours to relax, have a beer, and chat. Later in the afternoon, the campfire was renewed, and arrangements got underway for our group evening meal. Between conversations with fellow campers scattered around under the pavilion and adding logs to the fire, the aroma of grilling hamburgers began to permeate the air, while people bustled in and out bringing side dishes and dessert. While the activity was coming to a boil, Annette, our organizer, was collecting funds to cover the meal costs and for raffle tickets supporting Rally for Rangers, a group that provided resources, particularly motorcycles, to forest rangers in far-flung and impoverished parts of the world. In return for the raffle funds raised, Rally for Rangers supplied some cups and a grand prize of a bottle of special Mongolian vodka for the lucky winners.

With afternoon giving way to dusk, dinner got underway, and we all scattered from the food line back to our perches in the pavilion to eat. When everyone was satisfied and busy digesting the meal, the pulling of the raffle tickets began, with me, alas, receiving neither cup nor vodka, but the charity receiving a couple hundred dollars toward their mission.

From the pavilion, the group migrated to the blazing campfire as darkness fell. Our friend, Dale, had died recently from Covid. As we settled into our new locations, Annette began to recount stories of Dale and reminded us of her vivacious way of living and how she always wanted others to be happy. Dale had been the life of the party and founder of the "Tequila Swilling Whores," a tongue-in-cheek name for a bunch of us who had been initiated. Her husband, Mike, who had also contracted the virus but had survived, next told the story of how the name and tradition came about when Dale and her friends had been together at their house, and he had come back to find his tequila shelf empty. Chuckles and tears followed, being slowly replaced by light banter flowing into the chilly night, while the flames licked the cold air.

## THE PUSH HOME

On the following morning it was time for me to start the several hundred-mile ride back to Florida. I grabbed a breakfast biscuit and a couple cups of coffee at the office, then settled my bill, climbed onto the Tiger, and crunched across the gravel out to the road, bound for Valdosta, Georgia, by the end of the day.

I didn't bother with maps, as much of the territory I'd be covering I had ridden many times before. I did turn on the GPS and punched in "Valdosta GA" and hit "GO," in hopes that the Avoid Highways option would keep me well clear of Interstate 75 and the huge and busy area around Atlanta and get me south of the Interstate 85 corridor, running between

Atlanta and Greenville, South Carolina. If I could avoid those areas and get south of I-85, I would be on familiar roads, which would make navigation easy. But as I rode south, it became obvious that the GPS was sending me straight into the very area I had wanted to avoid and I was getting dangerously close to the Atlanta traffic. I abandoned the GPS route and headed southeast toward Dahlonega, where I could pick up US Highway 129, and from there, no map or GPS would be needed at all.

Getting past Athens, using its simple and familiar circular bypass, sent me straight into the heart of Georgia farm country and eventually to Macon.

This day was the longest distance I'd cover on the two-day jaunt home, so I decided, to save time and ensure an arrival before dark, to take the Interstate south from Macon all the way to my friend Julie's house, just west of Exit 18 in Valdosta. I ramped up the throttle, set the cruise control at five miles per hour under the speed limit to minimize my fuel consumption, and sped south in the right lane.

I started to regret leaving my sweatshirt on under my riding jacket as the day warmed into the 80s. Luckily, other than a stop for gas, the continuous wind from my forward motion kept me cool enough to make it all the way without a wardrobe change. It had been eleven days since I'd left temperatures in the 80s and had headed out into ever increasingly chilly air.

I rode into Julie's driveway just as the sun was setting and parked the Tiger in the open garage. Inside, I shed my outer layers, was handed a beer, and ordered to relax, while Julie grilled thick steaks. Her brothers, Dan and Steve, and I chatted until the call to dinner, when I hungrily wolfed down the hot sirloin, potatoes, and vegetables.

Julie had an early class to teach in the morning at Valdosta State University, and I was exhausted, so we called it a night early, and I trundled down the hall to "Mike's Room."

Julie was already at the university when I woke up in the morning. I gathered all my things, geared up, and loaded the bike for the last time. I got on and started backing it out of the garage. The Tiger felt odd, like it was heavier than normal, although it was loaded exactly as it had been when I'd arrived. It took considerable effort to roll the bike backwards out to the driveway. I had the same feeling I'd had back at Rainbow Family Restaurant on the way north on the first day. I got off the Tiger to find a flat back tire and a shiny spot of metal in the tread.

I'd taken my time, getting up late and loading the bike in no particular hurry. After all, I was only twenty miles from Florida and 267 miles from home. I thought I had plenty of time to spare to get home before darkness. Now that had all changed. I knew from the first day of this ride, when it had taken from nine o'clock in the morning to two o'clock in the afternoon to get the tire repaired by a shop, that a dealership may not be a timesaver.

I filled up the tire, and it seemed to be holding air. The nearest motorcycle shop was only a few miles away, so I thought I could ride there and get it repaired much more quickly than I had before, having had to wait for a tow truck for hours to be taken to a shop quite a distance away. I gave the closest shop a call.

"Nope, don't have a tube that size." I tried calling other shops, one a dealership further away, but had no success. Still hoping to ride to a shop, I called a dealership when they opened at ten o'clock, only to be told by the service department that they did not have the tools to work on a Triumph. "Yeah, right," I thought, "They don't have metric tools in a motorcycle dealership service department—unlikely." They offered to look for a seventeen-inch tube—no luck. I started work to remove the wheel, thinking if Dan would drive me to a shop wheel-in-hand, then I might have more luck. As I worked I called another shop with no success, but they referred me to one that did work on tires and was not too far from where I was. I rang them—closed on Mondays.

Soon, I had the wheel completely off. I do carry the tools to fix a flat, in case I'd have one in a very isolated area where

I would have no other options . . . and that seemed to be the place I was currently, even though I was in the relatively large city of Valdosta, on a weekday.

By then I'd decided it was up to me to fix the tire. I sat the wheel down on the old carpet I'd been given to use as a workspace and got ready to pull the valve core to deflate the tube completely. I reached for my tire tools—no valve core tool. I always have at least one, but now that I needed one, it was gone. I suspected that when my experimental, tire tool-tube I had suspended from the pannier rack's rear crossbar had cracked, which I had discovered two days previously, the tool must have shaken out. I had abandoned the tool tube and relocated its contents to my left pannier, not noticing the missing tool. I had my doubts that I could get enough air out of the tube to enable me to pull it out to repair it by only depressing the valve, but I gave it a shot.

Easily enough, I popped the tire off the bead on one side, then began the struggle to pull it over the rim so I could access the tube. When I'd try prying it over the last bit, the tire would constantly reseat on the bead on the opposite side, instead of staying in the middle groove of the rim that would give me room enough to get the tire over the rim's edge. With the opposite side in the wrong position, no prying would pull the tire over.

Again and again, I tried, constantly paying attention to the location on the opposite side, trying not to let it reseat. Finally, after an hour or so, it suddenly plopped over the rim, and the innertube could be reached.

There was the tube, still inflated enough to defy my pulling it out through the narrow slot between rim and tire. All I needed was the section on the far side from the valve pulled out, because, luckily, the puncture had been there and so could be repaired without completely removing the tube. I tried letting out a little more air by depressing the valve and squeezing what I could reach of the tube inside the tire. I did that several times, until with a final mighty tug, the tube came out.

My driveway workshop

I'd not lost my patching kit from the tool-tube when the valve tool had made its escape, so after pulling out the offending nail from the tire, I roughed up the area of the puncture on the tube, coated it with cement, waiting for it to dry as instructed, then placed a patch on top, rubbing it vigorously to ensure good adhesion. I waited a few minutes, then tucked the tube back in, crossed my fingers, and hoped for the best as I spooned the tire back over the rim.

Now all together again, I attached the little portable compressor and plugged it into the bike's power lead. The tire expanded slowly, and finally, with a couple pops the beads on both sides were seated. I continued airing it up until I had reached the recommended pressure, and then waited, and waited some more. When I applied the pressure gauge to the valve, I got the same value I had when I had first inflated it—success! It had been a dirty job and had consumed a couple hours, but I was satisfied with it and my ability to get it done on my own. It had been the first time I had unmounted and remounted the wheel on the Tiger, but I didn't run into any snags. In fact, it had been easier than the same job had been on the Bonneville.

It was well into midday when I had reloaded the Tiger and had climbed back on board, bound for central Florida and home. It would be a challenge to make it in before dark. I headed back to the Interstate and decided that accepting the lower gas mileage that would entail was worth the time savings I would get, so I stayed on it, flying past the many "We Bare All" strip club signs approaching Micanopy, Florida, and continuing almost to Bushnell, where I struck out across the flat countryside, once again on old familiar roads all the way back to Lake Wales.

The sun was down when I first sighted Bok Tower on the horizon, and by the time I rolled into the driveway at home, 4,461 miles from when I had left, the skies had darkened into night. I'd been as far west as the Mississippi River and as far north in Michigan as it was possible to go. Other than the two flats, I had no problems with the Tiger and had become quite acquainted with its features and accustomed to riding it. The best part was simply getting back on the road for an extended time after the long recovery of doing virtually nothing motorcycle-related after my crash on the Blue Ridge Parkway in April. The only regret I had was not having more time to ride further and to explore more in-depth some of the places I'd gone. In time, though, there would be more opportunities to get away and more places to see. I was looking forward to that.

H stayed in hotel

# Florida Interlude

## Rally in Crystal River

The VJMC had been having a Florida Rally at Crystal River the last couple of years in November. It was only a hundred and thirty miles or so from home, and I normally tried to attend so I could get photos of the event for the magazine. In 2021 I had been asked to also lead the rides through the Florida countryside surrounding Crystal River. It was an easy enough ride up and back, leaving Lake Wales on a Friday and returning on Sunday. The club normally got a block of discounted rooms at a hotel, where they staged the rides, and my friend, Norm, who was riding up from Bradenton, was willing to share a room, making the cost of attending very economical.

On Friday, I loaded up and headed northwest through the Green Swamp, which I traversed on almost all my rides going anywhere north out of Florida, riding the twenty-mile, almost arrow-straight Highway 33, lined with forest on both sides and occasional houses set near the road with wetlands close behind them. Exiting the swamp on the north side, I turned northwest in Groveland, meandering on quiet country roads past Bushnell and toward the west coast.

I arrived in Crystal River just in time for the first ride of the day. After my old Suzuki had, surprisingly, refused to start that morning, I'd had to transfer all the gear I had on it to the Tiger and took it instead, resulting in my last-minute arrival. So after checking in quickly with the hotel desk, I was back outside to meet up with the riders. I would be leading a dozen riders on vintage Japanese bikes while in the saddle of my British adventure bike, but it couldn't be helped.

I'd laid out routes and had printed the resultant Google Map pages and inserted them in the clear top compartment of my tank bag, but I'd found the details way too small for me to see clearly as I tried to simultaneously navigate the road and peruse the tiny details of the printout. Before we got off the main highway out of town, I decided to try setting my GPS on Adventurous Routing, so I would easily know ahead of time where I'd need to make my turns, hoping it would provide a decent route. As the screen came to life, I was surprised to see it had mapped almost the same route I had so carefully planned, making my task much easier. So, following the Garmin's prompts, we headed off the busy main highway the hotel was on and turned south onto an empty road that led along the west side of Citrus Wildlife Management Area.

We turned on West Stagecoach Trail, which continued east to Floral City and our lunch destination, the Shamrock Inn. After a lunch of some of the best burgers and onion rings to be found in Florida, we were off again, riding east through a tunnel of Spanish moss-festooned oak trees out of Floral City bound for Trails End Road, a twisty excursion through the bayous skirting Flying Eagle Preserve.

We took a rest stop at what used to be Sleepy Hollow, a popular biking destination that had burned down a couple years before and was now a grassy parking area with a food truck and open space beside a portion of Tsala Apopka Lake. The lake was part of the Withlacoochee River Basin, stretching top to bottom for over twenty miles and across for at least ten, looking for all the world from the air like a coarse sponge charged with water. Islands and land arms extended everywhere, creating a labyrinth of passages with Wildlife

Riding through a tunnel of trees in Floral City

Management Areas on the north and the south ends and Flying Eagle Preserve in the middle. We took a few minutes to watch the airboats drift by and get a photo of the group before continuing our loop back to US 41 and heading back to Crystal River.

That evening we all ate at Dan's Clam Shack, less than a mile east of the hotel, one of my favorite spots for fresh seafood. Getting a group as big as ours all into a restaurant in that area was a challenge, but Dan's welcomed us with open arms and served up some great fare, with bay scallops being my favorite. The Nature Coast of Florida is a perfect habitat for those little shellfish. I'd spent some of the best afternoons of my life snorkeling and chasing after them as they squirted ahead across the grassy shallow areas of the Gulf trying to evade me. In Crystal River you could not get much closer to the source of those tasty bivalves.

Taking a break at Sleepy Hollow

Saturday morning, after a complimentary breakfast at the hotel, we gathered in the parking lot, mounting up for another ride into the countryside. The goal was to make a stop at each of the Coney Island Grills in the west central Florida region, with a challenge to have a hot dog at each of the three locations.

The original Florida Coney Island, in Brooksville, is a popular spot we often used as a starting point for rides. It is famous for being one of the places Elvis Presley had satisfied his hunger years ago. It had become so popular they had expanded into two other locations. They had the original in Brooksville, another in Crystal River, and one in Zephyrhills.

Our first stop in Zephyrhills just happened to be at the southern end of some of the best riding in Florida. Between it and Brooksville is a very hilly area that, if you didn't know better, might make you believe you were no longer in flat Florida. I let the GPS lead again as we rolled happily along on some great country roads to the Brooksville location. The last Coney Island was back in Crystal River, a little west of our base at the Holiday Inn, but most of the riders peeled off at the hotel as we passed it, having been thoroughly filled up at the other two stops. A couple other riders and I made sure to get our third hotdogs before joining the rest at the hotel, returning a little heavier than when we'd left. At the hotel we all had time to hang out together, and later, those that were not too full of hot dogs went out in search of evening meals to finish off the evening.

I had planned on heading home Sunday morning, but some members had expected a ride on Sunday to another favorite spot, Yalaha Bakery, a German bakery and deli plopped down on a hillside in the middle of nowhere. They served fabulous sandwiches and pastries and had live music on their patio on the weekends. I had no need to hurry home, and Yalaha was on one of the routes I could take in that direction, so I volunteered to lead again. Luckily for me, the stop also happened to be near my son's place in Lake County, so he was able to meet us there, giving us a chance to catch up. After a great sandwich and a wickedly delightful dessert pastry, I headed south toward home, my son drove back to Eustis, and my fellow members rode back to the hotel. The stop at Yalaha capped off a great weekend of food, riding, and fellowship with members of a great community of vintage bike enthusiasts.

## THE VJMC AT DAYTONA BIKE WEEK

As we were emerging from the winter doldrums, I had another chance to get out and ride a little. The VJMC had shifted their annual bike show, held during the first weekend of Daytona Bike Week, from Eustis to a spot much closer to the Bike Week action at the Volusia County Fairgrounds, just twenty miles from Daytona Beach and near the famous, or infamous, depending on your point of view, Cabbage Patch. All sort of nonsense went on at the Cabbage Patch all weekend, including bikini-clad women wrestling in huge mounds of coleslaw. No one claimed Bike Week was the epitomy of refined entertainment.

Again, my friend Norm agreed to share a room to save costs. He rode his Honda CB750 over on Thursday night and stayed in our guest room so we could ride together to the event the next morning and so we would only need to split the cost of a hotel room for one night.

Friday morning we left Lake Wales, and rather than deal with the heavy traffic on US Highway 27 and the even worse traffic we'd encounter on I-4, we headed up through the Green Swamp again, catching Highway 19 in Groveland and riding up into the Ocala National Forest where we could turn off and take minor roads east toward the fairgrounds, avoiding most of the traffic.

US 27 to Interstate 4 was by far the most direct route between home and the fairgrounds and would have been the most logical route had it not been for the traffic mayhem that we'd have to pass through in Orlando and the requirement of riding on one of the most dangerous freeways in the United States. Another benefit of our route was that it would pass through Umatilla, where my son was working, and I could bring him a pile of mail that had been building at our house ever since he had left home. We found the fire station easily enough and met Jacob outside for the hand-off, then we were on our way again, north into the National Forest for a short distance before turning east toward Deland and toward the fairgrounds.

The gathering of bikes and categorizing them into their classes for the show, to be held the next day, was already underway when we arrived. Norm took his place at the table promoting the club, where those who wanted to join could do so, and I went to work getting photos of the bikes already there. After working inside the large building where the show was being held, I headed out to the small swapmeet area to continue working.

Swapmeet bikes

By the end of the day, many of the motorcycles were in place, and the club members who had gathered there all headed back to the hotel, a sixteen-mile ride down the freeway to Lake Monroe. The group was gathering at a restaurant adjacent to the hotel. Norm, not being one for anything more exotic than a hamburger, headed back to our room, while I walked over and joined the rest for a steak and beer at the nearby steakhouse before heading back to the hotel.

On Saturday the building was filled with activity as the remaining motorcycles poured in before the registration deadline. This show was an unusual one for the club. Not only were vintage Japanese motorcycles welcome, but antique bicycles as well. There must be as many people owning, restoring, and showing vintage bicycles as there are doing the same with vintage motorcycles, because lined along an entire wall of the large hall were almost as many bicycles as were motorcycles in the other rows.

This bicycle had wooden "tires"

I worked through the afternoon and through the awards ceremony before deciding my work was done for the weekend and I could relax and enjoy the rest of my time there. Norm climbed back on his 750 and headed home.

Kawasaki class in the bike show

I had run into my friend, Andy, who lived in Kitty Hawk and had ridden down for the event, so decided to stay another night, sharing a room with him. We both went to dinner and afterward went looking for some entertainment before calling it a night. We walked to a nearby strip mall, passing an open door to a crowded room filled with spectators surrounding a ring and a pair of fighters duking it out. Further along we found the biggest pool room I'd ever seen. There must have been over twenty tables scattered across the huge, raucous space. We wound our way around them and found the bar at the back of the room, ordered a couple beers, and sat back to watch the people.

Sunday morning, I took a pass on riding into the mess that Daytona Bike Week had become, having been there, done that. I bid adieu to Andy and some of the stragglers from the event who had not left yet and were out in the parking lot, either loading up trailers or climbing on their bikes for their trip home. I headed out the way I had come in and made my way back home by early afternoon, arriving to a quiet house and backing the Tiger back into the garage until I'd have a chance to stretch her legs again. I didn't know it then, but I would have a chance soon enough to do some real miles on another adventure.

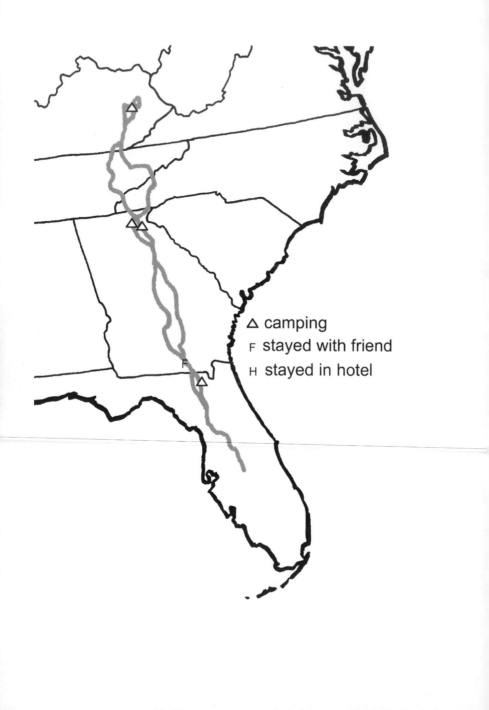

△ camping
F stayed with friend
H stayed in hotel

# Super Happy Fun Times

## Introduction

After my Upper Peninsula ride, I'd returned to my normal life in central Florida. I did manage to ride to those two club events, at least holding off my cabin fever and my blues for a while, but I found the time after returning from that long ride north awkward in some odd way. Travel changes you, but it doesn't change those to whom you return. They expect the same person they knew before, but you are no longer that person. What you experienced and felt they do not; they cannot. No one is going to share stories of the road around a blazing campfire with you or know the feeling of isolation you felt while in the northern wilderness all alone, with the strange mixture of fear and exhilaration that filled you at the same time.

So, instead, I set aside those feelings, and it was a rush back to business, trying to catch up on the thousands of emails that had come in during my absence and ramping up to gather and edit all the articles for a new magazine issue and get back to work on different books I was designing, editing, or publishing. There was not any time; between riding into the quiet driveway after so long and getting back to the business of making money, paying bills, and fulfilling obligations; to sit back and absorb what I had experienced, somehow putting it in perspective and appreciating the uniqueness of the journey. Oddly, it was a bit of a let-down returning home after accomplishing a personal goal. I always got the feeling that something was missing, and I think what that missing thing might be is pure motion, movement. I never felt truly alive or completely awake in my work-a-day world like I did on the back of a motorcycle, where goals were made daily and were distinct and solitary. There was no question to answer, other than "Where to next?"

I'd been staying in touch through weekly Zoom meetings with my friends with whom I'd camped for a short weekend on my way back home to Florida from Michigan. A Facebook group was formed, cheerily and optimistically called Super Happy Fun Times, as a place for us all to stay in touch regularly. To keep the fires alive, we were occasionally gathering to camp together, as we had in the fall. Another campout was planned for June at a different campground in eastern Kentucky called Lago Linda. Getting there and back would be a reasonably short ride: a couple days up, a couple days there, and a couple days back. I cleared my schedule and got ready to get back on the road after a long winter of being almost sedentary.

## BACK ON THE ROAD

I liked to pack and load the motorcycle the day before departure whenever I was doing rides of any significant distance. And on June sixth, all I had left inside when I went to bed were any clothing I'd be wearing the first day, my riding pants and jacket, helmet and gloves, and boots and socks. When I woke up the next morning, I simply brushed my teeth, took the one blood pressure pill I had retrieved from the already-packed pill bottle and set aside in the medicine cabinet, got dressed, and walked out the door to the waiting

Tiger. All the prep of the bike had been already completed: oil level check, water level check, tire pressure check. Other than opening the garage doors, rolling the bike outside, and climbing aboard there was nothing to do except hit the start button, thunk into first gear, and ride out of the driveway.

I'd decided I'd take two days to get to Lago Linda, stopping the first afternoon in White Springs, Florida, several miles south of the Georgia state line. I took the scenic route up, diverting from the main north/south route of busy US 27 and taking my frequent route through the Green Swamp, with a breakfast stop, again, at Rainbow Family Restaurant in Mascotte.

Time and again I'd ridden through the that area, and once on US 41 at Floral City I'd not leave it until I had arrived in White Springs. I'd traveled that course so many times before, maps and GPS were superfluous. I'd not see much I hadn't seen before, but I would be free from most of the traffic that plagues the direct route from home to the little town on the Suwanee River.

I made my way through the green horse country of Florida west of Ocala, north under shady oak trees, stopping only for gas once. The path took me back under I-75, through Lake City, one of the only busy towns I'd pass through the whole day on Highway 41, and on to White Springs.

I knew on a weekday there would be no food available at Suwannee River Resort, so I pulled into Fat Belly's Bar-N-Grill for a bite before riding to the campground. Fat Belly's is the kind of diner I always look for on the road: small, quaint, popular with the local folk, and not part of a chain. The food had always been good when I'd stopped there before, and this afternoon it was no different: simple, inexpensive, and satisfying. The only other requirement was a beer or two for camp, which I procured from the convenience store across the street. Libations squirreled away in my baggage, I turned left off the main street, crossed the brown, slow Suwannee River, and turned on the other side toward the resort.

Suwannee River Resort was a naturist campground and RV park where I liked to stop and camp on my way out of Florida, being ideally situated geographically for the final push out of the state when I was heading anywhere within an arc from due north to northeast. I had taken advantage of those types of resorts several times in the past as I'd traveled. Often, camping at them is inexpensive, and there are usually amenities like pools, hot tubs, and even restaurants, which you would rarely find at a regular campground. And a great bonus is not having to struggle getting dressed in the mornings inside a tiny three-foot tall tent before climbing out into a new day.

There is something so liberating about being outside without the "uniform" of clothes draped around you. I mostly became an advocate of freedom from clothes years before when I was sailing solo on my little twenty-five-foot boat in the Bahamas. Until then, wearing clothes was something I had just accepted. Of course, in the hot Bahamian sun, clothing was often merely a swimsuit. But the more I sailed solo, getting up in the morning, donning a suit, soaping up on deck, and jumping overboard for my morning "shower," the more absurd it seemed putting anything on—for the sake of who? I was alone. Without clothes there was no sticky salt-encrusted cloth sticking to your skin. Being bare was just more comfortable. Eventually, I just did away with what I did not need.

I imagine that when clothing was first donned by humans, it was a tool, a very useful tool. It allowed people to move to colder latitudes and hunting grounds in areas that would be too cold without some insulation. They provided a kind of moveable shelter. They also provided protection during certain tasks. I'd never dream of not wearing a riding suit when on my motorcycle; clothes are one of the tools that keep me safe, so I use them when I need them. But for much of life, they're unnecessary.

Clothing was adopted for practical purposes, but society, as society often does, developed other, more sinister purposes for it. It became a uniform, a symbol of social status, a way of separating one person from another, an outward sign of higher or lower value, elevating or lowering someone's status based purely on some material or animal skin draped over their forms. I rejected that perversion.

I also rejected the notion that something is bad about our bodies, so much so that they must be hidden from others. Perhaps it was a way for me to stand up against that mentality that was driven into me when I was a kid, that somehow who and what I am was not good enough and intrinsically bad. The Church and the scriptures had taught that God and all creation was good, so how could the bodies of the very beings that were part of that creation, who were created naked, be bad? It was all contradiction. The logic escaped me.

As soon as the bike was switched off, I was off it and stripping down in the late afternoon heat, shedding my oven of riding gear, and soon was feeling the cooling sensation of the breeze over my bare skin as I set up the tent.

Once camp was complete and all the gear I'd need for the night was zipped up inside the tent, I grabbed a towel and headed to the inviting pool, which even in early June, proved to be a refreshing reward after a long day of riding in the hot Florida sun. I sat neck-deep in the cool water with a beer in hand until it was time to wander back to the tent for sleep. The night was warm, and all that was needed was a sleeping bag liner on which to lie.

## SERENDIPITOUS DAY

I am always reluctant to put the trappings of civilization back on after some time dressed in freedom, but protection when riding was one of those times that clothing fulfilled its true function, keeping me as safe as possible as I faced the inevitable vagaries motorcycling always presented. I waited until everything was packed, slipped the riding gear back on, and rolled across the pine needle-strewn sand out of the park and back onto the pavement, bound for northern Georgia.

The ride north would be straightforward and familiar. US 41 would join US 129, of Tail of the Dragon fame, several miles north at Jasper before I crossed into Georgia. After that, all I'd have to do is follow 129 north through the sun-drenched and hot heart of Georgia, around Athens, then out the north side, into the Appalachians, all the way to Cleveland, the destination for the day. Once there all I'd need to do is find Serendipity Park, another naturist park.

The heat was almost overwhelming as I blasted north through the eastern Georgia back highways, past groves of pecan trees and fields of young corn, soybeans, and cotton plants that had only been planted recently. The agricultural activity that was, and always seems to be, in action was tree cutting and transporting. Truck trailers loaded fifteen feet high with ridiculously slender tree boles rolled past me in both directions as I rolled north. I wondered how they could possibly get much lumber from trees taken so young. I suspected that most were bound for chippers, the result to be made into the ubiquitous OSB panels used almost everywhere in construction or perhaps to be packaged as mulch or ground into paper pulp. Whatever their ultimate destination, their cutting and transportation through the hot Georgia air lent a familiar, pleasant, balsam scent to the atmosphere, a smell I specifically associate with Georgia.

Most of the ride was on almost empty US highways. The ones further from the centers of population were usually two-lane with passing lanes offered in alternating directions every few miles. As the highways flowed through more populated areas, despite the still light traffic passing north and south, they were designed with four lanes and grassy medians, as if they were Interstate highways. That made making progress easy and fast until approaching Athens, when the traffic picked up. It still flowed efficiently, however, and hopping onto the circular bypass, I soon found myself on the north side of the city and headed toward my crossing of Interstate 85, which served as a transition between Georgia's flat farmland to the south and the foothills of the Appalachians to the north.

After crossing I-85 the traffic abated, The highway I'd been on all day took me directly to Cleveland. A right when I arrived in town had me headed east on a minor state highway for just a few miles, where I turned again onto a small local road that turned into gravel as I approached the gate of the resort.

Once inside, I quickly stripped out of my hot riding gear and set up camp. Even at that little bit further north than I had been at Suwannee Valley Resort, the air was slightly cooler but still very comfortable. I'd picked some food up before arriving, so I wandered up to the pool area to have my dinner. There were a few others in the pool and on the deck. One fellow was from near where I lived in Florida, and we chatted for a while after I finished my meal.

Serendipity had nice walking paths through shady woods that led downhill to Blue Creek and back uphill back to the park. I decided to take a quick walk and "forest bathe" for a while, to stretch my legs, feel the cooler air on my skin, smell the earthy fragrance of the forest, and to listen to the subtle sounds the forest made. I wandered toward the creek, taking advantage of the short time I had before it got dark. In the shade the air was cool and comforting, a nice contrast to the heat I'd ridden through all day. I'd walked the trails there before, so I had a good idea how to snake my way down to the creekside, remembering most of the turns I'd taken before on the dirt trail. I walked slowly and as quietly as I could, hoping not to startle any wildlife hiding out under the tall trees or in the undergrowth of brush beneath them. I found the little stream bubbling and gurgling over flat heaps of rocks. I was hoping that the water would be higher than before, so I could find a little spot to swim. Arriving at the creek, I found the water level was unchanged, but I dipped my body anyway into a tiny pool for a moment to cool down before climbing the bank to the trail. I'd not seen any wildlife on my way down, but I continued to walk slowly and carefully, making sure to make only a minimum of noise as I crunched over the carpet of leaves, and kept a sharp lookout for whatever might show itself. I was rewarded when a deer appeared ahead of me, further down the hillside. It made its way quickly over the trail ahead of me and into the trees on my left. It did not appear to have noticed me, ambling along only fifty feet from the path I was walking on and made no sign it might dart off as I passed on my way up the hill.

I emerged after the sun was already behind the hills and trees, and the sky was darkening. The air temperature was dropping quickly, but it would not get cold, and I'd be able to be comfortable just in my sleeping bag liner, keeping the bag near to hand if the forecast proved to be overly optimistic.

## OVER THE SMOKIES AND INTO KENTUCKY

In the morning, I made my way east toward US441, there turning north toward Tallulah Falls and the North Carolina state line. Before I left Georgia, I stopped in Clayton at a diner called the Rusty Bike Café, where I recalled having had great breakfasts on earlier trips I'd made through the area. And just as I'd remembered, the food was still delicious, but what had transpired since the last time I'd eaten there was the 2016 election. The place was festooned with Trump signs and a signed photo from Don Junior himself, thanking them for their support. I had remembered the place as being eclectic and quaint with a friendly atmosphere, but it now had a definite vibe of "If you're not for Trump, get out," which some of the signs declared, in not so many kind words. I ate my breakfast in silence, not really wanting to believe what I was seeing. One of my favorite stops had become a den of partisanship. I get political differences, but don't understand the hate to which they had recently seemed to have given birth. I was glad to get out of there and back on the road.

The challenge of the day's ride would be to get around the busy traffic concentrated around the Great Smoky Mountains National Park and Gatlinburg on its north edge. While a stunningly beautiful area, because of that beauty and its location near the East Coast and proximity to large interior and coastal cities, it was also the most visited National Park in the country. With that came traffic, slow traffic. The straightest and shortest route between Cleveland and Lago Linda was straight across the Smokies on US 441, which split the National Park into an eastern and a western half as it climbed over the mountain ridge, but it was also the only route into Tennessee for at least fifty miles. Avoiding it meant circumnavigating the park around the southwest by means of Deal's Gap and the Tail of the Dragon, also chock-full of traffic, mostly motorcycle, challenging themselves on its 318 curves, or by means of Interstate 40 on the northeast side. I chose the latter.

I made my way north toward Cherokee, which sits on the southern edge of the National Park where US 441 starts its ascent to Newfound Gap. Before I reached Cherokee, I turned northeast at Franklin toward Waynesville and I-40. Traffic was heavy on the freeway, with it being the preferred truck route between Asheville, in North Carolina, and Knoxville, in Tennessee. It was also climbing and winding its way over the mountains, with the truck traffic slowly chugging up in the right lane while cars blew past at high speed in the left. It was a white-knuckle ride, but the least of the three evils I had to choose from.

I kept my speed up and watched my mirrors like a hawk, blasting around trucks when I could or matching their slow progress uphill until I could pass them safely. I-40 rounded the corner of the Smokies and, once on the north slope, turned west toward Knoxville on its way to its distant end in Barstow, California. I turned north onto Interstate 75, away from the city. Although I was still on a freeway, traffic thinned out considerably as I made my way into Kentucky and toward the town of London, where I would turn off and once again be on quiet, two-lane state roads all the way to the campground where all my friends were already gathering.

The further north I'd ridden, the cooler the air became, until I was riding along in beautiful high-70s under sunny, early-summer skies. As I approached my destination, the Garmin displayed my icon floating over fields, valleys, and hills. I realized its maps had not caught up with new road construction in the area, as I was rolling on new, black asphalt roughly parallel to the road the GPS showed nearby that I thought I was on. I figured out the discrepancy and had no trouble quickly re-orienting myself and becoming comfortable with the GPS showing my icon flying over a roadless countryside.

It was perfect weather when I arrived at Lago Linda, a beautiful, over four-hundred-acre campground, formerly used for equestrian purposes but now a quiet country campground for both RVs and tent campers, and especially motorcycle travelers. The campground had hosted over one hundred riders during the Red River Scramble just the previous September and would host it again in 2022. It was close to the 29,000-acre Red River Gorge Geological Area, where the river had gouged out a deep canyon in the sandstone, creating cliffs, waterfalls, and more than a hundred natural arches, and within which was a lacework of trails and both paved and unpaved roads. In other words, a dual-sport paradise.

Most of our group had already arrived and had set up their trailers or tents around the property. The tents had taken advantage of the roofed, re-purposed stables, whose floors were now covered in soft sawdust with one side open to the pavilion and fire ring area up the hillside. There were two of these buildings below the pavilion where everyone would be gathering. The lower one only held one tent, while the top one had already been filled up, so I rode the Tiger down to the second and set up in the opposite end from my campmate's tent.

After pitching the tent and getting my camp clothes on, I wandered up to the pavilion to greet and be greeted by my family of friends. It was after six. Most of those who had been out riding had returned, and everyone was gathering for conversation, beers, and preparation of dinner.

Next to a hot, cooking fire pit, a long table was covered with pulled chicken, cheese, and peppers, while a cast iron skillet filled with corn and other goodness sizzled on the grill. I grabbed a couple freshly-grilled tortillas and loaded them up. We all gathered in the pavilion for our repast, washed down with more than a few beers. Conversation flowed along with the beers through the rest of the afternoon and into the night after we had all relocated to the nearby campfire. The rest of the evening was spent in conversation, joking, and tall tales until tiredness crept in and we slowly dispersed to our tents, RVs, or cabins.

## Tasty and Twisty Exploration

I took my time getting up and dressed and then joined my friends up the hill, where conversation was already bubbling up here and there. I brought my Dragonfly stove up, and borrowing some water, put it on to boil to make a pot of cacao. I got the water boiled and in the French press before a leak from my supply connection began a small fire on the picnic table on which it had been sitting. It was caught quickly and put out before any damage was done. I'd have to remember to repair that when I got home. I poured myself a cup and offered some to my companions, Theresa and Tracy, who gave it a taste and a thumbs-up.

It was discovered that the kitchen was open at the campground office, so we wandered up for some breakfast there before people, singly or in small groups, wandered off to explore the area. Having ridden so far just to get to Beattyville, I did not want to do a long, hard ride, but I did want to take a short jaunt to do a little scrutiny of the area on my own.

I looked at my maps and decided on a road that looked squiggly enough to be entertaining that would form the western leg of a roughly triangular loop, eventually returning to camp. Most of the group had already ridden off when I headed northwest on Kentucky 52 toward Ravenna, where I came across an unusual diner in an unusual building with an unusual name, and a parking lot filled with my fellow riders' motorcycles.

The Wigwam

I parked up in front of the Wigwam among my friends' bikes and entered the little eatery crammed in the wedge between the highway and a little side road that ran back into a residential part of the tiny community. The Wigwam had been there for almost as long as I'd been alive, having been opened in June of 1957, just a couple months after I was born. The feature that stood out, and which explained the name, was the cone shaped roof above the entrance. Apparently, the highway it sat on had been a popular cruising road for teenagers back in the fifties and sixties, and these days many come from miles around to eat there on weekends, due to its history, ambience, good food, and low prices.

My friends had mostly finished their meals, but I sat down with a few stragglers who were finishing up while I ordered a huge burger and fries. As riders trickled out, I decided I was going to have dessert, having seen butterscotch pie on the menu. I was slightly disappointed when I was told they had sold out of butterscotch, but undaunted, I ordered blueberry instead, which I calculated had to be good as well. "I'm on vacation, so why not?" I justified to myself. But what arrived at my table was not a slice but a full quarter of a pie. I was already stuffed from the burger, but in the spirit of adventure, I ordered black coffee to wash it down and tucked into it, until even I was surprised when I pushed an empty plate away from me and asked for the check.

When I left the diner, I was once again alone and set out in search of the squiggly line I had spotted on the map earlier. I rode further west to the adjacent little town of Irvine, looking for the bridge I'd need to cross the Kentucky River, where I'd pick up McKee Road, also known as Kentucky 89, for a run south on the west side of the triangle. As I approached the bridge, I saw a sign declaring "Bridge Out!", so I adjusted my course back onto the main highway for a short while until I found the next bridge over the river. Once across, I made my way back along the river's edge to where the closed bridge had crossed, then turned onto McKee Road and headed south out of town.

I twisted and turned along valleys, tracing the edges of the hills, climbing up and down ridges toward Foxtown. Eventually, I emerged into the narrow valley that contained

Bill's Branch that spilled me and the creek into Pigeon Roost Creek and the little town of McKee. I turned left onto US421 following the creek just a couple miles to a small state road that curled up and away into the hills again and back to Beattyville and Lago Linda.

Back at camp, we gathered under the pavilion roof for beer and talk, while waiting out light showers that passed through from time to time. By mid-afternoon, the riders had returned, and we turned our attention to dinner. Again, food was laid out and we partook with gusto, although I kept it light after having gorged myself at the Wigwam.

The showers soon dissipated, and evening darkness overtook the grounds as we gathered around the campfire once more, sharing stories of where we'd ridden that day and sharing ideas for the next. Theresa had taken the opportunity of being in eastern Kentucky to bring back a bottle of fine Angle's Envy bourbon. Soon, cups were passed. The warmth of the fire in front of me matched the warmth inside brought on by the bourbon as the night wore on and conversation was passed through the licking flames of the campfire. Another cup or two and I was ready for my sleeping bag.

## RED RIVER GORGE

The morning brought sunshine and another breakfast at the campground office, and again, riders began heading out on various routes to discover what they could of the area. I decided to head north that day. After breakfast, I mounted up and headed north toward Slade, on the southwestern corner of the Red River Gorge Geological Area. There, the Bert T. Coombs Mountain Parkway sliced across the south edge of the Red River Gorge, with its western terminus intersecting I-64 near Winchester and ending in the east at Salyersville. The parkway was a modern Interstate-like highway that charged east, straightening out the natural curves it passed through. Instead, I chose Compton Road, the old route that bounced along the mountains beside, under, and above the parkway, following the ancient curves the parkway ignored.

I had only gone less than five miles when I spotted a sign for Tunnel Ridge Road as I passed it. I'd heard the others talking about an interesting single-lane tunnel in the Red River Gorge, so I made a U-turn back, hoping I'd found a route to it. Crossing over the parkway, I found myself on gravel and winding my way into the forest. I didn't recall anyone mentioning the tunnel was off-pavement but decided, based on what the name of the road suggested, that it must be the way. The gravel was not deep and the sub-surface below it was solid, so the only thing to have concern for was not slamming into the numerous potholes scattered along the road.

I rode surrounded by trees on both sides and overhead as I climbed and descended, twisted, and turned my way through the Red River Gorge for miles, passing turnouts for campgrounds and hiking trailheads. There was no sign of a tunnel, so I pulled into Pioneer Parking Area, figuring I must be near the gorge, to look around. There was also a sign indicating a waterfall, so I hiked into the woods on a barely discernible path, but only found a few tents and other spots that obviously had been used by campers, but no signs of either the falls or the gorge. It didn't matter much, though; it felt good to just walk and take a break from the saddle for a while.

Back at the parking area, I took advantage of a bathroom there, on the side of which was posted an official-looking notice to "TAKE CAUTION! HIKERS AND CAMPERS BE AWARE" of an "unclassified wild creature," with a centered photo of something akin to a great ape or a sasquatch. Its legitimacy was attested to by it having been posted by the Department of Zoology of Miami (Ohio) University. I didn't feel too vulnerable there but had decided I was not going to find the tunnel on that route, anyway, so turned around and found my way back out of the woods the way I had come in, off the gravel, and onto Compton Road.

*Be on the lookout for Bigfoot, Sasquatch, or the the Skunk Ape*

I rode east to Compton, where I turned off to make my way north along the east side of the gorge area. At Denniston I turned west again, catching State Highway 77 south toward the Red River and its gorge. Highway 77's bridge leaped across the gorge where it also become known as Nada Tunnel Road. I was in luck and had found the right route to the tunnel and saw it only a couple miles after crossing the river. I pulled over onto a narrow strip of gravel just before the dark tunnel ahead and beside the yield sign where motorists had to wait until the tunnel was clear of oncoming traffic. I climbed off and took a couple photos before continuing through the ragged and raw hole in the rock and under Tunnel Ridge Road, which I now understood had, indeed, reached the tunnel but had passed over the top of it on the gray rock towering above me now.

The road spit me out at, where else, Nada, where I rejoined the highway on which I had ridden up. At Zachariah, I diverted onto another, smaller route that shot me south through a series of valleys and over ridges toward Big Sinking Creek, northwest of Lago Linda. From there it was a very short ride beside the stream before I was back at camp and opening a cold beer.

Nada Tunnel

It had been a glorious day of riding and a great chance to get practice on the Tiger off pavement and to see a little bit of the natural wonders that attracted so many people to the Red River Gorge area. I'd missed a lot. Looking back over the maps I saw I'd missed a couple natural arches, waterfalls, and what looked to be what must be a spectacular road running through the gorge directly beside the Red River. I made a mental note to make sure I revisited that area again one day.

Back at Lago Linda, rain had appeared and fell in light sprinkles for just a couple hours. When it had stopped, I decided to take a walk down the hill to the lake and work a little on my writing. I discovered Heather at the shore, trying her hand at fly-fishing and catching a few small bream. I sat on a small dock and wrote and watched, while a few others wandered down, including Brent, the fly-fishing expert among us, who joined Heather, giving her some tips and guiding her to possibly good fishing spots. I decided to take a short hike along the creek that was spilling out below the pond. I put my stuff away and wandered down the path below the levee that held the pond back and into the woods on a two-track trail into the cool shade of the forest. I meandered down the path for a mile or so, making short investigatory jaunts here and there down to the little creek I was following, then back up and continuing along on the two-track, which dwindled and narrowed as I found my way further and further downstream. I didn't come across any wildlife, but just being soaked in the atmosphere of the woods was enough. Satisfied with my exercise, I retraced my steps uphill to the pond and back to the pavilion.

As the afternoon wore on, other riders straggled back, and a big feast was planned, for which we all pitched in. Everyone was involved in something: cooking, laying out plates and utensils, or having beers and chatting. After eating, another ring around the campfire was formed and we settled into chairs or on logs close to the warmth of the flames as the night air cooled. Talk went into the night, and more bourbon appeared as we all shared the camaraderie only a group of like-minded motorcycle riders could provide. But the next day was Sunday, and it would be time to head back to our homes, so I left the circle before it got too late and walked to my tent and sleeping bag.

## SOUTH TO SUCHES

As the sun came up, I crawled out of my tent and headed up the hill. The first order of business was breakfast, which I found at the office, where other campers had gathered for a bite and hot coffee. That gave me the chance to say my goodbyes to my fellow riders before I returned to my campsite. I packed up my dry tent, thanks to the overhead shelter the stable had provided, eliminating the otherwise inevitable dew. With everything gathered up and installed on the back of the Tiger, I rode up toward the pavilion across the grass and rolled up the gravel driveway, waving goodbye to my friends as I passed them on my way up the hill and out into the warm air already suffusing the eastern Kentucky air.

I was gifted with good weather as I rolled south through the soft, rounded mountains of Kentucky on small highways. I aimed for Sweetwater, Tennessee, between Chattanooga and Knoxville, where I could jump across the I-75 and US 411 corridor between the two busy cities into the Blue Ridge with a minimum of traffic on Route 68. Once across 411, I was almost immediately in the major mountain ridge of the Blue Ridge Mountains and in quiet, forested hills. Tellico Plains lay ahead and would be an option for camping, as I knew of two campgrounds there, both of which I had used before, that catered mainly to motorcycle riders and would be conveniently on my way.

I'd made better time than I thought I would, and by the time I reached Tellico Plains, there was still plenty of afternoon left to ride, so I made the decision to continue south into Georgia before stopping for the day. From Tellico, Highway 68 ran south, and I had a fun ride on one of my favorite mountain backroads, taking the turn left at Turtletown onto an even smaller twisty road heading southeast into Georgia and toward Blairsville.

By the time I reached Blairsville, it was late in the afternoon. I decided to stop for the night in Suches, not much further south. When I spotted a busy barbecue restaurant, I pulled in to have some dinner, so I would not have to run a meal down in the little town of Suches, which was comprised of a smattering of houses, the campground for which I was bound, and a convenience store and gas station. I wanted to have a light dinner after the feasting we had done at Lago Linda all weekend, so I ordered a salad with pulled chicken, but what arrived on my table was an acre of greens with a mound of steaming meat balanced on top. So much for a light meal, I tucked into the hill of salad and chicken and somehow got it all down. I couldn't complain; it was delicious.

Back on the pavement, I chose US 129 for the ride out of Blairsville. Tail of the Dragon was miles further north from where I was now, but south of Blairsville was something similar: a section of highway running south to Turner's Corner where the curves were plentiful but which were curves that could be taken at much higher speeds than those on the Tail. That section brought many sport bike riders to it, where knee-dragging was the norm as fast bikes and riders raced to Turner's Corner, where they could meet up with other riders and share stories of their high-speed exploits. Before I got to the more intense section beyond Vogel State Park, I turned off on a slower, but no less technical riding road called Wolf Pen Gap, which twisted and turned all the way into Suches and to Two Wheels of Suches, the motorcycle-only campground I had been aiming for.

I decided to treat myself and took a small cabin for the night, allowing me to bypass setting up the tent and all that entailed and, even more so, avoiding all the repacking I'd normally have to do the next morning.

It being late afternoon at the end of a weekend, the grounds were quiet, with only scattered tents still pitched here and there across the large grounds. The afternoon was almost gone by the time I deposited my stuff in the cabin. As the sun dipped behind the western ridges and the air began to cool, I wandered over to the convenience store to see if I could get a beer to have back at the cabin, but it being Sunday, beer was not an option, so I grabbed a coconut water instead and headed back across the road to Two Wheels, where I sat on the diminutive cabin porch sipping my cold drink as the day turned into night before I turned in.

## Going to See an Old Friend

Getting the bike ready to roll that morning was easy, with no need to reattach all my camping gear. I went down to the bath house to brush my teeth and take my medicine, and then all that was left to do was throw the toiletry bag in one of the panniers and cinch it up. I was on the road early, heading south on Highway 60, which ran past Two Wheels and caught back up with US 129 after exiting the mountain ridges at Gainesville.

Riding through Gainesville toward the eventual meet-up with 129, I spotted a little roadside diner, Stan's Biscuits, and pulled in, having worked up an appetite over the last forty miles. Armed with new energy I went back out to the bike ready to face the rest of the ride in the hot Georgia sun to Valdosta and my old high school friend's place.

Before I'd left town, I was back on 129 and running southeast toward Athens, now on an increasingly crowded highway as I approached the city. I'd ridden that route so many times before it was almost second-nature. I easily found my way around Athens on the loop road and was quickly leaving it behind and reentering the Georgia farmland I'd ridden through a few days before.

I continued following US 129 south away from Athens and through Madison, which was filled with an eclectic mix of white ante-bellum homes, early twentieth-century houses looking much like our four-square 1914 bungalow in Florida, 1960s houses, and contemporary mobile homes. I passed Eatonton and Gray and finally the big town of Macon, where I often jumped on the Interstate for the run down to Julie's place. This time I skipped the Interstate and stayed on 129 in the countryside east of I-75 all the way to Ocilla, where I turned southwest toward Tifton, where I'd finally connect with the big freeway for the short ride south to Valdosta. Passing through Tifton, I noticed a huge, fenced yard full of rusting motorcycles, metal, and chrome. Motorcycles were packed so closely they might as well have been stacked on each other, and probably some were. I made a note of its location and a plan to return one day to rummage through the priceless artifacts in hopes of finding a gem, in part or whole, of a vintage motorcycle.

At Exit 18, I turned off onto a small Georgia State Highway for the short run west to Julie's. After four miles, I rolled off the road and into Julie's small quiet, pine-shaded neighborhood and into the pine straw carpeted driveway to Julie's garage.

Julie greeted me with a big hug and a beer. I finally grabbed a much-needed shower while Julie prepared dinner. The rest of the night was spent in conversation, the kind that only old kindred spirits can have, who've experienced much of their formative lives together and who share similar outlooks on life and art. We didn't stay up late; we had the entire following day to spend together. I had decided one afternoon with my friend was just not enough.

## A Day Off

There'd be no riding this day. It was set aside for just Julie and me, and anything we might want to do. It started with hot, black coffee in the early morning behind her house staring into the woods that filled her back yard and thickened along the back of the property. We sat for a long time, drinking the black liquid and talking, while watching little russet cardinals flitting here and there, fighting over seeds Julie had provided. After we'd had enough coffee, Julie whipped up a quick breakfast for both of us.

The grass in Julie's front yard was getting high, and I noticed a riding mower sitting there. Earlier I had noticed a mower sitting in the back yard as well, so I asked Julie what was up. She had borrowed the mower in the front from her brother, who lived just a couple doors over, when hers, the one in the backyard, had quit working. She thought the belt must have snapped on hers. And apparently, her brother Steve's, which she'd borrowed to finish up the yard, had quit working too. I decided mower repair would be my afternoon task.

We wandered outside to the disabled mower in the front yard. I opened the hood to see if I could figure out what had gone awry. There was an obviously blown main fuse, so I expected a repair could be accomplished easily. I hopped into the passenger seat of Julie's Honda Ridgeline, and we headed into town to find an auto parts store, where we found a fuse that would work and brought it back to install it. But no luck. I investigated further and, by process of elimination, ascertained that the only possibility left was a bad starter solenoid. Steve would have to pick that up himself later but could install it himself easily and be back in business. So, the front yard mower mystery being solved, if not fixed, I turned my attention to Julie's in the back yard. I laid down beside it and looked underneath. The belt was all there and had only jumped off the pulleys. Fifteen minutes later, I had the belt back on. It felt good to do something to help Julie after she had been so kind and welcoming so many times when I had passed through on my way north or south.

Mower work behind us, we opened more beers and cooked more food then hung out the rest of the evening, simply enjoying each other's company.

## HOME . . . FOR A WHILE

The next morning, after a coffee and quick breakfast, I was back on the road, leaving the quiet street of Julie's neighborhood behind and rolling southeast toward I-75. Highway 41 went in the general direction I was headed but was several miles east of the Interstate and required me passing through the city to get to it. I'd decided to make some time and jump south on the slab, rather than go out of my way to the east, but only as far as Lake City, a little over seventy miles away, where 41 would eventually cross and flow southwest into the mostly empty pine woods and horse country of northwestern peninsular Florida.

By one o'clock the heat was on, and I needed a rest and something cold to drink, so at Williston I pulled into a McDonalds for iced tea and a little time off the bike. Back on the highway I was on a route I knew intimately, and so I ignored my GPS and navigated my way south by memory. I turned off Highway 41 at Floral City and once again rode the tunnel of trees in that little village, in reverse of my ride up. I hurtled toward Bushnell, passed under I-75, then followed my usual route through Center Hill to Groveland. Twenty more miles of straight and boring road got me to my cutoff to Haines City, where I turned south on Highway 17 for the rest of the way to my hometown.

Arriving in Lake Wales, I only had two turns through our little neighborhood before I was parked up in the drive and was unloading the Tiger at 4:30. It was the 15th, and I had yet another journey to make on the 21st, this time to Arkansas on a working ride to document the VJMC National Rally being held in Eureka Springs.

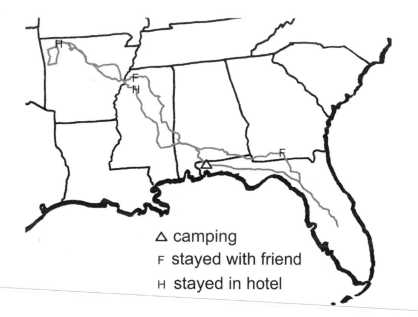

△ camping
F stayed with friend
H stayed in hotel

# This Time Northwest

## And I'm Off Again!

I'd not been home long from the Super Happy Fun Times camping trip before I had to prepare for another ride, this one to work, not that I would not have a lot of fun while there. The VJMC was holding their national rally in Eureka Springs, Arkansas, and of course, I'd need to be there to do the photography. I was glad they had chosen a venue located more in the middle of the country than they'd been held for a while, giving those in the West and the Midwest the chance to attend without too long a trek to get there, not to mention the beautiful riding to be had in the Ozarks. In addition to meals and a big bike show, a highlight of these rallies is group riding, and Arkansas would not fail to impress.

I'd just arrived home from the camping trip and needed to catch up on business before leaving again for the rally in Eureka Springs on a Tuesday in order to arrive on the first day of the rally, Thursday, June 23. That gave me only a week to catch up and to prepare for things that would have to be done while I was away. Luckily, I had already completed publishing two books and had no other irons in the fire in June, so the publishing work would not be demanding. The June magazine issue had recently shipped, and work had to begin on the next issue, but I would not have to have the articles to the designer until around the first of July, which meant I could squeak this ride in without upsetting the scheduling apple cart too much.

By Tuesday morning, I was ready to ride again. It would be a three-day ride to Eureka Springs. I consulted the ADV Tent Space List and found a host in southern Georgia on the general route I'd take toward Arkansas. I messaged Josh and got the green light to stay at his place the first night. So, I set my sights on Thomasville, Georgia, a bit less than three hundred miles from home.

I was out of my driveway and on my way before eight o'clock and worked my way via my usual route toward the northwest, making a stop in Mascotte for a quick and cheap breakfast. I cut across the state until I reached US 98 for the run north-northwest along Florida's Nature Coast, but instead of running all the way to Perry before peeling off, I turned north at Old Town, taking less familiar, small country roads across the root of the Panhandle, across Interstate 10, which dips its toes in the St. Johns River, in Jacksonville, then runs across the US to dip them again in the Pacific in Los Angeles.

I crossed the state line less than fifteen miles north of Madison and rolled into Georgia aiming for Quitman. From there it was twenty-five more miles to Thomasville and my refuge for the night.

Josh had the garage of most riders' dreams, with everything you'd need to work on or store your motorcycles, while enjoying cold beers pulled from the garage refrigerator, and one door away from a bedroom and bathroom. I rolled the Tiger in, and Josh and I immediately hit if off over a couple beers, sitting in the garage on the overstuffed couch and talking bikes and motorcycle travel. Josh obviously leaned toward dirt riding, attested to by the dirt bike perched on a work stand in the middle of the space.

After I'd deposited the gear that I'd need for the night in the bedroom and having changed into shorts and a T-shirt, I headed through the bedroom and out the other side to the backyard and pool, where his kids were soon frolicking while we cooled off in the refreshing water. It had been a hot day, and we lingered in the pool until we got hungry. Josh whipped up some tortillas and fillings for burritos, and we all sat down and ate until we were full.

After dinner the kids got out a card game, gave me a quick introduction and synopsis of the rules, then Josh and I played with them until it was time for sleep.

### DESTINATION UNKNOWN

I got up early, and with Josh's help, I rolled the Tiger out into the already warm South Georgia sunshine. I bade farewell to Josh, reminding him that if he ever was in Florida, he would have a place to stay at our house, then rolled back out of the neighborhood and onto the highway heading southwest.

Josh had said that Thomasville was known for its many plantation houses, and there was no shortage of large, white, pillared mansions as I whizzed past them angling back toward Florida, where I'd loop under Lake Seminole, fed by the Chattahoochee and Flint Rivers and nestled in a little notch in the Florida Panhandle. I left US 379 and made my way west below the lake on a variety of small state and local roads until I rejoined Highway 90 at Chattahoochee, on the southern extremity of the lake where the two rivers flowed out as one, now as the Apalachicola, which would finish its run at the Gulf of Mexico, seventy-five miles away.

I stayed on 90 until Marianna, where I succumbed to the temptation of The Waffle Iron and pulled in for breakfast. It was another of my ideal kind of breakfast joints, filled with locals talking about the peanut harvest and other matters of interest to the citizens of Marianna and with cheap, basic breakfast fare served up with hot black coffee. I knew a peanut farmer from the vintage motorcycle club, so as I checked out, I asked if they knew him, as it was obvious most of their clientele were or had been local farmers. Surprisingly, they didn't know him, but unsurprisingly, it was not surprising when I found out later I'd had the name of the town where Larry lived completely wrong.

Back on the road, I veered off 90 into the west-northwest toward Graceville, a village barely four miles from the Alabama state line. From there, I turned due west on a little state road for about thirty miles, where I turned right and shot quickly into Alabama.

I had a reason for going that way instead of more directly northwest toward my final destination of Arkansas. Andrea had been watching Hometown, an HGTV show about a couple slowly working on restoring the homes in their hometown, Laurel, Mississippi, and I was on my way to see if I could spot any of their work there. It was not far out of my way, and I thought I might be able to get some photos of some of the places we'd seen renovated on the show, and who knows, perhaps even catch them working on one. Once I had gotten several miles into Alabama, I turned toward the west-northwest and the town of Opp, sticking on minor state and local roads as I rode through fragrant pine woods and through tiny settlements. At Opp, I caught US Highway 84, still a relatively small, two-lane back road, which I followed all the way across the Mississippi state line. Within forty miles I was in Laurel.

The television show portrayed Laurel as a tiny, traditional, southern town, While it would still be considered a small town, I found it bigger than I'd imagined. Unlike so many other small southern towns that usually have the main highway as their main street with neighborhood side streets branching off left and right until the highway exited on the far side of town, US 84 ran into the city whereupon a spiderweb of roads wriggled in every direction, with 84 being swept down and around the south side of the center of town. I rode straight ahead until I found a parking lot with a shady tree where I cold stop to figure out how I might go about finding one of the homes from the show. By then it was blazing hot, and I was glad to have shade under a lone, miniscule tree planted near a sidewalk in a relatively empty, large parking lot adjacent to Pine Burr Apartments. The show had done a couple episodes on commercial projects, and the name sounded a bit familiar, so I took a photo, but nothing else looked familiar. Where were the quiet residential neighborhoods the show portrayed? I saw only malls and commercial districts. I called home and let Andrea know where I was but that it did not look hopeful for finding any of the places we'd seen in various episodes. Besides, the heat had gotten so extreme that to just sit still meant my clothes would be saturated with sweat quickly. I decided the quest was not worth the effort and pulled back out into traffic, bound for the far side of town. I still kept an eye out, but I was not going to try to chase down any of the places in that heat.

Once past the middle, at least what passed as the middle, as I never did find a "downtown," I turned north out of Laurel, aiming for Memphis, where I considered crossing the Mississippi River the next day. I'd not planned out my stopping point for the day and was now in the steamy afternoon hours. I rode smaller state roads, and as I got further north, I started to look for those iconic brown, tent-icon camping signs. By the time I had crossed the Choctaw River, near Philadelphia, I'd still seen no signs and the sun was heading for the horizon. By Kosciusko, where I crossed the famous Natchez Trace Parkway, the situation was the same.

It was close to sunset. By Grenada, my luck had run out as the sun had retreated behind the trees on my left. Not willing to risk another deer strike in this forested state, I jumped over to Interstate 55, thinking that the chances of having wildlife leap in front of me would be less on the big, divided freeway than on narrow, tree-lined, rural roads. By then, I had given up all hope of finding a tent space and figured that at least along the Interstate I'd eventually find a hotel. The Interstate proved not to be much of an advantage as far as wildlife went, because other than it being a divided highway, it had little traffic, no lighting, and was passing through the same forested areas I had been in earlier in the day.

At Batesville, just a hundred miles short of the crossing of the Big Muddy, I spotted a Hampton Inn and exited to find a room. I was not happy about the unexpected expense, but it was my fault for not planning better. Fortunately, on the same sideroad beside the Interstate was a Cracker Barrel restaurant, so I didn't have to go far to get my dinner. Back at the room, I got a shower and settled in for the night, knowing I'd not have to worry about finding a place to sleep the next day, as I had already made reservations at the Eureka Springs Best Western where the all the activities of the National Rally were being held.

## EUREKA!

By morning I had reconsidered my choice to cross the Mississippi River at Memphis. My originally intended route would have been faster, but I'd also have been dealing with Interstate traffic all the way from Batesville to the western bank of the big river in Marion, Arkansas. I decided, instead, to cross at Helena, Arkansas, the next bridge south of the large city of Memphis. It was just fifty miles away on the far side of the river from the Isle of Capri Casino that I had passed several times before. The route would entail riding north after crossing the Mississippi, then turning west, crossing above Little Rock to avoid city traffic, and staying on a series of minor state roads. It would be out of the way compared to a direct route and more complicated to find the many turns, but I'd ridden through the area before, so that second part would not prove to be too difficult. Once past Little Rock, however, I could catch US Highway 65 all the way to Harrison, which would connect to Route 62 for the final run into Eureka Springs.

Both highways kept me chugging northwest along a narrow passage between the taller main body of the Ozarks on my left and smaller hills in the range that reached north toward the White River, which zig-zagged in and out of the Arkansas and Missouri border.

The mountains started growing again as I approached Eureka Springs in a branch of the Ozark Mountains reaching northwest across Dick's Creek, which after flowing through miles of tortuous twists and turns, many lakes and dams, would eventually become one with the White River far west of where the creek had begun.

After a little confusion and an accidental tour of the popular tourist town, I eventually found the Best Western Inn of the Ozarks, where the rest of the membership was gathering. I popped into the office, picked up my keys and found out my room number, and was soon unloaded. I changed into my off-bike clothes and wandered down the hill through the series of parking lots to the convention center.

At the club desk, I checked in and spent some time catching up with friends who had come for the rally. Many bikes were already inside the building, although the bike show would not be for two more days. Trucks and bike trailers were scattered across the parking lot adjacent to the building, and members were gathered in the shade of awnings next to their vehicles and trailers. There was not much for me to do until dinner, when we would all be together inside the center for a communal meal and fellowship, so I climbed back to my room, laid on the bed, and relaxed in air-conditioned luxury.

Evening brought me back down the hill to the convention center for the meal. No one ever loses weight at a regional or national VJMC rally, and this one was no different. I entered the dining room to find a buffet of barbecue and sides thirty feet long stretching across one end of the room, while white, tableclothed, circular tables, each able to seat a dozen, filled the rest of the huge room. I got to work documenting the buffet and crowd in photos while people trickled in and occupied the tables. Dinner was soon underway. Table by table proceeded to the buffet and wandered back to their seats with plates overflowing with some of the best food I remembered ever having at one of those rallies. The rally's first night's dinners are usually informal, a time to gather and get back up to speed with friends who may not have seen each other for months or even years. So other than a couple announcements, the night was one of conversation, jokes, and more pie and hot coffee until the wait staff had to start cleaning up. Members ambled out, either walking to their rooms or assembling near trailers in groups where the camaraderie continued, along with drinks.

No one loses weight at a VJMC rally

I called it a night early and headed back to my room to get some sleep before all the activity started in earnest the next day.

## OUT AND ABOUT IN THE OZARKS

Morning found me at the on-site restaurant in search of a hot breakfast and coffee. The large restaurant was filled and overflowing, and wait time was expected to be an hour. I didn't want to wait that long. A group of my friends who had travelled to the rally together from Indiana didn't want to wait either, so we all piled into a truck and rolled down the steep hill into downtown to see what we could find there. We lucked into arriving at the Main Street Café fifteen minutes before they normally opened. Apparently, the town didn't wake up very early there, and so downtown was nearly empty when we'd arrived. We'd gathered outside the door to the café when a waitress noticed us, opened the door, and let us in early. Breakfast was superb and surprisingly inexpensive. I made a note of where it was located, so if the same thing happened the next morning, I could walk down steep Benton Street to the café on Main Street, only a half-mile from the hotel.

After breakfast, I went back down to the convention center to get started on the photography. More bikes had arrived, and it was a good time to get individual bike pictures before they were crowded side by side later in the weekend with spectators gathering around them and making my work more difficult. Once I had enough images for the time being, I turned my attention to the schedule. I was in the Ozarks and did not want to miss out on doing a little riding in them when multiple group rides had been organized for the weekend. I'd need some representative photos from the group rides, and there was nothing like joining one to get what I needed. I decided on one that was heading south out of Eureka Springs on the "Pig Trail," also known as State Route 23. I'd ridden that road many years ago, and while it was not super technical, it had enough curves to keep you on your toes, along with stunning scenery of the surrounding mountains.

I climbed the hill once more, got my riding clothes back on, and rolled the Tiger down to the convention center where other riders were getting ready to roll out into the Arkansas countryside. I took a few photos of a group heading out then joined my group, with the members already climbing aboard their bikes and warming them up. I joined the queue at the back, and we all pulled out, a snake of over twenty bikes, roaring through town and out the south side and onto Highway 23.

It was June, and all the hills were a vibrant, youthful green, with trees growing close to the edge of the winding tarmac. We were all having a brilliant time until we came upon road construction with a one-way section and a stop light that glowed red for almost fifteen minutes. The day had grown hot, and we were all sweating in our riding suits atop our heat-producing motorcycles with no moderating breeze flowing over us and our machines.

Finally, the light changed to green, and the bikes ahead of me moved on. But I had noticed a dual sport behind me that, like me, had pulled to the shoulder in front of the light, and which was now refusing to start. Most of the other bikes had moved on, but a couple other riders and I waited with the disabled bike to make sure the rider would not be abandoned. The rider guessed that it was vapor-locked from the heat, and after many kicks, he decided to call a friend with a trailer back at the hotel to come pick him and the bike up. Russ and Amy, the other riders who had stopped, and I could not do anything more to help. The rider insisted he would be alright and that his friends would be there soon and insisted we go on and enjoy our ride.

The light had turned red again while we were seeing if we could be of any help to the disabled rider, but when it finally turned green again, Russ, Amy, and I headed south on the Pig Trail, miles behind the pack we had been riding with. That was not so bad. Usually in big groups you need to slow down to the pace of whatever rider is the least experienced, which means more accomplished riders could not enjoy the experience at the higher speeds they were capable of riding safely. With the crowd gone, we had no hindrance to our fun on the winding trail south. Russ and Amy were accomplished riders, and it was a spirited ride through the heart of the Ozarks to the wide Arkansas River and Interstate 40. As we had approached the Interstate, we passed the group we had been riding with, who were gathered outside a restaurant on the side of the road. We'd been delayed enough that if we'd stopped, by the time we had ordered our food the rest of the gang would have been ready to take the Trail back to Eureka Springs, so we decided to wave as we passed and continue on, charting a ride of our own for the rest of the afternoon.

Riding the Pig Trail

Interstate 40 paralleled the Arkansas River, which divided the mountain ranges, with the Ozarks to the north and the Ouachita Mountains to the south. We jumped on the freeway for the short twenty miles to Alma, where we exited north, back toward the mountains. We wound our way north on the minor US Highway 71 along the narrow and shallow valley formed by Frog Bayou, which ran south to join the Arkansas. Another Interstate, running to Fayetteville, mirrored our route to the west, but when we began to trace the western shore of Lake Fort Smith the two diverged, with our route riding a mountain ridge north to Winslow, eventually also ending up in Fayetteville, less than twenty-five miles from the Oklahoma state line, where we took a short break before heading east and away from the city and all its traffic.

We had considered riding into Oklahoma for a bit before heading back to the rally headquarters, but by the time we hit Fayetteville, it was hot and late in the afternoon, so instead we started our trek east back toward Eureka Springs. We headed into the hills again, passing Goshen and then Hindsville, where we turned north on a minor road that would rejoin the Pig Trail for the final run into Eureka Springs. By the time we had arrived, it was almost time for Friday's dinner, leaving only a short while to be in my room getting cooled down in the air-conditioning and stripping out of my riding gear and replacing them with my regular clothes.

Spirits were high among the members after their fabulous day of riding, and while we waited for the Italian buffet to open, there was a lot of joking and hijinks among the many tables. The serve crew joined in and contributed to making the night a dinner filled with laughter. After all the guests had eaten their fill, trivia games followed, with more laughter erupting as one group or another either won by answering a question brilliantly or failed dramatically. Dinner over, it was time to wander out to the parking lot and gather in groups for drinks and more conversation until we were all too tired to continue and scattered to our rooms for the night.

## A Walk to Breakfast then Work

I got up early and walked over to the restaurant looking for some breakfast, but the situation was the same as it had been the previous morning. I looked around for my friends from Indiana, expecting them to probably be wanting to look elsewhere for food as well, but I was too late and found they had already left for the Main Street Café without me. I poked around on my phone and found the restaurant on Google Maps and decided to follow its lead downtown, where hopefully I could catch up with my friends, or in any case, get some breakfast.

I crossed the main highway and headed down steep Benton Street in the cool shade under the overhanging branches of the surrounding woods, which prevailed, even though I was less than a half-mile from downtown. As I neared the bottom, just before homes started appearing on each side, a deer walked across a few yards in front of me and into the trees on my right, taking its sweet time and obviously not bothered by my presence. It was a beautiful way to start the day.

Once I'd reached Main Street, it was only a few store fronts to the café, where I found my friends gathered around a big circular table at the back, with room enough for me to squeeze in. I must have just missed them back at the hotel restaurant and they had only, just minutes before, ordered their food, so I flagged down a waitress and did the same as she poured me hot coffee.

After breakfast, my friend Steve, who also lived in Florida not far from us, decided to skip the truck ride and walk back to the hotel with me. Going up Benton Street was quite a bit more work than walking down it, but the quiet and the shade made it a worthwhile trek. We didn't see any more wildlife but took our time and explored a little trail off-shooting from the street that ran uphill into the trees. There were signs of an old stone foundation that looked interesting, but we didn't dawdle there, as it also looked like someone might have been making a home in the woods nearby, evidenced by the debris they had used to make a little shelter.

Bikes crowding the entrance to the bike show

At the hotel, I gathered my camera equipment and headed down to the convention center. Saturday was the day of the big bike show and would be the day I had little time to do much other than work. When I approached the front of the building, there already were bikes overflowing the display area inside and ranged along both sides of the entrance under the overhang. Inside, last-minute entries were being signed in and rolled into their spots. Even the lobby was full of motorcycles. I began my work trying to get good shots of individual stand-out bikes and groups of bikes that were related to each other in one way or another. I wove in and out of the lines of motorcycles and in and out of the building entrance until I finally had all I thought I'd need and could relax a bit and sit and chat with members.

Vintage Yamahas

The voting started about midday. I grabbed a ballot and pencil and floated around the rooms and outside picking my choices for Best Honda Pre-1970, Best Yamaha, Best Competition, and on. After casting my vote, I was asked by the event coordinator to do some specialty shots, so I went back into photography mode and made sure we had what he wanted.

I had a few moments in the afternoon to return to the room and take a little break before dinner started, when my photography work would start again. I killed a little time mindlessly watching TV and relaxing on the bed before climbing back down the stairs and hill.

Saturday night's dinner was the main event, and everyone lined up for southern cuisine at the biggest buffet I think I'd ever seen at a VJMC event. The fare was delicious, and more merriment ensued while we all partook. Following dinner, the awarding of the bike show trophies required my services, so I left the table and got in position to make sure I had individual photos of each winner, then at the end of the ceremony, I gathered all the winners up for the group photo that would go into the magazine. The evening wound up with a Zoom call from the club president and discussion about upcoming events, followed by a lightning-fast raffle of items ranging from T-shirts to helmets.

More vintage show bikes

With the final dinner behind me, I was able to remove the ever-present camera from around my neck and relax. I shuffled outside and joined Russ and Amy and a gaggle of other members clumped up next to one of the trailers, opened a beer, and got busy doing nothing. A few stories and beers later, I said my good nights to all in the circle and headed back to the room.

I'd arranged to ride as far as northern Mississippi with a club member and friend, Marty, who lived in Coldwater, less than ten miles south of the Tennessee state line, with Memphis hovering just on the other side. It was nice for a change to have someone to ride with and who knew the area roads well. The first order of business was breakfast, so we aimed our bikes for Ozark Café in Jasper. I'd accidentally run across that little gem of a diner years ago when I was wandering around the state, and it was still all it had been back then, with plate-sized, delicious blueberry pancakes that I remembered clearly from my last visit. I not only gobbled down a stack, but before that, I had a full breakfast of eggs, bacon, and potatoes.

We waddled back outside to the waiting motorcycles and resumed our course southeast toward the Mississippi River and the Delta, the birthplace of so much iconic blues music. We rolled through the Ozarks on US 65, jumping south to Jasper on little country roads, back to 65 for the run to Bee Branch, then switched back to minor highways and backroads into the Delta and to the Big Muddy at Helena. We passed Isle of Capri again then ran north for fifteen miles, where minor side roads took us east into Coldwater, at the southeastern tip of Arkabutla Lake.

Marty and his wife put me up for the night and even took me out for some great Mexican food at a nearby restaurant. I'd been spoiled on that ride so far, not yet having broken out my camping gear. The next day would be the only night the tent would get used.

## FIRE ANTS AND HIDDEN LAKE

Morning found me squinting into the rising sun, heading east for a short distance, then cutting south across the east end of Sardis Lake and through the alternately wooded and tilled land of north-central Mississippi on a tiny rural road. I grabbed an early lunch at Louisville, then continued generally southeast toward the Alabama line. Entering Alabama, I got on US 84 for the run east about fifty miles north of Mobile Bay until Monroeville, where I dropped south, once again on minor backroads into Florida.

I'd made an early start, knowing I'd have nearly four hundred miles to go before I could rest again in the Florida Panhandle, passing between Atmore and Brewton, Alabama. At Flomaton, which straddled the line between Alabama and my home state, I stopped to pick up a sandwich and snacks for the evening's meal and to fill my water bottle.

Hidden Lake Resort, another naturist campground I had visited before, only lay a little over fifteen miles away, and soon I was registered and pulling into a tent space. I got off the Tiger and looked around for a relatively level spot on the uneven site, picked what looked like the best near the brush at the back of the site, and threw up my tent. As I did so, it became clear the site was infested with fire ants. I move the tent, but again the fire ants appeared as I stepped into their territory. With every footstep I took, the ground would ooze out thousands of ants. The entire site was crawling with them, and I had no choice but to go back down to the office and ask for another site.

The attendant was understanding and let me ride back up with her in her golf cart to pick up my still-pitched tent and camping gear bag and carry it downhill to a more suitably flat and ant-free spot. Then I went back up the hill and retrieved the bike, parking it in the shade next to my tent in the new location.

Now in a safe and much better spot overall, I peeled off my hot gear and finished setting up camp. The new site was flat, in the shade of pines trees, and just a short walk from the lake, a dock filled with chairs and tables, and a clubhouse with cooking facilities, so being driven off the slanted, unshaded, and ant-overrun previous campsite was a blessing.

When I'd been at Hidden Lake before I had taken a long walk on trails through the woods in a huge circle encompassing the resort, but this day I'd have to skip the hike, with it already being late in the day. I only ambled down to a small swimming hole that had been created below the dammed lake. It was ringed with a sandy beach and lounging chairs. From the swimming pond a tiny trickle of water flowed, I assumed, eventually to Blackjack Creek, which after many more miles would become Blackwater River and find its way into Pensacola Bay and the Gulf of Mexico. Instead of a long hike, I walked back up to camp, picked up the food I'd bought earlier, and headed to the deck on the main lake to eat my dinner as the sun sank lower in the west just above the line of tall, southern yellow pines on the far side of the lake, lining the gravel road I had come in on.

The entire campground was seemingly deserted, with not a soul stirring anywhere that I could see, although I knew a few must be sequestered away in their trailers and air-conditioning. I sat and ate in solitude and silence while checking in on friends on my phone on Facebook and by Messenger.

By the time I'd finished my meal, the sun had dipped below the horizon and the sky was darkening quickly. I walked up the incline to the bath house and took a shower and brushed my teeth before settling back down in camp in my tent on top of my bag liner, with my sleeping bag nearby, in case I'd need it later if the temperature fell, and went to sleep.

## ANOTHER FINAL DAY

I got up with the sun and found my way back to the bath house and took care of my morning ablutions before returning to the tent to pack up. The day was already warming, and I waited until the last moment, after everything had been packed on the Tiger, before I climbed back into my riding gear for the last time on this trip.

I rolled back to the south end of the lake and crossed on the levee above the swimming hole to the other side, then turned back along the lakeshore and out of the park, crunching on the stones under my wheels. The riding on the gravel drive did not prove difficult, and I was soon back on pavement and heading east on a peaceful county road for a couple miles. I turned south on Walling Road and made my way to another road that led southeast, following the north bank of Big Coldwater Creek, where the water that flowed from the campground's miniscule source had found its way on its run to Blackjack Creek and Blackwater River. In a few miles the creek and my route parted ways, with mine heading east and the creek meandering south toward the bay.

I finally met up with a US highway that mimicked the path of I-10, which ran a few miles south of it. The route brought me into Crestview, where a stop for breakfast was in order at a Waffle House, where I scarfed down my usual of eggs scrambled with cheese, grits, raisin toast with apple butter, and hot black coffee.

Breakfast over, I headed toward Choctawhatchee Bay and Freeport, where the route continued east and the coastline swept away to the southeast toward Cape San Blas. I rolled toward Tallahassee until I'd passed over the Ochlockonee River near Lake Talquin, where I took a smaller highway across the north side of the Apalachicola National Forest, finally joining US 98, that old familiar route, for the run south-southeast long the Nature Coast to Goethe State Forest. I blasted down the shortcut through the State Forest to Dunellon through an empty corridor of asphalt between stands of pine forest ranged out for a couple miles on either side of the highway.

Now, it was just a quick run through areas of Florida I knew well. The GPS was superfluous. I rode to Floral City, back under overhanging oak tree branches hung with flowing Spanish moss, across the low land to Bushnell, then hopped down to Highway 50 and into Groveland. Before reaching Clermont, I turned south and ran along the eastern edge of the Green Swamp again, cutting across east from the new roundabout to my shortcut to Haines City. After a couple miles south on US 27, I turned west off of it to catch Scenic Highway for the final stretch home along "The Ridge."

I'd ridden almost another four hundred miles that day by the time I rolled into the driveway. I unloaded the now-silent Tiger in the sweltering Florida afternoon heat, rolled it backwards into the small garage reserved just for my motorcycles and walked into the house.

△ camping
F stayed with friend
H stayed in hotel

# A Ride around the Block

## Planning the Big One

After the camping weekend with the Super Happy Fun Times group, I started toying with the idea of getting away and doing something more substantial than just darting north, then darting south again—something that would be a longer-lasting break from immobility, more than a quick gulp at life, but a long, deep breath of living.

By late spring, I had finished up a cabinet job that brought in some extra money, and in general, our financial situation had improved, so I was optimistic about being able to do something a bit more epic. Being self-employed, it was hard to ever know which months would be good and which would be bad, or what last minute thing, like having to print another couple hundred books to restore inventory, would snatch any gains away. Many times before, I had planned grand trips, only to have had to cancel them, literally a week before departure. I knew that could happen this time as well, but I kept my hopes up and made plans despite the challenges. Meanwhile, in June, I had covered the VJMC National Rally in the Ozarks. While not allowing much time for personal exploration, it did give me the opportunity to test out my equipment on the Tiger in anticipation of an extended ride on my own and just for myself later that summer.

The plan for that big ride was to start in Iowa. I had a VJMC event called Meetin' In the Middle to attend in Atlantic, Iowa, to make sure we had adequate photos for an article in the upcoming issue. This was a new, major regional rally, and I wanted to show the board's support by being there personally and making sure it had a prominent place in an upcoming issue. Once I was there, I'd be halfway across the country, and might be able to use it as a springboard for further adventure after working the rally. Luckily, the time of the event coincided with that crucial gap between magazine issues as well. If the money held out and nothing surprising intervened, I hoped I really might be able to make the big trip happen.

I'd be in western Iowa, not far from Omaha, Nebraska, so riding west seemed to be the logical direction. Even though I'd been out west years before traveling through Colorado, Wyoming, Montana, and even British Columbia, those trips had stopped there. I'd never been to the West Coast or explored much of the southwestern states, only having passed through the northeastern corner of Utah on my way into Wyoming. So, my goal was set, and plans started to percolate in my brain. I'd have to do it on the cheap. That summer's gas prices were as high as they'd ever been, which was a bit of a worry. On the other hand, the Tiger got about sixteen miles more to each gallon compared to the fuel mileage I would have gotten from my old Bonneville, almost offsetting all but the most egregious prices I'd find in California, so the cost of fuel would not be much different than if I had traveled on the Bonnie. Also, camping would be a necessity most of the time, and when possible, in National Forests or Parks, where my Senior Lifetime Pass would get me in the parks for free and half off the already low camping prices. And to reduce the costs further, I'd need to do more cooking on my own, rather than dining in restaurants, although if I was careful, I could still enjoy meals out from time to time.

When the time for departure had arrived, for once all the finances and timing had worked out, and the ride was on.

## PREPARATION

I had four weeks to prepare for the ride. I had been in Eureka Springs until June 26, headed home, and had arrived in Lake Wales, in central Florida, on the 29th.

I had to scramble to get things caught up before leaving again on the 19th of July on the new adventure. A new magazine issue had to be assembled, edited, proofread, sent to layout, then back to me for another final proofreading and approval before that departure date. And hopefully, that would be early enough that my stipend for the magazine work would be in the bank before I left, ensuring I had sufficient funds for the journey.

There were plenty of things to accomplish at the house as well. I had to hang a new screen door I had made in the woodshop some time before and still had to install cabinet latches on the set of kitchen cabinets I had built and installed for my neighbor before I'd left for the Ozarks. On top of all that, the yard was a jungle, having exploded in the Florida summer rains during my absence on the previous trip and had to be mowed.

There was publishing and book design work to do as well. I needed to wind up the interior of two new books I was going to publish, and two other book designs for independent authors had to be completed. And, of course, all the bills had to be gathered and paid before I could leave.

Things were going well enough, but then there was another complication. My wife had driven to the coast to spend some time with her sister, Cindy, at a beachside hotel during my last week at home. She was just supposed to stay over one night. When she arrived at Cindy's room, her sister was sick and tested herself for Covid—positive, as was obvious from her symptoms and inability to get out of bed. Andrea was contaminated, and I would have to take care of business, work around the house, and our college-age daughter, who was still living at home, on my own.

Somehow, everything was accomplished, or at least done enough to let go of what was left undone. I departed for Iowa and the West Coast at dawn on Tuesday morning, the 19th of July.

## A Dash to Troy

I slept fitfully and woke while the sky was just starting to lighten in the east. I brushed my teeth, climbed into my riding gear, and took the last few items out to the Tiger, which had been almost completely loaded and prepped the night before.

It was seven, and the sun was not quite over the horizon when I rolled out of the driveway. I made a quick stop for fuel and was off into the gathering day of central Florida. I'd done the ride out of Florida so many times I think I could have ridden it in my sleep. I veered off the highway and onto the backroads that would lead me north on my traditional route through the dark and still shadowy Green Swamp, northwest of Lake Wales.

After about sixty miles, in the little village of Mascotte, I crunched across the parking lot of my favorite breakfast diner to get a bit to eat, an oft-repeated ritual. The Rainbow Family Restaurant fed me grits, eggs, and coffee while I chatted with the server about where I was off to this time.

By the time I left Mascotte, the day had been fully born, but at least it had not reached the boiling temperatures we had been having all that summer. The skies looked dark to the west and north, foreshadowing a day of riding in and out of rain. For at least most of the day, the rain moderated the temperatures a little, and the day turned out not to be an unending scorcher like I'd experienced on my trip to the Ozarks.

I rode well-known backroads, cutting across the state in a generally western direction to US 41, where I turned decidedly north for the short distance to Dunellon, then turning west again, leaving the busy traffic behind, continuing on quiet rural roads. I cut northwest on my shortcut through Goethe State Forest that joined the main coastal route north on the other side. After following the empty, pine tree-lined highway almost a hundred miles along the Nature Coast to Perry, I took a branching road to the northwest into the territory below Tallahassee and north of the Apalachicola National Forest and Tate's Hell, a large wilderness area stretching southwest to the Gulf Coast.

It wasn't until the little village of Blountstown that I stopped for an iced tea and a break from riding. It was midday and the very same McDonald's I had stopped at on the way home a few weeks before, where my knobby front tire had sunk and left a perfect impression an inch deep in the hot asphalt. The rain had moderated the propensity of the asphalt to mold around anything parked on it this time, and all that sunk in a millimeter or two was the "puck" I'd placed under the sidestand, just in case. I pried the puck out of its impression in the pavement, climbed back on board, and rolled back onto the road.

I made my way north and west into Alabama. Distances are misleading in Florida, and the state is much bigger than it appears on a map. From Miami, in the south, to Pensacola, at the west end of the panhandle, it is around 700 miles. So, although I had just barely left Florida, I had already ridden close to 400 miles when I hit the state line and started looking for a campground for the night. I had seen one on GoogleMaps near Troy, Alabama, so I aimed for that. I punched the address into the Garmin GPS, and it sent me to ... nothing ... just trees and empty fields. I rode a mile or so down an adjacent gravel road, but never found anything other than the same. I tried calling the campground, but the number was disconnected.

It was getting late, and I had to reconsider what to do. At those southern latitudes in the summer there is not much between late afternoon and darkness. The transition is like a switch had turned off the daylight. I didn't have much time. I'd have to eat something, anyway, and not being sure where I'd be stopping to camp now, I pulled into a restaurant on the main highway, where I thought I would consult GoogleMaps again on my phone for alternatives and perhaps ask if any of the wait crew knew of a place to camp nearby.

I called a couple campgrounds I'd found on my phone that were around forty miles away and left messages. While eating dinner, one of the campgrounds called me back and said they could accommodate me and told me how to find a spot when I arrived after-hours. Meanwhile, the restaurant manager I'd talked to knew of the original campground I had been looking for and gave me directions to its actual location—good news. I'd turn around and backtrack the couple miles and see if I could still get a spot there, and if not, I'd have a backup plan for a place an hour's ride further along my route.

The next time I punched the campground in on GoogleMaps, it located the place exactly where the manager had said it would be. Who knows the mysteries of that electronic brain? But now it clearly showed the right place, in a completely different location than it had when I'd typed it in earlier in the day.

I returned east onto the highway I'd come in on and finally found the campground, although its name had changed, and the only way I could make certain it was the right place was to ask a man who was cutting the grass beside the road I was on. There were trailers and mobile homes in varying, mostly poor, states of disrepair scattered here and there on a series of low grassy terraces, along with a smattering of small shed-like cabins. I paid twenty dollars for a spot of lawn between two travel trailers, one without wheels and up on blocks and the other with broken windows. Everything was out in the open and in the sun, with no picturesque settings, views, or trees. But the trailer to my west cast a long enough shadow at that time of day to make it pleasant enough where my tent was planted.

The campground owner had told me where the bathrooms and showers were when I had checked in but hinted it was not a good idea to "go down there at night." "People who don't live here go down there after dark. If it was me, I wouldn't go down there." Yikes! I'd stay put after the sun went down. The bathrooms were far enough from my site that, hopefully, the night visitors would not be a problem.

I wanted to brush my teeth at least before bed, so I walked down a couple terraces to the big red metal building where the restrooms and showers were supposed to be, "on the back side." I walked around the opposite side and tried a door. It opened into a huge open space that may have once been used as a gathering place. It was hard to tell in the semi-darkness, the only light the late afternoon sun filtering through filthy small windows perforating the steel walls at long intervals. I noticed an interior door on my right and opened it, thinking it may lead to the bathroom I was looking for. As the door creaked open, I was immediately hit by an overwhelming smell of death. It was a smell I remembered from a time when the refrigerator in my shop had quit, unbeknownst to me until I opened its door and the rotten reek of all the extra venison and other meat we'd stored out there hit me in the face. In the almost darkness, I thought I saw the gray outline of a big fridge, or at least that's what I told myself it was, and quickly I closed the door and exited the building without investigating further, not really wanting to know what was dead in there.

Outside, I turned the corner to the other side of the building facing away from camp, found the correct door, and opened it into a dark and musty space. I found unflushed, or perhaps unflushable toilets, one with its tank lid laying on the floor beside it. The faucets took herculean effort to turn on and were impossible to completely turn off. I managed to get my teeth brushed, and then I glanced at the curtainless and showerhead-less stalls, with nothing but a small pipe sticking out of the back wall and a ninety-degree elbow that would shoot the water straight down the shower wall, only two inches away from it. With the sun almost down and the possibility of vagrants, or worse, showing up soon, I passed on the shower.

Back at the tent there was not much to do while the sun was setting but sit in my camp chair and check my phone.

I was sitting in the shade, phone in hand, when a dog trotted up to me. It seemed friendly enough at first, so I pet it. It kept wanting more and started gently nipping at my arm, but soon it got more aggressive and had my elbow in its mouth and was biting down harder. Every time I pushed it away, it came back for more. Finally, I got aggressive myself and shouted at him to shove off. He quit his nibbling on me and casually walked away, stopping at the side of my tent to piss on it, while looking over his shoulder at me with a defiant expression, before sauntering off to wherever he'd come from.

During this, my neighbor, a grizzled old woman came out of her travel trailer and sat for a smoke on her miniscule stoop. I looked over at her and asked her if it was her dog. She said she didn't have a clue where it was from. She told me where I could get water, and I filled up my bottle and poured it over the tent where the mongrel had peed on it, before it had a chance to set in.

The lady turned out to be friendly, and I ended pulling my camp chair over near her trailer while we talked about bikes, which she and her deceased husband had owned, and about his various airplanes while she told me all about her family.

Soon, the sun was down, and the sky darkened. The clouds looked benign. The rain had stopped before I had arrived in Troy, so I hoped for a dry night. It was still warm, and there would be no need for a sleeping bag that night. The liner alone would suffice under me. Not being in a sleeping bag would also make it easier for me to spring to action in case I had any visits in middle of the night by interlopers. I went to sleep with one eye open.

## ACROSS THE MIGHTY MISSISSIPPI

I was still alive in the morning and decided to chance the bathrooms and shower, now that it was light. Whoever might have been in there in the night must have scurried out before daylight, because when I entered, I had the place to myself.

I needed to use the toilet, but when I reached into the toilet paper holders, all I found were spiderwebs. There were no paper towels or soap in the dispensers either. I decided I really had to use the toilet, anyway, having passed on that function the night before, and would just have to use the shower as a bidet. So, upon completion of my task, it was an awkward scurry directly from the toilet stall to the shower stall. I turned on the shower spigot, and as the stream ran down along the wall, I backed my rear up to the wall to clean myself as best I could in the vertical column of, of course, cold water. That part of my ablutions completed, I soaped up quickly and shoved whatever body parts I could under the stream to rinse off, and for the parts I couldn't get fully under, I used the splash method, then dried off and got out of there as quickly as possible.

Despite the favorable appearing evening before, it had sprinkled for a short time in the night. The tent had not dried, so I shook off what I could and shoved it into its compression bag wet. Soon, camp was broken down and loaded back into the bags and onto the bike, and I was rolling out across the crunching gravel, glad to have survived for another day, and back onto the highway to Troy.

Once west of the town, I joined the innumerable logging trucks loaded with bouncing pine boles for a ride through the still shady Alabama and, later, Mississippi forests, past abandoned neighborhood general stores and many forlorn, forgotten, and vacant attempts at gas stations.

It was July, and everything was in full growth and green. Views varied from dark glimpses into wet forests to sun-illuminated fields of corn, sorghum, soybeans, and I think, tobacco.

The day started cool and pleasant, but by half-past-ten, the heat struck again fully. It was sweltering. As I rode through the forests, I could smell the balsam of recently cut pines mixed with an increasing odor of sweat floating up out of my riding clothes, out of the collar and up into my helmet. The skies did not forecast rain, and all there was overhead was a scattering of blue-gray-bottomed cotton balls floating on the southwest breeze. There would be no rainfall that day.

The day's ride took me along some Alabama and Mississippi state routes, but mostly on tiny county roads, with a US Highway trying to imitate an Interstate highway thrown in now and again to make a connection to yet another backroad. I scrapped my plan to cross the Mississippi River in Memphis, not wanting to deal with traffic and Interstate speeds, so I pointed the GPS toward West Helena, Arkansas, the next southern crossing from Memphis. I had been across there a few times before, including only a few weeks previously. As I rode, I recognized bits and pieces of former routes I'd followed before. The river crossing was the first goal of the day—get into Arkansas. Once arriving there, I stopped at a McDonalds for an iced tea and a phone reconnoiter of possible camping spots in the southeastern part of the state. There weren't many, and most were RV campgrounds, but I hoped I could talk one of those into letting me set up my little tent on some scrap of their lawn.

I set the GPS again, this time for the area where two highways converged ahead on my general route. There seemed to be a few GoogleMaps' camping icons in the vicinity. But it was getting late when I arrived, and I could not find any place to camp at all. I was running out of time. Darkness was not far off. I spotted a police officer sitting in his SUV on a side street and rode up to ask him about the area and the possibility of a campground. "Nope, no camping around here at all." I told him if I didn't find something soon, I would be forced to get a hotel to avoid riding after dark, which I should not do with the less-than-perfect vision in my right eye. He told me where to find hotels, which were plentiful at the next main highway exit, but more importantly, that he would not stay at any of them there, but a few more exits west would provide lodging that was safe. I headed on, hoping I'd find a brown camping sign or even a campground or RV place along the way as I rode, before having to resort to a hotel room. I had been keeping an eye out for possible stealth camping spots, even before running into the officer, but I was in the Delta. Along the sides of the roads and around the rice fields were moats of water keeping anyone from leaving the road. I didn't spot a camping option, stealth or otherwise, and it had become all but dark.

I finally got on the Interstate-like main highway heading west and passed the exit to Bald Knob, where I'd been warned not to stop. Full darkness caught up with me near Searcy, where I ended up signing for a hotel room. I'd run out of time. I hopefully anticipated that camping spots would not be so hard to find out in the West, where there was a lot of public land, unlike this area and in the states east of the Mississippi River.

The room price was horrendous, especially considering I was nowhere near any kind of tourist area, but there was a Mexican restaurant next door that I just made it to before they closed, after quickly dragging my gear into my room—not bad; my meal of three enchiladas, beans, and rice cost only $10.25 before the tip. I couldn't complain about that, and I'd save buying breakfast the next day, as the hotel had a full breakfast included. Those two fortunate things at least usually took a tiny bit of the sting out of paying for a room.

After dinner I trekked back to my room. I was exhausted and hit the bed immediately, too tired to do anything else and leaving showering for the morning.

## MISSOURI BOUND

I was a bit discouraged the night before, having had to settle and pay for a room, but morning brought a new and, hopefully, better day. Breakfast was typical hotel fare: scrambled eggs, some variety of sausage, and potatoes. There were also waffles, but I passed on the temporary sugar rush it would give me and, instead, grabbed some fruit.

After eating, I went back to the room, finally got a shower, packed all my things, put on clean clothes, and headed out. While loading the Tiger, I had a short conversation with a fellow travelling by car but wishing he was on a motorcycle. He said he liked adventure bikes, but because of his short legs he was limited to lower motorcycles. I understood. I had been trying to get used to the seat in its high position on the Tiger for a little more relaxed position while riding, but which had me tippy-toeing at stops. I'd regret that later.

I set the Garmin for Holden, Missouri, hoping to catch up with my second-cousin. Cindy, who lived there. She was sister to another of my cousins, Bonnie, who had moved from Missouri and now lived near the Gettysburg Battlefield in Pennsylvania. I'd visited Bonnie's farm several times and always had the greatest times with her and her husband, Bill, but had never met Cindy, so was looking forward to getting to know her. By around noon, however, when I stopped for a break, Cindy had not responded to texts or calls, so I directed the GPS instead to Knob Noster State Park, a little to the east, where I had confirmed a tent space for the night. If I eventually heard back from Cindy, we could still possibly meet for breakfast somewhere before I headed north into Iowa and on to the rally, just two hundred miles away.

I rolled alternately north and west through Arkansas into Missouri. In the Ozarks the riding was beautiful, with high-speed sweepers. The only problem was that for forty miles I was behind a semi and an RV going twenty-under the speed limit. The RV finally pulled over after around twenty miles to let people pass, but when I stopped at a dam for some photos later, he passed me again, and I was stuck behind it once more, amongst a string of cars for miles. It was a shame, because that had happened in some of the best motorcycle riding sections in the Ozarks. Eventually, we parted ways, and the riding got better. As I rode north, the twisty mountain corners gave way to gentle curves and hills and cultivated fields. The "ABC" county roads, called that for their alphabetic names such as "V" or "BB" or "PP" and the like, were a rollercoaster up and down most of the day, with fewer and fewer attempts to wind around the hills as the rises and falls grew smaller.

By 4:30, I found the nicely wooded state park and secured a spot before heading into the tiny town of Knob Noster to find something to eat or perhaps food to bring back to camp. In town, I spied an almost obscured, out of the way Subway tucked behind an auto parts store, which had air conditioning and a place to sit. I soaked in the coolness inside while eating a Philly wrap and having a cold drink. By the time I left, I was so full I decided not to stop at the convenience store to pick up something more for back at camp. But out of the corner of my eye I spotted a "Tap Room" in the miniscule downtown and turned around, almost getting rear-ended by an inattentive driver behind me as I did so and parked up across the street from the pub. I found the small, quaint place crowded with people and filled with stacks of pizza. I just wanted a beer, as I'd not had one since leaving home, but the friendly folk, who were celebrating the first Social Security check received by one of their own, offered me a slice. Too bad I was too full to eat. If I'd spotted them earlier, it would have saved some of my scarce funds I'd set aside for the trip that I'd just spent at Subway. I allowed myself one beer only, as I had to ride back a few miles to the campground, but I enjoyed that sole brew almost as much as the friendly conversation with the locals.

Back at the park, I had camp set up in a few minutes and walked to the shower, not to bathe but to rinse myself off with cold water, leaving myself wet so I would cool down, as the day's heat had barely diminished.

Still, no call came from Cindy, so unless there would be a message in the morning, I'd head straight for Atlantic the next day. It was only a couple hundred miles away, and for once, the day would be an easily managed short ride with time to spare.

### Iowa on the Horizon

It had been hot the night before, but by midnight it had cooled enough that I could crawl into my light sleeping bag liner. As I was pulling the liner up over myself, I heard "footsteps" outside the tent and very close by, along with soft purring sounds. I grabbed the lantern and flipped it on, simultaneously shaking the sides of the tent and yelling, "Get out of here!" There was a scramble outside, and I clearly saw the distinct silhouette of a racoon scuffling inches past projected onto the tent wall. It must have scared the scroungers sufficiently, because I never heard or saw them again. With them foraging elsewhere, I could only hear the aircraft taking off and landing at the nearby Air Force base and the faint sounds of occasional distant traffic passing on the highway.

I awoke about six o'clock, when the sky was just beginning to get light. By seven, the clear sound of "Reveille" emanated clearly from the base, just as had "Taps" as darkness had fallen the night before. I could not check out until nine, so I took my time getting camp picked up and cleaning myself at the bath house. By nine o'clock, I had pulled up at the gatehouse, paid for my night's stay, and was back on the road.

I'd not heard from Cindy, but in the last text I'd sent I suggested meeting for breakfast at Warrensburg, which was, more or less, halfway between where she lived and where I had camped. It was roughly on the way, so I headed there for breakfast, thinking I might hear from Cindy in the meantime. I pulled into the parking lot of the Country Kitchen, which the gate keeper at the park had suggested as a good breakfast place, went inside, and ordered a hearty breakfast. Midway through my meal, Cindy rang. She could be there in thirty minutes. I asked for more coffee and settled in. I did not have far to go, so I could afford the time.

In a little while, Cindy appeared, recognizing me from the self-description I'd given her as the "only hippy in the place" when she asked me how she could recognize me. We had a great talk about life and family, and although it meant I'd be riding in the hottest part of the day, it was worth it to meet such a wonderful person and to connect with a long-lost family member. We had a lot in common, and we talked until at least half past eleven, before I finally had to leave in order to get to Atlantic well before dark, as I had planned. We both expressed our hopes to see each other again and said our goodbyes, sharing a hug before I climbed back on the Tiger and pulled away.

The mountains of southern Missouri were far behind me, and I was now in the farming heartland of America, covered with rolling hills. Everything was some shade of green, with dark-green trees trimming the lines between expansive light-green fields of soybeans.

The day was brutally hot. A friend in Kansas City had texted me, telling me 103 degrees Fahrenheit had been forecast. I'm not sure what it was where I was riding, but at minimum, it was in the high-90s. I was sweating.

At one point, even though I was on a relatively minor local road, the speed limit was sixty and the road was four-lane with a grass divider, one of those fast-paced boulevards that ring most bigger cities to avoid traffic on the major highways, and which end up being as heavily trafficked as the highways they were meant to avoid. I spotted a car broken down in the left driving lane and a worried woman next to it on her phone. I pulled to the right shoulder, climbed off the bike, and carefully made my way across traffic that had stopped at a light just ahead of us. I pushed her car into a left turn-lane, just beyond where her car had expired. I could not get her completely off the highway, but at least she was not in the high-speed travel lane, where other drivers would not expect a stopped car to be sitting. From there it was uphill, so she needed professional help, but at least she was in a safer position. I gave her some cold water from my bottle so she would have something to allay the heat until more help arrived before I braved recrossing the highway back to my bike.

I sped north under bright blue skies fading to a light rose on the horizon all around. The GPS had done a good job of keeping me on backroads before, but with Kansas City and St. Joseph in the way, I had to deal with lots of traffic, even on their outskirts. Once past St. Joseph, I was back in the countryside and made good progress again. The Garmin said I'd arrive at four-thirty, and it was true to its prediction.

I made a quick stop at the hotel the club members would be staying at, to see if anyone had arrived yet, but I only saw one vintage Honda Nighthawk in the parking lot, with the rider nowhere to be seen. While in the lobby in the air conditioning, I looked up the location of the fairgrounds where I'd be camping. It was only a couple miles from the hotel and maybe a half-mile more to the dealership where the bike show would be held the next day.

I made my way through the little town and arrived at the campground in a few minutes. I queried a fellow who was painting a fence rail at the entrance on how to proceed. He told me that he was retired and volunteering there as camp host while his wife, a travelling nurse, was working nearby. Ten dollars a night dropped into a slot was all that needed to be done, and I could pick any spot I liked.

Although it was getting late in the afternoon the air was still brutally hot. I quickly made phone calls home and set up camp, then rode back to town to find a place to eat, have a beer, and sit in air conditioning until it cooled down outside. I found a friendly neighborhood pub just a few blocks away where I ordered chicken nuggets and beer and was soon chatting with my bar mates about what I was doing, where I was from, where I was going, and where they had travelled as well. Soon, we had a group of a half-dozen sitting and conversing along the bar. I left with an hour or two remaining before dark but with the promise of a drop in temperature soon. My oasis had rescued me from an uncomfortably hot afternoon in the summer sun at the campground.

Back at camp, I found the bath house, but there were no lights, or so it seemed. I guessed they were serious about closing at sunset as the entry sign had stated. I quickly brushed my teeth in what very little light was left and hopped into a cold shower, then walked back to the tent site wet, again letting the cold water cool me as it evaporated from my clothes, becoming my own kind of personal swamp cooler. That kept me cool enough until the sun had set and the air started to cool. Later, I noticed light shining from the bath house, so assumed they must have been on a light sensor and not simply shut off, as I had thought, so if I had waited, I could have done my evening ablutions while being able to have seen what I was doing. I wrapped up the day writing in my journal while the temperature slowly moderated. It was still warm at sunset but not even close to what it had been on the previous nights. By the time I climbed into the tent, it was warm but comfortable. Over the last few days, I'd ridden halfway across the US south to north. There was something to be said for latitude.

## Meetin' In the Middle

It started as a pleasant night, warm but comfortable if I slept naked on top of my bag liner. It wasn't until 2AM that it had cooled enough to make being inside the liner comfortable. Despite the chatter of distant campers talking loudly until two o'clock in the morning, I eventually slept soundly and didn't have to scare away any critters in the night.

Morning was cool as the sky was lightening and I was climbing out of the tent. I knew the bike show would not be until at least nine o'clock, so I took my time and prepared cacao using my gasoline stove and French press. The last time I'd used the stove the gas had leaked out around the burner control, and I'd had to abandon using it. When I got home from that trip, I'd dismantled it and found the likely culprit—two tiny O-rings in the valve stem. I couldn't source them locally, so bought a bag of fifty from Amazon, having measured the old ones with a caliper, and hoped they'd work. They seemed a bit thicker than the originals, but I coated them with assembly grease and was able to lock down the nut over them. My work paid off, and I didn't have any leaks on this first test as I made my pot of hot cacao and had a small granola bar for breakfast.

I took a leisurely shower under the cold water in the bath house, making sure the grime and smell from the road were gone, and then donned clean shorts under my riding pants, so I could simply take off my jacket, remove my boots, drop my pants, don the light shoes I had strapped to my tailbox, and be comfortable in shorts and a T-shirt while at the bike show, as I expected another hot day.

I arrived at Nishna Cycle, where the event was being held, as the bikes were being put into long shiny, multi-colored rows. I began taking photos of each bike and then groups of bikes by their class, while also getting good overall shots of the venue and the guitar player/singer, who entertained everyone in the welcoming shade of several popups.

Mark, one of our Missouri Field Reps and a customer of mine, for whom I had designed a couple books, was there. We caught up on the club, book news, and common interests. At lunchtime, Mark bought me a meal at the adjacent food truck. I dined on some of the best brisket in sandwich form I had ever tasted, along with equally good pasta salad.

Once I had most of the photos I'd need for the magazine, I suited back up and followed on the Tiger behind Mark and a fellow club member who were in a van to Marne, just eight miles away, to Baxter Cycle, the place that had first put the idea of eventually getting a Tiger into my head. My deer strike crash had accelerated that idea, and I was now on the back of the same bike I had drooled over in their showroom a couple years before, although an older 800cc version, rather than the newer, and expensive, 900cc model the owner had shown me. We soaked in the air conditioning in the Royal Enfield and Triumph showrooms and then had a look at their backroom stuffed with vintage British bikes. I thought I'd be able to pick up rubber footpeg inserts that were missing on my Tiger when I'd bought it, but the parts person was out sick, and if they had them, the remaining crew couldn't find them. I had hoped that using them on the highway may prove more comfortable and less wearing on the soles of my boots. I left empty-handed, although I had enjoyed our time there and having a chance to take a look at the new Tiger 1200 that had come out recently and looked positioned to possibly give the class leader of large adventure motorcycles, the BMW 1250GS, a run for the title.

A rare Norton Manx along with other vintage bikes at Baxter Cycle

When we arrived back at Nishna Cycle, the awards were about to be handed out, and once they were, I got several shots of the trophy winners' group for the article that would be in the upcoming issue, which Mark would be writing.

There was to be a get-together at the dealership owner's house for brats and drinks and for a look at his barnful of motorcycles. The cookout would not be until six o'clock, and the show was over at three—the hottest part of the afternoon. I sought out my tavern from the afternoon before and shared some beers and air conditioning with the locals, biding my time slowly sipping beer and avoiding the heat until time to go to the get-together.

After 5:30, I went back to camp for a quick check on things and to open the tent windows to let the breeze through in hopes of cooling the tent before evening and then headed to the party. It was only a few miles, but some of the roads were gravel, and a section was dirt, so I was able to test the new Shinko 705s appropriately that I had installed on the Tiger just before leaving home. They behaved wonderfully and felt solid, even on the dirt section. I was quite pleased with their confidence inspiring performance. It was fortunate to have a little test of their ability to bolster my confidence in them before getting out west and into rougher off-pavement conditions.

As promised, the host, Dennis, had brats on the grill and other foodstuff on the table. He had cold soft drinks and beer on hand in a cooler, but after my afternoon of sipping beer in town and knowing I had to ride back to camp, I only went for the former.

Dennis must have had a hundred bikes of all sorts, shapes, and sizes in the barn. While he grilled, we wandered around looking them over. Meanwhile, word spread that that there was a thunderstorm coming our way soon. I checked the radar on my phone. It looked like the worst would pass north and south, but as the skies darkened, I bid adieu and headed back to camp, not relishing the idea of riding back up that hill in that dirt section in a downpour. A short test of the tires was sufficient; an endurance test was not necessary or desired, especially when I might be immersed in mud as well as the tires.

It turned out I only got a couple drops of rain on my visor on my return trip. It was not quite ready to pour yet. I cleaned up a bit back at camp, wrote in my journal, and waited for the rain while the sky darkened and dusk settled in. I went to the tent early, and just after dark, the rain began. It never got very heavy. There were only a few big gusts of wind that threatened to roll my tent, but within an hour it was over, and the passing storm had cooled the air substantially. Apparently, the bulk of the storm had passed on each side of Atlantic, just as predicted. With the rain gone and the air cooler and more comfortable, I soon fell asleep.

## THE JOURNEY REALLY BEGINS

I'd found free camping on my phone, courtesy of the town of McCook, Nebraska, about three hundred miles to the west and about the same from my next day's destination, Littleton, Colorado, and Mountain Air Ranch. Two easy days—I was glad for it. There was no big rush now, with this being the true start of my ride, where obligations other than to the ride itself were behind me. My pace would be my choice. I broke up camp and packed leisurely. By eight, I was once again on the highway and heading west.

I waited until getting into Nebraska to start looking for a place for breakfast, but it was not until Lincoln, far into the Cornhusker State, that I found what I was looking for—a hometown, non-chain diner surrounded by vehicles, a sure sign of good food. I'd found Virginia's Travelers' Cafe on US Highway 6, also known as the Cornhusker Highway. It was the kind of place you'd have expected to find years ago on travelers' highways like Route 66. It was crowded, but I found what was probably the only seat left, sat down, and ordered an omelet and hashbrowns. It turned out that the diner was something of a legend and had been there for years offering good, simple, hearty food for a low price. It obviously was very popular, evidenced by the non-stop flow in and out of patrons. Breakfast there had been more of a meal than my body required, and so I promised myself to eat a light dinner to compensate as I climbed back aboard the Tiger.

So many had told me they despised crossing Nebraska and the other Plains states, but I found them pleasant and interesting. The first part of the day was crossing endless hills covered in corn, with each field bordered by tree-filled windbreaks. I'd first learned to hunt along windbreaks like those way back when I had worked in Kansas after my first stint in college. Game took cover in the windbreaks during the day and at night would pop out to fill themselves on the abundant grains growing in the nearby fields. As I rode west, I passed a few wind farms, getting a close-up view of the monstrous giants. By afternoon, the trees had become less frequent and the hills milder, not so much in height but in the gentle slopes I rode up and down on over their backs. As the trees disappeared, the landscape reminded me of the large ground swells I had witnessed six hundred miles offshore on an Atlantic crossing from North Carolina to the Virgin Islands years ago. I recalled the wave heights being impressive, but the wavelengths were long and at a low angle, which gave the sea a gentle character, despite the height of the wave tops, much like the feel of this rolling prairie.

I found the park in McCook, just east of town. A few travelers were taking advantage of the spot, with me being the sole tent camper. It was clean and well-kept, with shade trees scattered about. I chose a spot in the green, grassy circle formed by the ring drive, on the outside of which RVs were parked. My spot had a bench under a roof and thick lush grass to pitch the tent on nearby.

West of the Mississippi these city camping parks are common

I quickly got camp set up and then rode into town. I needed more cash and a few other things, so I was happy to find a Walmart there, which is usually the last place I'd be looking for, not at all being a fan of the huge and monopolistic chain. But it was a handy place to pick up what I needed while allowing me to get a hundred dollars back in cash easily, and luckily, McCook had been the first town on my route all day since breakfast that had been large enough to have a Walmart.

Shopping complete, I headed back downtown, where I had spied a "Family Restaurant" with lots of cars outside on a cobblestone side street. I pulled up, wondering where I could park, as all the spots directly in front of the restaurant were taken, when I saw a couple coming out. There was no traffic, so I stopped in the street, flipped up the chin bar of my helmet, and asked them if the place was good. They said yes, but it was impossible to get in. The woman said that they were doing Mexican food instead, on the same street but on the other side of the main highway. I took their advice and headed there too. I also noticed that another biker from the Christian Motorcyclist Association heard what I had, and all of us turned around to cross over to the Mexican restaurant. There was plenty of seating there, food was good, and as cheap as I was, I didn't have to spend more than ten dollars to be completely satiated by the huge meal. So much for my morning promise to myself.

As I was getting ready to go, the rider wearing his Christian Motorcyclist Association vest came over and asked me where I was heading. We chatted for a few minutes before I left, only a minute or so ahead of him. That was a good thing, because when I tried to do a U-turn on the oddly-sloped, cobblestone street, I dropped the Tiger. When I had tried to execute the turn-around, my right foot, on the downhill side, could not touch the ground until the bike was leaned over so far that I could not prevent it toppling over. The fellow rider was already outside and ran over to help, along with another stranger, to get it up and back onto its sidestand. Embarrassing; but no harm done. I'd absorbed some of its weight as it fell, and it had not hit the ground hard. It was good the bystanders had been there to help, because I was finding out the hard way that the Tiger was not easy to lift. I thanked them both, then executed the U-turn, this time successfully, and headed back to camp.

I'd not be taking a shower that night, as there were no showers at the park, but the bathrooms were otherwise fully functional. I could go without a shower for one night (later, I'd find out I could, and would go much longer than that).

Back at the park, I met Michael, a young man camping in a tent rig mounted over the bed of a Toyota Tacoma four-wheel-drive pickup. We struck up a conversation, and I learned he loved wild camping and being alone in the wilderness. He showed me his rig and how he had built sliding containers in the bed, where he stored all his gear under the camping platform. We hit it off instantly while we talked about camping and travel.

As the day was drawing to an end, the sky was overcast, but not threateningly so. The storm that had rolled through Atlantic had brought cooler temperatures behind it. It would be a comfortable night. Or so I thought.

The campground was comprised of a circle drive, with obvious paved pullouts and electric connections for RVs along the outside edge. In the middle were trees and wonderfully soft grass. I thought, "What a perfect place to pitch my tent." I figured that, with me in the middle, all those RV spots would be free for anyone who might show up later. What I didn't know, and which wasn't posted anywhere, was that the center grass was so green and lush because it was watered by a sprinkler system. That I found out about just when I had crawled into the sack. "Oh well," I thought, "They'll be on a timer and will eventually turn themselves off. I'll just close the windows and wait a bit." And they did turn themselves off, but then the rain I thought we were going to avoid rolled in and took its turn soaking the tent. The one bright spot was that at least I'd not pitched the tent directly over one of the sprinkler heads; that would have been interesting. The rain continued into the early morning. The inside of the tent was dry but the outside was drenched and would have to be put away that way. Packing wet was never pleasant, but it was sometimes inevitable, and the tent would be back up in the evening early enough to dry out before being used again, if it didn't rain again.

## FINALLY IN THE ROCKIES

I only had to cover three hundred miles, so I was not in a hurry to get on the road. I fired up the Dragonfly stove and invited Michael over to try some cacao. He'd been looking for something to replace coffee, and he liked the cacao enough he thought he might have found a good substitute.

Soon, Michael was heading east, back to Pennsylvania, and I west, toward Mountain Air Ranch, near Denver. As I rode further west the landscape changed again. The dominant crop changed from corn to wheat, and the landscape became more reminiscent of old TV Westerns, with gulches and even a butte or two sticking their heads above the prairie.

In a tiny town in far-western Nebraska, I passed a diner that was the epitome of the kind of homegrown places I loved to visit. Even though I had decided to skip a big breakfast and just make do with the cacao and granola bar I'd had at camp, I couldn't resist turning around and trying this diner's fare. As expected, a good, hearty breakfast was provided for a pittance, and plenty of local charm diffused the place. I was tempted to try their undoubtedly delicious pie but passed, feeling I'd already overdone my caloric intake for most of the day.

Back on the highway, within a half-hour I was in Colorado, home of the Rockies, although clocks had changed to Mountain Time already back at the diner, still in Nebraska. The road continued west into Colorado, then I turned south about midway between the eastern border and the mountains hiding somewhere over the western horizon.

I rode south for a while, then west again toward Denver across the high plains, watching my fuel range closely. Still fifty miles from Denver and thirty from the next gas station, the range fell to nine miles. I stopped on the edge of the road that headed west toward the city and removed my luggage, so I could retrieve my spare gallon of gas in the Rotopax under my left pannier. I didn't want to wait until I was completely empty with the fuel pump running dry, which is not healthy for the pump, because the gas flowing through it also cooled it.

The gallon would get me another forty-five miles, and gas was available thirty miles away, so disaster was averted. However, while stopped and refueling in those rolling high plains, it was clear that the cool morning start, having require my heated grips to be turned on, was now over.

Tapping my reserve gas on the way into Denver

As I headed toward Denver from the gas station, having refilled the Tiger and the Rotopax, I was surprised I could not see the Rockies yet. I had to be only forty miles away, yet they hid in a bank of haze in the west. Finally, on the outskirts of Denver, the blue mountain silhouette appeared, the peaks now growing larger and more distinct as I rode toward them.

There was no avoiding Denver traffic coming in from the east to get to Deer Creek Canyon, where Mountain Air Ranch was tucked away, southwest of Littleton. I'd been having problems with my eyes. They both would water easily, I assumed because of the trauma both had been through. Most afternoons on hot days they would start watering and then begin to sting. When the tears flowed, they brought with them salt from my sweating skin into my eyes. Often it would get bad enough that I simply could no longer see and would have to stop and wipe them dry before riding on. Now, on the high-speed roads around the south side of Denver, I was almost to the point of being blind, but there was simply no place to pull over out of traffic. I was beginning to panic as the cars I could barely see rushed past me. I kept swiping at my eyes with my left hand. I was relieved when I somehow managed to navigate off the highway and onto the familiar side road leading away from the city. My eyes had cleared up by the time I got on scenic Deer Creek Canyon Drive, with its red boulders and hoodoos rising up on each side of the twisting and climbing road. I took it slowly, just enjoying the rhythm of it all, and soon I'd arrived.

I'd been to Mountain Air Ranch years ago on my way to British Columbia and had really liked the vibe of it but had only stayed one night. Now that I was heading through the area again, I wanted to stay a couple nights and enjoy a whole day of relaxing there. It would give me a chance to get in a different state of mind after working all weekend in Atlantic, now that my only purpose from here on out was to enjoy the ride, with no work, no hard schedules, and in anticipation of jumping off into new territories when I left.

At Mountain Air Nudist Resort, I checked in for two nights, rode to the tent camping meadow, got out of my broiling clothes as quickly as I could, and instantly felt the relief of the mountain air on my bare skin. There was enough sunshine and breeze that the tent would be dry by bedtime, so I left it to dry and headed up the steep hill to the pool deck to relax and eat my wrap, chips, and beer I had bought in Denver before getting to the ranch.

As the sun sank lower, I climbed back down to camp, grabbed my toiletries, and took a quick but thorough shower outside, bathed alternately in warm water and the fresh, cool mountain air.

A young couple with a six-month old baby were camping next to me, and as I returned, the father said he hoped the baby would not bother me and wanted to apologize in advance if it fussed at all. I told him not to worry. I had raised two children myself and completely understood. We chatted, talking about the raising children. We agreed that the notion of there being a one "right way" was nonsense. We both concluded that as long as you loved them as you raised them, they'd turn out OK. He was interested in getting a motorcycle as well, so we had a lot in common, and we talked about bikes in general while sharing ideas of what might make a good starter bike that he might consider, which he could learn on but not outgrow quickly. They were a very pleasant couple, and his wife reminded me a lot of my daughter's girlfriend, who I liked very much.

As I was writing in my journal, the sun had settled behind the mountain ridges and an evening chill was creeping in. I was, after all, over a mile high in elevation, and the day's heat dissipates quickly at high altitude. I turned in before it got chilly enough to require putting clothes on—that's not why I had come.

## In Nature Au Naturel

I got up late, letting the chill of the early morning evaporate before climbing out of the tent, as being clothe-less requires a bit higher temperature to feel comfortable. I had the entire day, so there was no need for haste.

I headed to the community kitchen just up the hill, where I made some oatmeal and a pot of cacao on the provided stove. I took my time as the air warmed up outside. While walking to the kitchen, I had passed a completely unalarmed mule deer grazing in the meadow. I walked within eight feet of it without it flinching. While cooking my breakfast, I could see it continuing its own breakfast among the bushes just feet from the window.

Breakfast completed, I decided to walk some of the trails, hoping I might get a cell signal at the "Denver View" or "Panorama" spots marked on the park map. Down in the little vale where I was camping, I had not been able to call home the night before to report that I was in safe and sound for the day, so getting a call out would be good, and a hike and some forest bathing would do me good after sitting so many hours on the Tiger. The trail was very steep in sections, but for some reason, I didn't really feel winded at all, even considering I was above 7,300 feet. It felt glorious to be surrounded by nature in my natural state, having only donned sneakers to protect my feet on the rocky trail. I headed east from the clubhouse to the ridge above it and was able to get a message out to home. Once finished with my call, I walked the northeastern perimeter of the 150-acre resort that was set in a "bowl" within encircling ridges. There were places in the woods where piles of boulders were stacked on each other, and here and there, someone had placed chairs to give hikers a spot to sit, rest, and contemplate the natural beauty around them. I took advantage of some of them to sit and feel the warmth of the sun on my skin and to quietly listen to the rustle of the pines and the subtle sounds of nature all round me.

By the time I'd hiked to the most northern point of the circle, it had become quite warm, and I was perspiring from my efforts, so I started heading back down to get a proper shower to cool off.

After cleaning up, I took my water and the few snacks I had left and went to the pool, where I relaxed in the shade for a while. There I took advantage of the sauna and showers before deciding to do more hiking.

Forest Bathing at Mountain Air Ranch

This time, I was determined to walk the western rim starting at the trailhead adjacent to the camping area. I climbed a very steep trail to the ridge then walked north until I'd almost reached the place I had stopped on my last jaunt. Then I retraced my steps, continuing south until arriving at an old mica mine, which was marked on the map at the southern end of the circuit, close to the entry office.

A view from a hiking trail at Mountain Air Ranch

There was a huge gouge in the side of the mountain where miners had obviously extracted the mica. The entire hillside sparkled with glints of the shiny material. Opposite the gouge was a pile of rubble filled with pieces of glittering mica. I picked up a couple nice pieces to bring back to my daughter, who had an interest in minerals and gems. Mica is silvery and is layered in thin sheets, which can be spilt into even thinner translucent pieces. I recalled our old pot belly stove we used when I was growing up in Michigan, with "eisenglass" doors made of the same material but in sheets so thin you could see the flames inside the stove through them.

Leaving the mine behind, I walked north again a short distance on a different trail that led back to camp. Another shower was required after the hike, then I returned to the pool deck and, eventually, got into the hot tub, where a fellow named Gary was enjoying the hot water. He had lived in Colorado all his life and shared stories of work life and everything under the sun. We were soon joined by a young man who, it turned out, was getting started in standup comedy in the Denver area and who was hoping to expand. We all got on well and talked for an hour or two, sitting on the edge of the tub when we got too hot, and dipping back in when we had cooled down. The comic left to buy some weed, which was legal, of course, in Colorado, and Gary and I were then joined by Stacy and David, who both worked at Mountain Air Ranch. I told Stacy I had mentioned the resort in my last book and had sent them a copy as a thank you for their hospitality when I was on the northwest leg of those two trips I'd written about. She was not aware they had a copy and promised she was going to find that copy and read it.

After having had enough of the hot tub, I returned to the kitchen to see how good, or bad, the freeze-dried dinners were that I had bought for the first time to try on this journey. I chose the "Mac Beef and Cheese" and, after trying it, gave it a C. Perhaps the other two would be better; I'd find out sooner or later.

Our comic friend showed up later, and he and I spent the rest of the evening checking out the lounge area, where we talked while he played the piano and I checked my phone until it was almost dark, when I set out again for the tent and my sleeping bag.

## HOORAY FOR OURAY

I woke up to a munching sound and unzipped the window to find myself staring face to face with a deer cropping the lawn a foot outside my tent door. It was early, but I searched for my phone to get a photo, although by the time I'd managed to drag it out, the deer had moved twelve or so feet away. I pulled the sleeping bag up to my ears and tried to relax for a few more minutes. I only had about three hundred miles to go that day to Ouray, and there was no point going while it was still chilly and deer, like my visitor, would be near the roads.

Eventually, my bladder demanded my rising, but by then it was slightly warmer. I began the task of packing the tent and its contents back onto the Tiger, then slowly and reluctantly started to pull on my riding clothes. This time I'd need jeans and long sleeves under my riding suit, as I'd be passing over some high and likely cold passes.

Back in the uniform of the adventure rider and back on my bike, I started rolling up the grassy meadow, doing a U-turn to exit the camping meadow when I felt the weight of the bike falling to my left and downhill. Again, my foot found the ground too late to stop the bike from tipping. Down it went again, and this time, despite me trying to ease her down, the clutch lever tip broke off where the relief cut was near the outer end, and the hand guard of that side was loosened. Both wheels were off the ground as it lay on its engine guards and panniers.

The drop was embarrassing and shook my confidence, especially when I tried to pick up the Tiger and found I could not lift it from its prone position. Picking a bike up when both wheels are not on the ground is especially difficult, and I was finding out that was the Tiger's preferred napping position. To get your butt against the seat to lift the bike using your legs is almost impossible when the seat is laying on the ground. If you can get down there, then your legs are bent at such an extreme angle it is very difficult to straighten them out as you lift.

I was about to relieve the bike of all the luggage when a fellow, who had been parked in his truck nearby, came over and helped me get it upright again. My seat was still in the high position I had mounted it in, thinking it would be more comfortable riding with my legs not bunched up quite so tight, but I was beginning to doubt the wisdom of that decision. When the bike tilted, there was too much of a drop before my foot would catch it, and in that position the weight would be too much to hold, especially when the bike fell toward a downhill slope, as it had here and in front of the Mexican restaurant earlier.

I tried to shake off the loss of confidence I was having as I was leaving Mountain Air Ranch behind and riding further up Deer Creek Canyon Road. I had found a way to avoid passing through the mess that is Denver traffic upon leaving and now was heading northwest out of the canyon. I took Wild Turkey Road, and that brought me out onto my main westbound route, US Highway 285. I stopped for a quick coffee and breakfast sandwich as soon as I hit the highway at Indian Hills before moving on.

Everything was going well as the day passed until I connected with US Highway 50 and was riding along the Black Canyon of the Gunnison. This was an area of outstanding beauty, but there was road construction on the highway and a flag man. At least a mile-long line of vehicles and I waited in the blazing sun for no less than a half-hour before being permitted to move along the single open lane. It was one of those turn off the bike, get off, and walk about moments, but eventually I could see oncoming traffic, so I remounted my GPS, phone charger, and myself and got ready to roll again. We finally started moving, and I followed in the dust of a semi and trailer for what must have been twenty miles of torn-up tarmac and gravel.

About the time we'd gotten past all the construction, rain set in, then it poured heavily, like so many heavy summer downpours we have in Florida where you can't see your hand in front of your face. There were a couple places that a river of muddy water was flowing over the highway a foot or more deep. I rolled through with my axles just above the raging water. Luckily, the passages were brief and the rain had slacked off to a drizzle by the time I got to the flash flood crossings. I emerged on the other side upright but muddy.

Black Canyon of the Gunnison

By the time I got to Ouray, the rain had diminished, and after I'd found the last available tent site at the Ampitheater Campsite, it had stopped completely. The campground sign had said "Full," but a couple I had stopped to ask said some campers had left their reserved spots, and suggested I check with the campsite hosts and then showed me where the hosts were located. The host I talked to was genial and said the first-come, first-serve sites went quickly. I was beginning to fear my construction delay might have cost me a site because of my late arrival. Luckily, he said they often get tired bikers who simply needed to stop for the day, so they kept a site for them, just in case, and I could have it.

I gave him the fifteen-dollar fee and went to set up camp. Meanwhile, the couple I'd spoken with earlier, Mike and Debbie, were walking their dog nearby, and we got to talking again. They asked me if I liked beer, and they didn't have to ask again. I accompanied them to their site for a porter and some chips. That was a godsend, as I'd resolved myself to going hungry that night. I'd decided not to return to Ouray to eat that night, as the road up was wet, steep, and slippery and the slanted streets in town made it look like a chore to find a suitable and safe place to park the bike. Everywhere had seemed to be unlevel. Now, the bottle of porter and the chips had been just enough to satisfy my hunger, and Mike and Debbie were marvelous, kind people. We kept talking until it was almost dark. They were from near Denver, and it turned out that I had ridden past their weekend getaway cabin on my way to Ouray that same day.

Looking down on Ouray from the Amphitheater Campground

Back at the tent, I wrote in my journal until I couldn't see any more and then hit the sack, but not before stowing my food and toiletries in the hosts' shed, as I was now in bear country and wanted to avoid having one visit my tent or my bike in the night.

## MILLION DOLLAR HIGHWAY TO MOAB

I got up at a leisurely seven o'clock, only having 230 miles or so to go to Moab, my next target, by way of Durango. I'd be riding the Million Dollar Highway, also known as US

Highway 550. Once I was packed up, I walked up to retrieve my stuff and have a cup of coffee, provided by the hosts inside the little shelter where I'd hidden my smelly stuff away for the night from the bears.

I had just finished loading the bike and was about to leave but walked across the parking area in which the Tiger was waiting to take in the view from a vantage point and to sit still for a moment on a bench placed there to allow visitors to take in and enjoy the views across the mountains. The area and its scenery came as close as anything I'd ever seen to being comparable to the mountain ranges in British Columbia, one of my most favorite areas I'd ever ridden through.

While I was sitting there, one of the camp hosts walked up, and we sat and talked for a half an hour. I'd seen on Facebook that someone had posted that US 550 had been closed due to a mud slide, but the host was able to confirm that had happened the day before and the road was already cleared—good news, because I'd have hated to miss the fantastic ride that I'd heard so much about and was now about to experience.

550 went south past Silverton to Durango, where I'd turn west toward Utah, and surmounted 11,000 feet in a couple places. It was winding, with no guardrails alongside most of it separating you from thousand-foot or more drops into the valleys below. The views into the valleys were beautiful, and the ride was spectacular as the sliver of highway wove its way south cut into the sides of the mountain ridges.

My dad had a passion for the West and Southwest and a longing to move there, which unfortunately never happened for him. I think he had fallen in love with the Southwest when he and a couple of his brothers-in-law had driven out to Arizona from South Bend to retrieve my uncle's effects and his mourning wife after he had died in Tucson under mysterious consequences, back when I was no more than ten. After that, Dad always talked about the West, dreamed about the West, and watched just about every old Western movie set in its romantic grandeur. When we were a little older, Dad took us out camping as far as Colorado a couple times, but he never did make it to Arizona again. I couldn't help thinking about him and how he would have loved to be doing what I was doing. Not that I am a believer in the metaphysical, but in an odd way it felt almost like he was there with me. I wished I could have somehow told him about what I was experiencing. I know he'd be grinning from ear to ear.

View from the Million Dollar Highway

The camp host had told me about a good breakfast place in Silverton, but somehow, I missed it, despite looking for the distinctive red building he described situated right beside the highway. So, it was not until ten miles before Durango that I found a place to eat. It was too late for the huevos rancheros I had been hoping for, but they had a good burger list. Most had two quarter-pound patties—a half pound of beef was too much for me—but then I spied a patty melt with just one patty and ordered that with a side of fries. It was a fabulous burger, and the mountain of fries that were delivered to my table were delicious, rolled in some delicious spices. I tried to clean my plate but still had to leave half of them. It was certainly a spot I'd have to revisit if I ever found myself in the area again.

It was not far to Durango, where I turned the bike westward, then northwestward, toward Utah. As I crossed into the new state, there were ominous clouds brooding over the massive wall of the Abajo Mountains ahead, beyond the high prairie. The Garmin showed a turn to the north before I got to the range. I hoped the rain would stay put until I made that turn. The mountain rain clouds didn't move, but then others appeared ahead and to the west and above the north edge of the mountains. Although I received a few sprinkles across my face shield, I outran most of it and was riding through patches of sunlight as I approached Moab.

Once in Moab, I stopped for beer, a couple granola bars, and iced tea to bring with me to wherever I'd camp. I was checking out my options on my phone beside my bike when a helmeted fellow approached and commented on how far I'd come. He introduced himself, and it turned out that we'd met before. He owned a company called MotoSkivvies, making motorcycle-specific underwear to make sitting on a bike for hours more comfortable. They were similar to bicycling shorts but designed specifically for motorcyclists. I remembered chatting with him at a booth at the first AIMExpo, a huge motorcycle equipment convention that's first venue was in the convention center in Orlando years before. I had been there with the VJMC, who were putting on a vintage bike show during the event, and I was browsing the circuit of booths when I had run into the MotoSkivvies spot.

The man lived somewhere else in the Southwest, but had a place in Moab, where he kept a couple light dual-sport motorcycles that he used from time to time to explore and play in the desert around Moab. Having local knowledge, he filled me in on several good camping opportunities, but what appealed the most to me that he'd mentioned was along a small road, Utah 128, to the right off the main highway, just before crossing the Colorado River, north of town. The road ran along the river's south bank for miles and had numerous campsites alongside it. I decided to check it out before going back to a less primitive spot I'd seen closer to Moab. His advice was spot-on, and I found Grandstaff Campground on the very edge of the river, just a few miles upstream. It was part of the National Park Service and there were plenty of vacant sites, each with a fire ring and a table—perfect. I filled out an envelope at the bulletin board, inserted a twenty, and dropped it in the box.

Camping on the Colorado River in Moab

The campsite was ideal, on the narrow shore tucked in between the road and the river, with towering red rock cliffs across the water and on the far side of the road I had ridden in on. I quickly set up the tent and sleeping gear, then struck up a conversation with my neighbor, Doug, who was riding a Honda CBR250. He was a handyman from Canada but had lived in Moab for a while in the past. His diminutive bike was rigged with a box for his tools, in case he found any work along the way, and a unique homemade rack for his camping gear, He was on an open-ended ride and had been in Moab for a couple days and expected to be there a couple more. He had just turned sixty-five, which I had done about a half-year earlier, and gotten his Senior Lifetime National Park Pass, as I had done, and informed me that I could have saved half on the campsite fee if I'd only written down my card number on the envelope. I knew there was a discount at in-park campgrounds but didn't know the special rate extended to all the National Forest areas as well. I'd not make that mistake again.

The rest of the day was spent watching the river flow by with rafters, kayakers, and occasional shallow-draft jet boats scooting along on its waters and by writing in my journal. The sky cleared, and as the air warmed, by late afternoon, it was clear and sun-filled, promising a rainless sky the following day.

Doug said that nearby Arches National Park was open only by reservation, a recent phenomenon caused largely by people having been cooped up so long during the Covid pandemic and now wanting to get outside. I hoped that would not be something I'd have to deal with much on the rest of my ride, which included plans to visit several more popular National Parks. I'd skip Arches the following day and head to the next park, Canyonlands, just fifteen miles further up the highway, which I knew was open to regular visitors. Doug was going to try to get into Arches before daylight in the morning.

The sun set over the crimson cliffs on the far side of the Colorado, casting their shadows first across the water, then over my tent, and finally moving slowly up the face of the cliffs of the canyon on the other side of the road. Once it was completely dark, Doug and I shared red wine while watching a truck rolling slowly along the road above us, shining a huge spotlight on the cliff faces to the south as it moved. Doug said they had been doing that each night, but he hadn't discovered what the purpose was but just assumed it was some sort of light show for the campers. Whatever it was, it was impressive seeing the cliffs glowing in that spotlight in the otherwise black desert.

Lighting up the cliffs

## HOODOOS, RAIN, AND ANCIENT PICTOGRAPHS

I heard Doug ride off in the morning very early in the darkness. He was determined to get to Arches before everyone else and slip in with the handful of others who didn't have reservations but arrived early enough to gain entrance. I fell back asleep but woke again about 6:30. I didn't lay awake in the tent very long before I was packing up and getting ready to leave for Capital Reef, with Escalante or Bryce National Parks as my day-end destination options, depending on how long it took to get there after a stop at Canyonlands National Park that morning on the way out of Moab.

Within three-quarters of an hour I was packed up and ready. I decided not to take the time to make breakfast but to get something to eat on the way. Canyonlands National Park was just thirty miles north of my camp. When I spotted the turn-in, I also spotted a little enterprise that looked very much like a tourist trap, but which also had a sign that said,

"Café." I pulled into the empty parking lot and found a smaller sign on the café door saying it was closed. Because I had only had a couple of granola bars for my dinner the night before I was more than hungry. But breakfast would have to wait until after visiting Canyonlands.

The road into the park wound for a dozen or so more miles, until it came to an entrance gate with a fee taker. I showed her my Lifetime Pass, and she asked for my driver's license as well. I guess I should have stashed both the pass and my license in my handy right sleeve pocket of my Darien. I'd be ready the next time so I would not have to dig into my jacket and through all my cards while a line of vehicles waited behind me. While I retrieved my license, the ranger made small talk about how far I'd ridden, then upon seeing the driver's license, simply said, "Enjoy your visit!" and waved me in.

A scene Dad would have loved

That Lifetime Pass would prove to be one of the best bargains I'd ever found—eighty dollars for access to all our National Parks, plus usually a fifty-percent discount on camping fees. I recall years ago while passing through the

Tetons on the way to Yellowstone that they were charging fifty dollars just to ride between the two parks on the Rockefeller Parkway. I'd paid eighty for an annual pass instead, as I was going to be visiting more National Parks on that trip, but now eighty dollars for unlimited access for life was an easy decision. Once in a very great while it pays to be old!

When I'd planned my trip, I had hoped to visit Arches National Park, but I saw that there was an arch in Canyonlands as well, so I made that my first stop, having not been willing to try to get into Arches in the dark that morning with Doug. The many tourists in Canyonlands National Park didn't dim the magnificence of the park and the view of the canyons below the Mesa Arch from a sheer cliff that must have had a thousand-foot drop from its edge to the valley floor far below. It had been a long, hot walk to the arch, still in my heavy riding clothes, but it was well worth it—a thrilling sight across miles upon miles of the red, desert landscape. Dad would have been thrilled.

Mesa Arch

I climbed back onto the Tiger and rode to the furthest viewpoint in the park, Grand View Point. It was not as fantastic as the arch had been, but was still, in a less dramatic way, a beautiful vantage point. I hiked along the trail for a long way, thinking the sign in the parking area indicating the distance of the hike to the complete the circuit to the point and back had indicated one minute, but halfway along I began to realize that "1 Mi" did not mean a minute but a mile. I guess my brain was on a break when I had read that sign. I turned back to the parking lot the way I'd come in and climbed onto the Tiger's saddle.

Next, I went to Green River Overlook, just a mile and a half from where the main road split to each viewpoint, so I figured it would not take long to check it out. The morning was burning up fast, and I still had a long way to go that day. At the viewpoint I shot a few more photos before making my way back out to the highway and turning north.

I'd have to do a big, roughly upside-down U to get from the southeastern part of Utah to the southwestern corner, as no paved roads shot straight west across the state from the area around Moab. I had to take an Interstate highway twenty or thirty miles, which formed the top leg of the U and that would intersect my southbound route toward Capital Reef National Park, Escalante, and Bryce Canyon National Park.

Once on the southbound highway, I was passing through the San Rafael Desert. The route took me past an interesting park called Valley of the Goblins State Park that I'd seen in an episode of a friend's YouTube channel. I wished I'd had time to stop there and explore, but I didn't want to arrive too late at Bryce and have trouble finding a campsite. I could at least see a few of the odd structures the park was known for from the highway, but not the cool, individual hoodoos my friends had seen up close. Passing this by was one of the first compromises I realized I'd have to make, as seeing everything there is to see in the Southwest is impossible without unlimited time. I'd have to learn to choose, wisely I hoped.

I sped south toward Hanksville, where I finally found a diner, Duke's Slickrock Grill, and stopped for a break for lunch by that time instead of breakfast. I had a huge salad with some of the best brisket I've ever tasted piled on top. The stop was just what I needed, and the waiter was kind enough to add ice to my water bottle as well. I was learning the great importance of my water bottle there in the Southwest and not to ever leave a stop without topping it up.

I had lost my reading glasses that morning and had been having a difficult time reading the map in my tank bag, and I mentioned to the server that was the reason I was having a hard time reading the menu while he waited patiently to take my order. He said that he had spare readers, and while I was eating, he brought a pair and told me to keep them. I offered him money to replace them, but he refused it, saying he had plenty of others and would not miss one pair. I gave him a generous tip when I paid my bill. It was the least I could do and much cheaper than if I'd had to buy a pair—the kindness of strangers.

While at Duke's, I was planning my next couple days. I was going to visit a friend in Sedona, who I'd met back in Lake Wales when I'd spotted him and his BMW GS broken down beside the road and had helped him get a new battery so he could get back on the highway. He mentioned he lived in Sedona and, if I was ever in the area, I would have a place to stay. I immediately replied, "Well, as a matter of fact, I'm heading out there in the next month or so . . . " Now that I was looking over the maps, I realized that being there the next day was too soon, with planned stops along the way at Bryce and the Grand Canyon's North Rim. I called him up and let him know it would be two days, instead, before I arrived. The Grand Canyon would be, well, too grand to not spend a little time exploring it.

At Hanksville, I had left the previous highway that trended southwest, and now after lunch, I was riding west toward Torrey. There I turned again onto another road heading beside Capital Reef, which sat in the east, and directly to Escalante and Bryce in the southwest. Soon, I was stopped by a flagman and was contemplating waiting a long time in the sun again like I'd endured before in Colorado. So, instead, I took advantage of the delay to top up my fuel, as the flagman had stopped me

directly in front of a gas station. By the time I pulled back out
to the road with a full tank, it was only a couple minutes before
I could continue, and the flagger let me in at the front of the
line again.

I passed Capital Reef while storm clouds gathered ahead of
me, growing most ominous in the Dixie National Forest. The
sky was dark, and there were low clouds clinging close to the
mountains I was passing through while at over eight thousand
feet. It was growing chilly as sprinkles began. I knew by then I
would not make Bryce that day. It was already approaching four
o'clock, and I figured if I arrived at popular Bryce National Park
after six, there would probably be no campsites left. I spotted
a campsite in Dixie National Forest and hesitated, almost
stopping there instead, but I wanted to make a little more
progress that day, so the next day's ride would not be such a long
slog all the way to the Grand Canyon. Finally, after four, I was
northeast of Escalante and spotted Calf Creek Campground
on my right below me at the end of a steep plunge down off the
side of the mountains.

I pulled in while it was still sprinkling, but there were signs
of the rain easing. Luckily, there were many sites available, and
I used my discount this time, instead of paying fifteen dollars
only paying seven and a half. I didn't want to dig for change, so
I just put a five and three one-dollar bills in the envelope and
called it close enough.

Most of the campsites were encircled by bushes, and
although I was surrounded by other campers, it felt almost as if
I was alone in the bush in the little secluded alcove where I'd be
camping. After camp was set, I walked around the campground
a bit and saw a large overland truck camped nearby. There were
two men and a woman standing near the vehicle. I stopped
to say hello and asked if they had been northwest of Denver
a couple days ago, because I had seen a truck much like theirs
when I had stopped for my breakfast after leaving Mountain
Air Ranch. The guys just shrugged and grunted, while the
girl said they'd not been there. I asked where they were from,

and they replied, "Germany," which I'd already guessed by the accent of their grunts. That was about the most I'd get out of them. There were no attempts to talk or be sociable on their part, so I left them alone. I don't know if they were rude or just didn't understand a word I'd said.

The rain picked up, and I went back to the tent and crawled inside for a bit, reading the park brochure until the shower began to dissipate. In less than a half-hour it had stopped completely. Meanwhile, I had learned from the brochure there was a trail following the creek upstream, eventually to some falls, and along the way it would pass some pictographs and granaries created by the Fremont culture, some seven-hundred to three-thousand years ago.

The cliffs along Calf Creek Trail

I decided to hike the trail at least as far as I could go in the time I had before sunset, which was not a lot. I got a couple miles up the trail before I had to turn around, but I got to where the pictographs were supposed to be, on the cliffs on the far side of the creek, and near the granaries, in a gulch on the side of the stream I was on. I couldn't make out the pictographs but took numerous photos where I knew they should be, so

I could examine them more closely in Photoshop when I was home and possibly identify them that way. I never found the granaries either, but it didn't matter; the walk felt good, and the sun had come out too as I had been hiking. At home, I usually walked over two miles every morning, and I had been missing that exercise on the trip, so the hike was perfect.

I had to scramble to get back before dark—the Utah desert was not the place I wanted to be caught out overnight with no shelter or protection. I made it back in enough time to do most of my journal entry still in the light, finishing it by the light of my lantern before climbing into my tent and turning in. I figured the huge salad I'd had that day was enough for me, so I went to bed without supper, not wanting to stay up late messing with the stove.

## CAMPING AT THE CANYON

Bryce Canyon

I woke up about quarter-'til-seven and was out of the tent by seven. It had rained moderately for a long time the night before, and everything was wet outside. All the scrub, bushes, and trees were soaked with rain, and they emitted marvelous odors that permeated the morning air—rosemary, sage, and all manner of other odiferous greenery.

Bryce Canyon

    By 8:30 I was back on the road and continuing through Escalante and toward Bryce National Park. I found some breakfast in the sleepy town of Escalante. The usual neighborhood diner was closed, but I stopped at an outfitters that advertised coffee. The shop only had various coffees and a few pastries, but the lady at the counter said the mercantile, four doors down, had good breakfast sandwiches and that I could walk there and bring back the food to eat on their porch that served as their dining area. I walked over to the mercantile and ordered a large and delicious egg, sausage, and herb bagel and bought a cranberry scone as well. Back at the outfitters, I ordered a large Americano to go with it. The shopkeeper was very accommodating, even though all I'd bought from her was the coffee. She even brought me a plate and silverware for the food I'd bought next door, and instead of pouring my strong, excellent coffee in a paper cup, she offered me a ceramic one. When I was leaving and went to pay, she refused a tip.

Bristlecone Pine

At Bryce National Park's Visitor Center there was a wonderful diagram describing Escalante (the "staircase") as a series of strata starting on a plateau where I was and descending all the way to the Grand Canyon. I rode the ridge in Bryce and picked out a couple vista points to stop and take photos. At Bryce Point you could look south and see the staircase leading downhill to Arizona. At Inspiration Point I got another, less-complete view of the staircase, but which was also staggeringly beautiful. There, I also found some bristlecone pine, the oldest living tree on earth, living up to four thousand years, and made sure to get some photos. Bryce was a rather small park, but I still was there when the day had passed from morning into afternoon.

The "staircase" (escalante) to the Grand Canyon at Bryce Canyon

I headed south to Kanab, where I turned right and into the state of Arizona, a state I had never visited before, the first of several first-time states I'd be passing through on this ride. After a couple more turns, I was passing over the Kaibab Plateau and on my final road into Grand Canyon National Park.

I had spent so much time at Bryce, I stepped up the pace heading south to the Grand Canyon. I didn't want to arrive too late. Despite my efforts, I arrived at North Rim around five, late for obtaining a camping space, I thought. I'd seen a "Sites Available" sign ten miles north at Motte but thought I'd give North Rim Campground a shot, and if it was full, I could always ride back to Motte.

When I pulled up at the Grand Canyon entry booth there was a big sign saying, "Camping Full." I told the attendant that

I'd just turn around for Motte and come back in the morning to see the canyon, but she said there were often cancellations or people who left early, especially because of heavy rain, which they'd been getting throughout the afternoon that day just before I had arrived. She encouraged me to check out the campground to see if they might have any space.

From the entry booth, it was a ten-mile ride to the North Rim Campground, but I gave it a go, and sure enough, they had three or four sites, and I was offered one of them. My pass gave me half-off, so nine dollars, but their card reader had been down for a few days, and they could not take cash. I was told I could pay the next day at the Visitor Center if I wanted to, or not, my choice. The attendant matter-of-factly said no one was checking on campers, and if I wanted to skip paying, I could.

I found my space and quickly reassembled the still wet tent. The inside of it was dry, so the little dampness on the outside did not pose a problem. Drinking water was just a few steps away, and nice, clean bathrooms were nearby as well. The only thing missing were showers, but tomorrow, at Tim's in Sedona, I would have a chance to shower.

As soon as I got my cooking stuff out and was almost ready to boil water for another pot of cacao, the rain began again. I escaped into the tent, where I sat working on my journal for an hour or so until the rain stopped. By the time I emerged from the tent again, I still had enough light to fire up the stove and prepare the cacao. After the hot drink, it was dark, and I was ready for bed.

## FINDING HOSPITALITY IN SEDONA

I awoke before six and didn't wait long before getting out of the tent and making some oatmeal for breakfast. I left camp to dry out and walked to the end of the campground to connect with the nearby Transept Trail to Bright Angel Point.

View from Transept Trail

The path to Bright Angel Point

The walk along the canyon edge was stunning, with each peep through openings in the trees yielding another spectacular view. Bright Angel Point allowed me to see far to the west of the canyon as the Colorado River, which had started a thousand miles away, flowed below on its way to, almost, the

Gulf of California, the demand for its water from the adjacent states having dried it up completely just a few miles before it could reach its former mouth.

While at the point, I was near one of the Visitors' Centers, so I went inside to pay for my campsite. When I told the ranger what I had been told about paying there, he looked at me oddly and said he didn't know a thing about that and could not take my money. So instead, I picked out a sticker for my windscreen and paid for only that before heading back to camp.

Taking a break in the Vermillion Cliffs

Leaving the point, I hiked back to the tent by a less scenic, but more direct, route. Time was passing, and I still wanted to take in the view from Point Imperial, at the eastern end of the canyon, before leaving for Sedona and backtracking forty miles to the main highway. That route took me east around the end of the canyon, along the south edge of Vermillion Cliffs National Monument, and into Marble Canyon, where I crossed the Colorado River, flowing far below the bridge. I pulled off once I was across and walked back across the river on the adjacent pedestrian Navajo Bridge, from which I could see tiny rafts floating below, gathered up at a landing under the highway bridge.

Leaving the river behind, the route continued downhill until almost to Flagstaff, where the altitude began to increase.

Approaching Sedona

After passing through the river of traffic in Flagstaff, I continued south on the same highway, avoiding the Interstate that mirrored its path just to the east. It was a climb and then descent through woods and around cliffs beside Oak Creek in the Verde Valley, green because of the creek's waters that nourished the area year-round. But fun was about to end halfway to Sedona, when a one-way traffic light for road construction stopped me and a hundred cars for forty-five minutes, while another hundred cars zipped past us coming from the south. Eventually, we got our turn, which was lucky, because by then I was about to pass out from sitting in the sun.

Beyond the construction zone, where no one was actually doing any construction on that Sunday morning, the route was lined with campgrounds and picnic sites and, apparently, judging from the many young women dressed in bikini tops, places to swim or tube.

The route took me through the heart of the tourist district in Sedona. It looked interesting, but I later found out that everything there was very expensive, too expensive for me anyway. The city loved its roundabouts, and I passed through dozens as I threaded my way to Tim's house, south of downtown. By the time I got to Tim and Tara's, I was exhausted, but after a shower and getting a load of laundry in the wash, I was ready for dinner.

I offered to buy some pizza for delivery, but Tim asked me if I really wanted to spend a hundred and fifty dollars on pizza, because that's what it would likely cost coming from Sedona. Tim explained that the cost of living was so high in Sedona that most of the wait staff at the numerous restaurants couldn't afford to live there, and many lived in their cars in the surrounding desert, despite working full-time. Pizza sounded great, but that changed my mind, so I took Tim's advice, and we all, along with their young son, piled into their Toyota FJR and headed south to Cottonwood for dinner at a place they knew. Cottonwood was much less exclusive and expensive than Sedona but had a great choice of dining places, being larger than Sedona but less of a tourist haven, and we settled into a cozy pub for dinner, for which Tim refused to let me pay a dime, despite my offers.

Back at Tim's, I unloaded my now-dry clothes and packed them away and scoured my maps trying to find a route west to California that would avoid passing through Death Valley, as the temperatures everywhere in the Southwest had been very high lately and would be even more so in Death Valley. I finally realized I was too tired to think straight that night so left the planning for the morning.

## Two Deserts and Joshua Tree

By six o'clock I was up, and I had packed by seven. While I loaded the bike, Tim made eggs, bacon, and toasted croissants. After breakfast, we said our goodbyes. Tim helped me extricate the heavily-laden bike from the garage and onto the steeply sloped drive to a position that would make it easy to ride the bike out and onto the street. When I'd met Tim in Florida, he had been there working on a gyroplane that was being built for him in Zephyrhills, so as I was about to leave, I extracted a promise from him to let me return the favor and host him when his plane was finished and he returned to Florida to pick it up and fly it home.

I'd looked again that morning at the maps with fresh eyes and came up with a plan to go south and then west into California via smaller highways and avoiding any Interstate travel or large cities. I made my way further south, toward Prescott. Still on Highway 89A that I had taken into Sedona, I passed through Jerome, a city perched literally on the side of cliffs along a stretch of the highway full of hairpin turns and extreme grades as it crossed over Woodshute Mountain. The town reminded me of pictures I'd seen of isolated monasteries in faraway places perched on cliffs, dangling over deep valleys, but with a distinct American Western flair to the architecture.

After passing through Prescott and before reaching the town of Congress, I stopped to top up my fuel in Peeples Valley and have a coffee and a snack to wake myself up. A modern Moto Guzzi was parked at the gas station, but I never saw any sign of the rider, with whom I'd liked to have had a chat. At Congress, where I encountered my first saguaro cactus, I turned onto another road, now generally headed west. I chuckled to myself that I could easily remember where I saw my first iconic cactus because I had seen my first prickly saguaro in a place named Congress, a place which was also far to the east and full of pricks.

The highway eventually turned northwest, toward Parker and another crossing of the Colorado River. This time when I crossed the river, I would also be passing into California, my second first-time state. The route took me through what the map called a "cactus prairie" and the northern edge of the Sonoran Desert before crossing the Coloardo into the Mojave Desert on the California side.

As I rode through the desert, in the distance, around the foot of a mountain range, was a line of gray-blue dust or moisture floating in a distinct layer. I never discovered why that was or what it was, but it was an interesting phenomenon to see, floating ghost-like above the desert floor.

I had been wanting to get a photo of the Tiger in front of a saguaro cactus, that icon of the American West, but there'd not been any good places to park near any I had seen so far. Then, before I passed Salome, I spotted a huge saguaro on the far side of a set of railroad tracks paralleling the highway. A dirt road crossed the tracks, which according to a sign planted near the saguaro, went to Arizona Valley Ranch. It looked like the area in front of the cactus to the left of the road had recently been graded. I assumed the ground would have been compacted as well. Stopping there might be my chance for the photo, so I turned off the highway, crossed the tracks, and turned left to park in front of and below the huge saguaro.

As soon as I put my foot down, I knew it had been a mistake. There was loose sand everywhere. I didn't even try to put the kickstand down or climb off. I carefully started to do a large U-turn away from the spot and back toward the more solid road and tracks. I'd almost made it when I turned the front wheel a bit too far in some loose sand, and down I went, stepping off as the Tiger went down for a nap.

Fortunately, it was soft sand, or perhaps not fortunately, because if it had not been soft, I probably would not have been in the predicament I was in. I checked the bike, but nothing was broken. But again, now the bike was laying top-downhill with both wheels off the ground. I tried to budge it, to no avail. I unloaded the heavy dry bag from the pillion and removed the tank bag to lighten the bike and then noticed the front wheel had dug a deep trench under itself. If I had been able to stand it up, I would probably have had the same problem trying to move forward to get out of the newly-dug sandy hole. I grabbed the bars and spun the bike a foot or so on its side on the ground to reposition the front wheel above virgin sand. I then gave lifting it another go, and this time I got the bike almost to a forty-five-degree angle before I could not hold it anymore and had to let it back down.

The Tiger taking a dirt nap

I was discouraged. What was I doing out there, alone, at my age, when I could not even lift my own bike from the ground? It was not even that heavy of a motorcycle. What if I had been in a remote place and that had happened? I was doubting not only my strength but my wisdom to even be doing what I was doing.

But I could not dwell on that now; I needed to get the bike out of there and back on the road. Only a couple hundred yards away on a railway bed that paralleled the highway there was a group of men working on the tracks. I left the bike where it was, after taking the obligatory napping bike photo, and trudged down toward them, walking on the ties. As I got closer, I waved my arms and asked if they might be willing to give me a hand. One kind soul spoke up, fired up his truck, and instructed me to climb in. He'd help me. The very short ride was a bit of heaven with the air conditioning blasting frigid air across my sweaty body.

We drove back to the prone bike and put the bike luggage into the back of his truck. With both of us lifting, we quickly had it on its sidestand. The man steadied the bike as I climbed back on and then stayed nearby, in case I dropped it again during my attempt at escape. But I made it to hard ground without mishap and parked near the highway on firmer ground. The truck pulled up beside me, and I got the luggage out of the back and packed it back onto the bike. I offered to pay him something, even if it was only enough for a six-pack for him and his co-workers after work, but he refused, saying everyone in the desert had to look out for each other. We shook hands, and he rolled back down in his truck to rejoin his partners at the track.

I was a bit jittery after the fall and my loss of self-confidence, but I had a long, straight highway to ride with few distractions, giving me time to get myself back together. By the time I crossed the Colorado, I was feeling a bit better. I stopped at a gas station at Vidal Station, once I was in California, to refill my water bottle, which I had almost emptied while struggling with the bike. As I was leaving, I noticed a tow truck pull up and start dragging a disabled automobile up onto its bed. The Mojave would not be a good place to be broken down, and the person who owned the car was lucky it had happened at this junction, because for miles around there was literally nothing but desert baking in the blazing sun under a cloudless sky.

As I shot west toward Joshua Tree National Park, I spotted a man sitting on the side of the road at an emergency call box. These were placed every couple miles in case someone was stranded, because the desert heat could quickly kill anyone who was unprepared, especially if they had no water. I'd seen him at the last second and had passed him, but I could not let him sit there in the heat, which was climbing rapidly, now that we were in the middle of the afternoon. I turned around and pulled up to where he was sitting. I asked if he had any water, and he said he had some, but very little. I gave him half of my two liters. He said his car was west of us, down a dirt side road, and that he was out of gas. I had a full extra gallon under my pannier in the Rotopax and had sufficient range without it to make it to Twentynine Palms, a city ahead on the north side of Joshua Tree, so I offered him the gas.

He indicated to me where the car was, a quarter of a mile away or so. I left him there and headed down to the car to put the gallon in his tank. The minivan was parked about a half-mile down a dusty gravel road in a bit of a wide opening. The ground was sufficiently solid for me to be able to use my kickstand and get off the bike without another incident. About the time I had finished pouring the contents of the Rotopax into the van's tank and was in the process of remounting the Rotopax to the rack, the tow truck I had seen earlier in Vidal Station pulled up with the same car on its bed, now with both the owner of that car and the stranded man in the cab, along with the driver. Apparently, there was more wrong than just lack of fuel, and the minivan's battery was dead as well. The man operating the tow truck was friendly and gave me enough water to refill my bottle, plus a bottle to drink on the spot. Water was precious there, and no one went anywhere without extra. The tow truck operator had things in-hand and more ability than me to help, so I got on the Tiger and got ready to leave. As I turned the key and waited for the fuel pump to pressurize the injectors, the ambient temperature gauge on the panel showed 106 degrees Fahrenheit.

I got into Twentynine Palms a couple hours later. The entrance to Joshua Tree National Park should have been on the left side of the same highway I was on, but I saw nothing that looked like a National Park entrance, Visitors' Center, or anything similar. The GPS sent me to a vacant building that had certainly been a Visitors' Center at some time in the past, but there was a sign outside saying they had moved and explaining, not very clearly, where they had relocated. Heading back out in search of the new location, I thought I had followed the instructions correctly but found myself back at the same spot at which I had started. Luckily, a couple young men were walking there, so I asked them where I could find the new center. They were very helpful, and finally with their help I located it, but by that time it had closed. However, there was a large map outside showing camping on Indian Cove Road at the aptly-named Indian Cove Campground. I found the gravel road and a ranger station near the highway, but the station was closed. I rode past to the campground, which was almost empty. There were reserved notes hanging on the posts of most of the sites, but it was late enough that if someone was coming, they'd have been there already, so I just chose a site and set up camp. I'd stop by the ranger station in the morning to check in and pay.

The campground was stark and beautiful as only a desert can be. A huge stack of red boulders towered above the camp sites with smaller ones scattered around its base and the tent sites sprinkled among them. I quickly set up camp and realized I had run out of water. There was a young couple camping nearby and they had a few gallons of fresh water, which they offered to share with me. I gladly accepted their offer and, after gulping down a liter instantly, I filled my two-liter bottle and thanked them for their generosity.

I wandered around the gigantic outcropping I was camped almost under and ambled toward the north side of it, which faced the highway, hoping to get a signal on my phone so I could call home, but I had to settle with just sending texts that would not go out until I had a signal, sometime the next day.

Camp in Joshua Tree National Park

I skipped dinner and sat back to watch the sky darken and turn red as night came on and millions of diamonds shined their pin-points of light down onto our little planet. The dome of the sky was the darkest of dark-blue with a ring of fire along the horizon in the west, which slowly grew dimmer until all was darkness between the sparkling stars.

I climbed into the tent and drew my sleeping bag up to my chin as the chill of the empty desert set in, and I nodded off to sleep.

## NORTH IN THE SIERRAS

The heat of the sun turning the tent into an oven woke me at 6:30. I was up, packed, and gone by seven o'clock. I stopped by the ranger station on the way out to pay, but it was still not open, so I headed back onto the highway I had come in on and headed west. Although I had been riding along the north edge of Joshua Tree National Park for a couple hours the previous day, I had not seen any of those unique trees yet, but now that I was at the western end of the park, Joshua trees become prolific and would be common along much of my route toward the Sierra Nevada.

Joshua Trees

I turned northwest toward Victorville and stopped for breakfast at the Highway 247 Diner, where 247 turned north toward Barstow and Highway 18 would take me west into Victorville. I'd not eaten anything since breakfast at Tim's the previous morning, so a hearty breakfast was in order. The place was almost alone in the desert, with just a tiny scattering of modest houses sparsely sprinkled on both sides of the highway nearby. The diner was certainly biker-friendly and looked to be a popular place for riders, especially the hard-core cruiser crowd. The food was basic but good, and the price was right. I did not leave hungry.

Soon, I was in Victorville, where I turned onto US Highway 395 north and crossed ninety more miles of the

Mojave Desert to Ridgecrest, with the Sierras rising in the west as I approached. There were still Joshua trees for a long distance until the highway started to climb, hugging the Sierra Nevada on my left. At Ridgecrest, the road veered northwest, hard up against the Sierras and began a slow ascent until, by afternoon, I was at over five-thousand feet in altitude. Eventually, I passed the western edge of Death Valley National Park and the Panamint Mountains.

Café 247

There was a sweet smell in the air all the way north and past Tioga Pass, which crossed the range at Yosemite, and on to the spot I would camp that night. The air had a smell like sandalwood but with a sweet, almost lavender, tone to it. It was a sensory delight.

Aaron, an author whose book I'd published, texted me while I was stopped taking a break and getting some iced tea at Lone Pine and suggested Convict Lake as a good, cooler, and higher campground along my way. Luckily, it was only about twenty miles further. I had started feeling weary, so it was perfect, if I could find a spot at four o'clock in the afternoon.

The campground was only two miles off the highway and was very popular. Despite the impending rain coming in from the mountains above it to the west there were many campers. But my luck held out, and I quickly found a spot. It was a bit pricey, thirty dollars, but my Lifetime Pass made it only fifteen for me. I only had tens and twenties left in cash, so I had to deposit a twenty instead, but I did not regret it, as I had not had to pay a dime at either the Grand Canyon or Joshua Tree.

The campground was very clean and nicely laid out. It had some open spots, while others were nestled among the brush, so you could have privacy if you wanted it. I chose privacy. To my surprise as well, there was both a flushing toilet and a sink, something I had been getting used to going without but now found quite extravagant. There was also a convenient nearby water spigot, so I could fill up my water bottle. I'd become very aware of our need for water during my desert crossing, and so I took pains to get it when I could, and here it was, as easy as turning a faucet. There were bear proof food boxes at each site as well, which were very useful, now that I was once again in bear country.

No zoom required

Walking through the campground toward the lake, I came across a fearless deer that wouldn't even take notice of me when I walked within four feet of it. It stood calmly as I snapped off some photos.

I got the tent pitched and was setting up the stove to prepare another freeze-dried meal, but the rain and wind set in, and I retreated to the tent for an hour or so. With the wind battering the tent and threatening to send it flying, I crawled back out in a lull and tapped in tent stakes at the corners, something I rarely needed to do. That accomplished, the sun decided to come back out, so I continued making my dinner. This time I had beef stew, which was quite good compared to the last packet I had opened at Mountain Air Ranch. Maybe they would not be so bad, after all.

Convict Lake

Next up was planning the next day. It was only about 250 miles to Roseville, on the northeast side of Sacramento, where Aaron lived. Aaron had written Asphalt and Dirt, and although we had worked together for years, we had never met in person, so he had invited me to drop by and stay with him and his wife for the night. I pulled out the Michelin Atlas, tore out the required pages, stuck them in the tank bag window, and then went back to the picnic table to write in my journal as the air quickly cooled. It would be a chilly night, but no rain was forecast.

### INTO NEVADA, BRIEFLY

I packed and left Convict Lake by about eight. The night had been chilly, but the sleeping bag did its job and kept me warm inside it.

*Topaz Lake straddling the California & Nevada state lines*

I continued north, with the Sierras on my left, and within an hour or so I entered Nevada. I could have turned northwest to connect with my planned route to Roseville more quickly, but I wanted to see Lake Tahoe, if I could. So, I continued past the Garmin's recommended turn and kept riding north until I was east of the lake. From there I turned west onto Highway 207 to cross the peaks between me and Tahoe in hopes of getting a good view of the lake from the top of the ridge.

The road was wild and twisting, with huge drop-offs and incredible grades. Once over the ridge, I expected to see the lake, but there were too many twists and trees to allow much of a glimpse, and the spectacular view I'd expected never materialized. When I got into the town of Lake Tahoe, the lake was still invisible. I passed through a tourist mecca, with music blaring from one club after another. I gave up on the view and veered off the main road onto a side route that would rejoin it later, beyond the party atmosphere and heavy traffic. In a short time, I was back in tranquil nature.

Instead of connecting with busy US Highway 50 for the ride toward Sacramento, the GPS sent me on quiet, paved two-lane roads, eventually recommending I turn off onto the Mormon Emigrant Trail. When I followed its bidding and turned off the highway, a large sign exclaimed, "WARNING You are entering a burned area. Debris may be in the road. Travel at your own risk."

Burnt forest on the Mormon Trail

Both sides of the road were lined with burned carcasses of pines and tree boles; cut, stacked, and waiting for pickup on the berm. The black, sooty remnants of a once verdant forest of tall pines went on for twenty or thirty miles, looking like a forest of charred toothpicks reaching for the sky. Despite the warning, I had no trouble negotiating the route and did not have to avoid debris in the roadway. The reward for taking the alternate route was a virtually traffic-free highway through the mountains on a gracefully winding road.

Eventually, the route reached Placerville, California, after which the land leveled out and the track zig-zagged around the east side of Sacramento. It was hot, and there was heavy traffic. I struggled to keep up with the flow and at the same time follow the Garmin's bidding, turn after turn. I passed Folsom Lake, and by half-past four I turned into Aaron's neighborhood, where I was out of the incessant traffic and could take my time finding his house without a mad rush of vehicles bearing down on me.

Aaron had said they'd likely not be home when I arrived, so they'd left a key under the welcome mat. But when I lifted it up on their porch, there was nothing there. I stepped back to the sidewalk to re-check the address, but it was the same house number Aaron had given me. I walked back onto the porch and rapped on the door, when Lisa's voice came back, "Who's there?" I replied, "It's me, Mike," and soon I was inside with heavenly air conditioning blowing over me.

Lisa had been able to come home earlier than she had expected, but Aaron wasn't home yet. He'd called to say he was on his way from the news studio where he worked. Meanwhile, Lisa showed me the room where I would be staying and the adjacent bathroom. I got a much-needed shower after the hot, sweaty ride into Sacramento and climbed into clean clothes for the first time since Sedona, three days earlier.

I called home while cleaning up and reported I was in for the day and then sorted out some family bill payment business with Andrea when I heard Aaron's voice in the living room.

It was great to finally meet Aaron face to face, after working with him for years never having met, like most of the authors I work with, who live scattered across the US, UK, Europe, and even South America. Out of the nineteen I had worked with, I had only met five before that day, having done all the work required to produce and sell their books electronically, working across oceans via email and DropBox.

Aaron, Lisa, and I all hit it off brilliantly while chatting around the kitchen table, having very similar ways of thinking. Lisa produced a delicious tenderloin dinner, and we all talked until we were tired and recognized we all needed to go to bed, with them going to work in the morning and me heading toward the California Coast.

## REACHING THE GOAL

I woke by six-thirty. By seven I was packing the Tiger, while Aaron was making breakfast and coffee. Soon, we all had to go our separate ways, Aaron to the television studio, Lisa to take care of business at the food bank she worked for, and I to face another scorcher of a day on the back of the bike. After breakfast, I finished the last touches of loading the bike, said goodbye to my friends, now not just business acquaintances but good friends who hoped to see each other again, and rode out of the neighborhood with the GPS pointing me toward Santa Rosa.

Years ago, when I had been a semi-pro woodworker, I'd attended a dovetailing class taught by David Marks, who'd had a television show called Woodworks on DIY Network for a few years. Later, after his television series had ended, David had started a fine woodworking school in Santa Rosa. The course I had taken had been in Orlando, Florida, and happened to be on a weekend that a group of my fellow woodworkers were all going to one of our buddies' home in the area for a gathering and a cookout, which we held from time to time, often at my place in Lake Wales. While at David's course, I had invited him and his wife, Victoria, to join us while he was in the area for the meeting and barbecue. To my surprise, they had accepted the invitation.

We ended up having a great backyard barbecue with the highly-regarded woodworker, getting to know both him and

Victoria personally. While everyone was sitting, chatting, and waiting for the food, a fellow woodworker and I removed ourselves to the garage and quickly built a Krenov-style smoothing plane out of some cherry wood as a gift for David (a Krenov-style plane is made of four segments of wood glued together: two sides and two inside pieces that form the bed for the plane iron and the throat, through which the cutting edge of the iron protrudes and where the shavings are expelled while planing). I'd known a fellow woodworker who had later taken a course from David at his Santa Rosa school, and he had remarked to me that he had seen the plane we'd built at David's school and that it had wood shavings in its throat, indicating the master had found some usefulness in it. I had been gratified to hear that. On this trip, I knew I was going to be passing very near Santa Rosa so looked up David's address on his school's website and thought I might drop in at the school, say hi, and hopefully get a tour.

When I arrived at the address, it was in a very typical suburban neighborhood, not in the country on a big piece of land that I had imagined would be necessary to host a school like his. I hesitated to knock on the door and considered that perhaps they only used their private residence's address for the school's correspondence, and the school itself might have been located elsewhere. It certainly didn't look like a school from where I was parked on the roadside, unless there was a lot more land behind the high, brown, privacy fence. I decided it would be rude for me to simply knock on the door of their home, and announce to them as the door opened, "Remember me?!" So, with that, I decided to move on and climbed back on the bike and headed back into traffic.

I reset the Garmin for Jenner, where the route west would meet the famous Highway 1, also known as the Pacific Coast Highway, and the vast Pacific Ocean, which I'd never visited before this trip. In a half-hour I caught my first glimpse of the ocean. Joining Highway 1 a bit north of the Golden Gate

Bridge and San Francisco, I turned right (north) onto the PCH and pulled over at the first turnoff.

The Pacific Coast at the Russian River

I had followed the Russian River to the coast, on the far bank of which lay the famous, or infamous, depending on your view of it, Bohemian Grove club, a private park where the wealthy and powerful go to "forget their burdens," or as some accuse, do much more secretive and nefarious things.

The Russian River's mouth pouring into the Pacific made for some dramatic photos. I posted a picture to Facebook, showing I'd finally made it and then headed north, forgetting I'd left my glasses on the tailbox. Just a quarter-mile on, I realized what I'd done and turned back for the place where I'd first stopped. A woman was there in her car. I told her what had happened. Sharon said she loved my rig. She helped me search around the lay-by and even up the highway for a short distance before we both gave up. Luckily, those glasses only enhanced my far vision, but without them I could still see perfectly adequately to ride. They had only helped me spot very small road signs much earlier than I might have been able to and to read them more easily from further away; they only "fine-tuned" my vision.

I got back on the Pacific Coast Highway heading north. At first, there were plenty of signs for campgrounds along the highway, so I thought I'd just ride until I felt tired or until it was late in the afternoon. I got to the point at around four-thirty that I wanted to stop, but meanwhile, the campground signs had disappeared. When I did spot one, I pulled in each time, only to find that each campground was full.

Camp at Caspar Beach

Back on the highway continuing north, I kept looking but was, by that time, well-past ready to stop for the day. At Caspar, I came across another camping sign and turned off, but instead of a National Forest or State Park Campground I had found a commercial one. I was anxious to get off the Tiger, so I pulled in anyway, knowing it would probably be expensive, but there were not other options. It did prove pricey, fifty dollars for the night to tent camp, but everything seemed to be expensive in California, so I decided I'd go ahead and take a spot. It turned out to be a nice, shady spot in a well-tended campground. Once camp was set up, I wandered down to the camp store, which was a nice convenience to have close by, for some wine. I'd been thinking about wine all day, since I had passed through the expansive wine country of Napa Valley and Sonoma County on my way to the coast. Of course, I had to have cheese and crackers to go with the wine. I made do with some prepackaged crackers with some sort of orange cheese squeezed between the cracker layers. Good enough.

I went back to my site and fired up the stove to try some freeze-dried chili mac that turned out to be very tasty, especially with the wine to go along with it. So far, the freeze-dried meals were two for three. I wasn't going to drink an entire bottle of wine, so I offered half to a couple pleasant girls who were camped next to me. I had to leave the bottle on a fence post between our sites to avoid stirring up their vociferous dog, who was making it difficult to get to know my neighbors better. From the little I had talked with them they seemed like lovely people, but I certainly understood them having a protector in their dog with them.

Mystery creature

Walking around my campsite, I came across an unusual creature. I had to stop to get a photo of it. It looked like what I remembered a nudibranch looked like, but this lived on the forest floor and not under the sea. It was about six inches long and a light yellow-green and blended in well with the fallen leaves scattered over the ground under the trees. Its disguise was well-suited to the woods, and when I'd look away from it for a moment and then look for it again, it would take me a few minutes to find it again. I made a mental note to ask someone about the strange creature.

I went to work catching up on my journal, which I'd neglected the day before, while the night set in, the air chilled, and the sea-fog came ashore.

## Coastal Cruising

I got up late and took time to walk down to the beach on the far side of the highway to explore it a bit before heading back up the hill to break down camp. While poking around in the beach sand, I found a couple small shells to bring back to Tess, to go along with the mica specimens I'd found in Colorado.

I made a pot of cacao from the last of the grounds and prepared some instant oatmeal for breakfast. I'd have to look for a place to stock up on coffee soon as a replacement for the rest of the trip, as it was very unlikely that I'd find ground and roasted cacao anywhere but online.

It was after ten o'clock before I got on the road. The fog had settled in during the night and had wet the tent, but the extra time that morning was sufficient for it to air out and it could go back into its bag dry.

Fog had been a constant along the coast, hanging out on the ocean horizon during the day, the gray banks of cloud hugging the water's surface and each night skulking back to shore to blanket the beaches and cliffs. It brought with it chilly temperatures and only retreated to sea again well after sunrise, but it was always hiding just offshore, waiting for the cycle to repeat. Only occasionally would an errant fog bank be bold enough to attack during the day, smothering the coast highway's cliff-side curves, but most would linger offshore.

The California Current, fed from the north by the North Pacific Current and pulling cooler water down from the Alaska Current, flows south, bringing cold water to the California coast. It changes the environment drastically. Hemmed in by the coastal mountains to the east, the current cools the pocket of air along the coast until it can be quite chilly. Fifty degrees

Fahrenheit was not unusual on my ride along the coast. If you come over the mountains from the east, from Napa Valley or especially the Great Central Valley in the center of which Sacramento lay, as soon as you crest the last coastal range and descend toward the coast, you will feel a distinct and dramatic drop in temperature. I was sweltering in Santa Rosa, less than thirty miles from the coast, but once on Highway 1 and heading north along the coast, I was looking for my sweatshirt to layer under my jacket.

California coast

Within fifty miles, California 1 turned inland to meet up with US Highway 101. The ride across the coastal mountains to 101 was easily a match for Deal's Gap, but the traffic was light, unlike the Tail of the Dragon on almost any day. 101 was non-stop twists left then right then left again, with some tight second-gear turns thrown in. As I rode away from the coast on it, the temperature rose.

Soon after Highway 1 had ended and I had turned north on the 101, I exited onto the Avenue of the Giants. What a spectacular ride through dark forests along a river, with massive redwood trunks touching the pavement on both sides. I stopped at Humboldt Redwoods State Park Visitor Center to buy a sticker for my windscreen, and while in the center, I asked about the yellow "nudibranch" I had found in my campsite. I was told it was a banana slug, and that I had been very lucky to have seen one.

On the Avenue of the Giants

I followed the "Avenue" for most of its length, rubbing shoulders with the giants trees, then rejoined the 101 highway to make up some time, because of my late start that morning. Other than a few curves, I could keep up sixty-five miles per hour and make good progress northward. I decided that once I crossed into Oregon, I'd take the first campground that presented itself, as it would be close to five when I got to the state line.

As soon as I finally crossed into Oregon, near Brookings, traffic in front of me slowed as we passed through a herd of elk bunched up on both sides of the highway, something I'd been hoping to see along many sections of road I'd been on with elk crossing warning signs. I'd always thought of elk as mountain animals, but although there were, indeed, mountains to the east, the road had returned to following the coast and was only three or four hundred feet above sea level. But the elk, in all their magnificence, were there, munching on the coastal grasses.

I continued north, but there were no signs of campgrounds, only the very occasional RV park, with no tent camping. As the afternoon grew late, I was starting to consider putting the tent up in one of the lay-bys along the highway. But virtually all of them were signed "Camping Prohibited," so I thought that, even if I found one with no sign, camping, especially in a tent, would likely not be allowed. I didn't relish the idea of being woken up in the middle of the night with a flashlight in my face, with an order to move directed at me.

While pulled over in one of those lay-bys and contemplating what to do, I put on a base layer, as I'd become cold and had resorted to turning on both the grip heaters and seat heaters on the Tiger. Once dressed better for the chilly ocean air, I thought I could ride for a bit more and see what I might find further up the road.

Finally, just before the bridge over the Rogue River, I saw a sign saying "Camping" on the right. I rode past some RV camps along the river but didn't see any tent camping spots. I rode a few miles in hopes of one showing up, but it was a futile search. I turned back and returned to a café at an RV park to ask someone about the possibility of tent camping there, but it had closed for the day. There was a gravel lot across the road from it with a grassy verge, a picnic table, and some information signs about the river.

It wasn't clear if it was a public area or owned by the RV park, but I was considering pitching camp there in an out-of-the-way corner, when I saw a woman walking toward the street from the RV park. I asked her what the deal was. She assured me there were tent spaces in the RV park, despite the sign in the nearby office window denying it. She was camping there, and she said one spot was empty next to her family's site, and there were two other motorcycle riders there who had just come in as well. She said I could just set up and settle with the office in the morning and that there was plenty of room.

I was glad to hear that, as I was too tired to go much further that day with the night and the chillier air coming on soon.

I quickly set up camp to claim the site, then ran back into a nearby town for pizza and a beer. I was hungry after only having my oatmeal early that morning and nothing more than an appetizer of jalapeño poppers during a midday stop. I also only had one more freeze-dried meal option on hand but wanted to save it for when I had no other options.

Earlier in the day, I'd texted Ron, a friend from Gig Harbor, who I'd put up at our place in Florida in my role as a Bunk a Biker host. Ron had headed to Alaska from our place in Florida, but before he departed, he had suggested I should drop by if I was ever in his area. And here I was, heading right for Gig Harbor, across from Tacoma on the west side of Puget Sound. Ron and his wife, Debbie, were headed south on a motorcycle along the same coastal route I was heading north on, and he offered me his place in Gig Harbor when I got up there. He suggested we try to meet somewhere on the road. By nightfall, we had decided on a rendezvous spot, which suited me fine, as it was not far from where I was and would make for a short and easy ride the next day.

Back at camp, I got out of my boots and riding pants and got a little more comfortable while I worked on my journal as the day drew to a close. Going to sleep, I was looking forward to a relaxed ride in the morning.

## ON THE OREGON (COASTAL) TRAIL

I woke up about seven thirty but lollygagged in the tent until eight. I knew I'd only have a ride of less than fifty miles to Florence, where I'd meet up with Ron and Debbie. They would not get there until late afternoon, so there was no point in getting there too early. I casually packed up the Tiger and then rode back out of the campground, stopping at the office to check-in and pay for the night. The lady in the office was surprised I'd found a space, as she was the one who had posted that the campground was full the day before. At first, I thought she might be a little upset with me, but I told her that when I'd pulled in, there were plenty of sites available, and she seemed to accept that without further question. I paid her twenty dollars and went next door to the Indian River Café in an attempt to get breakfast, but it was full, with a line out the door, snaking along the porch outside. I walked back out, planning to get a coffee somewhere down the road instead.

I crossed the Rogue River Bridge, bound along the Oregon coast for Florence, some forty miles north of Coos Bay. As I sped north, I kept the bike at fifty-five on the suggested forty-five mile per hour curves, which were perfectly fine at fifty-five, even though most of the vehicles slowed down a little bit for them. I saw a motorcycle ahead of me. In the foggy morning, I was gaining on a Harley-Davidson XR1200, especially in the curves. Eventually, there was a passing lane going north, and I scooted past him, waving as I passed.

Not long after that, I came into Port Orford, where I spotted a place on the right advertising food. I pulled over, and soon Grady, the fellow on the XR, was parked beside me. He was having trouble seeing in the mist because his goggles had been fogging up. He was from British Columbia and was heading home because he had discovered back in the Redwoods that his insurance had expired, and he didn't want to risk trouble about it in the US if he was stopped by the police.

We got to talking, and I offered to buy him a cup of coffee. But when I reached for the door and pulled on it, it was locked—closed. We both got on our bikes to look for another place, which, happily, appeared only a block further along. We went in and decided to have breakfast, not just coffee, because their offerings looked good. The "Special" was appealing to me—eggs, sausage, and blueberry waffles. Everything was excellent, and instead of me buying Grady a coffee, he insisted on buying both our meals.

We had a good time talking and decided, since we were both headed up the coast, we would ride together until I stopped in Florence where he would continue north. I like solitude, but it was a nice change of pace to have some companionship after eighteen days of being on the road alone. By the time we left the diner, the fog had lifted, and we had beautiful, sunny weather for the ride.

Our ride together didn't last long. At Florence, I peeled off the highway while waving so long, as Grady zoomed past yelling his unintelligible goodbye as he zoomed northward.

It was only one-thirty, so I had plenty of time to find a place to camp. Ron had texted saying they would not arrive until quarter-'til-five or five. At least I thought I had time. But stopping at an auto parts store to get a spare quart of oil, I searched the phone for campgrounds. There were plenty around, probably close to a dozen, but all I received in answer to all my calls was, "We're full."

It was Saturday, and weekends, I was told, were always busy, but there was also a "Dune Fest" going on in the area that weekend. I rode for fifteen or twenty miles north of town and stopped at the "full" campgrounds there to see if there were any cancellations or no-shows, but had no luck. Everyone was completely booked.

I tried a side road that I was told about by an employee at the auto parts store. He'd said he thought there might some campsites on it, somewhere further up the mountain, away from the main highway. I crawled up steep, winding pavement that quickly turned to gravel. As much as I liked the idea of riding off pavement, I'll admit it still intimidated me, especially when I was alone and had no knowledge of how a road might deteriorate. My recent bike drops had spooked me. I worried, being out in nowhere by myself, that I might drop the bike, even though by then I had learned from my mistakes and had returned the seat to the lowered position, making it easier to keep upright.

This isolated track led up into the coastal mountains. I followed it for miles after it had turned to gravel without seeing any campgrounds or even appropriate places to pull off and wild camp. All the time I was worrying about how I would be able to turn around on such a narrow and steep road and was watching and making mental notes of places I could possibly get the bike headed back the other direction if need be. If I did drop the bike, I still might not be able to pick it back up alone, and I'd not seen any other vehicles all the way up the mountain, so there would likely be nobody to help. The only marginally possible place I had found where I might have been able to set up the tent was steeply sloped, only three-feet wide, and directly beside the road on a narrow shoulder. I did not think it was a good idea to pitch the tent a foot or so from the path. If someone came up in the night, would they have any chance of seeing me before running me over?

I found a suitable place and carefully turned around, using a four-point turn with feet down the whole time, then crunched and swooped back downhill to the highway, breathing a sigh of relief once I returned to the pavement. Motel accommodation might be my only option again, but with Dunes Fest on, I was concerned that even those might be full.

I rode back toward Florence, thinking that I would have a cell signal there and could check out my hotel options, if I had any. On the way, I spotted a motel called "Economy Inn" and pulled up in front of the office. The price was shocking—$199 plus taxes—but looking at other hotels listed in my phone, they were all more expensive, and this one was only two-star, while all the others were more highly rated, making them surely more desirable and, therefore, likely to be without vacancies. Plus, I'd run out of time. Ron and Debbie would be there soon. Reluctantly, I coughed up the money.

The biggest bane of the entire trip once I had hit the coast had been finding campsites. The area was not suited to travelers on budgets who plan on the fly. Even the State Parks only had reserved sites that were booked months in advance, with no provision for setting aside even a few extra sites for travelers on the road, who might not be able to plan far ahead, like me. This difficulty was not a West Coast phenomenon only; the states east of the Mississippi River (and those along its western shore) are the worst at making life easier for the wanderer who only plans day by day.

The exception were the states in the West. Colorado, Utah, Arizona, and inland California had numerous campgrounds that were usually first come first serve and not on a reservation system. Camping there simply involved showing up, filling out a form on an envelope, slipping in a ten or a twenty, and dropping it in a slot in a metal drop-box. It helped to get in early, before they filled up, but usually they were less full compared to their West Coast and eastern counterparts. And in states like Utah, where seventy percent of the land is publicly owned, you can usually just find a place to pull off into on Bureau of Land Management or National Forest land and make a wild camp, with no one going to drive you off in the middle of the night. I had found, also, that the Midwestern states like Kansas, Oklahoma, and Nebraska, and even Texas to the south, often have small city parks where camping is allowed either for free or for a very small fee. I'd found the same to be true before on a ride across the Canadian prairies.

Outside those wonderful sweet-spots, the situation is not very rosy and traveling on the spur of the moment can be difficult. The situation was very discouraging, and it took away some of the joy of traveling for me, always worrying about finding a place to camp, although that joy returned to me when I passed through the more camping-friendly states.

I unloaded the bike below my room in the parking lot and hauled all my stuff upstairs to my second-story, two-star, non-airconditioned room. I had just gotten everything upstairs and into the room when Ron texted me. We agreed on a meeting place and time at a restaurant downtown.

The sidewalks were busy and the streetside filled with parked vehicles, but I very luckily found a parking space just big enough for the bike but not for a car almost directly in front of the restaurant. Ron was there to greet me and introduced me to Debbie as we made our way inside after just a short wait.

The food was delicious, and conversation flowed easily about motorcycles, traveling, and rides we'd both taken. They were heading south, and I was heading north. Debbie passed me the key to their place in Gig Harbor to use the next day while they would be still on the road. We said our goodbyes on the street, then Ron and Debbie walked back to their nearby hotel and I climbed back on the bike to head back to my motel, but not before having the inevitable conversation with a passerby about the Tiger and where I'd been and where I was going.

Back in the room, I got text messages from Ron with the address and all the information I'd need to get to their place and past the entry gate, along with ideas for eating places close by. I then worked on my journal before getting a much-needed shower. The following day I'd don my final complete set of clean clothes, since I'd not done laundry sine Sedona, a week before.

Fortunately, I was on the Oregon coast, and before I went to bed, the open window did what was required to air-condition the room. It would be an easy night of sleep, with an eight o'clock departure to enable me to make Gig Harbor in one day.

## Crossing the Olympic Peninsula

I woke later than I'd planned but still had time to make a couple cups of coffee using the in-room coffee maker while I packed. I was ready to leave by eight, as planned. I headed back up my old companion, US 101, past the familiar campgrounds that I had been excluded from the day before, but after fifteen miles I was in new territory. It was cold on the coast, fifty degrees Fahrenheit when I left the motel, so I layered up and turned on the grips and the seat warmer. The fog was heavy and brought with it the distinct smell of the sea, a mixture of both life and decay hanging in the air I was speeding through.

Most of the day was spent riding north along the remainder of the Oregon coast. I crossed some spectacular bridges but could not find safe places to stop and get good photos of them. Traffic was light once I was well-north of Florence and had passed a camper trailer and a truck that slowed unnecessarily on every curve. Fortunately, there were plenty of passing lane sections on the uphill grades where I could slip around the slower vehicles. I wouldn't have dared to pass into the oncoming lane even on the straightaways with the fog hanging thick and heavy, obscuring anything that might have been coming the other way.

Everything went smoothly until a jam up of traffic at Seaside. Once past the worst of that, I stopped for a coffee and breakfast sandwich at a McDonalds. Before leaving, I tried entering Ron's address into the Garmin, but the GPS did not recognize it. I'd had that happen before when I was too far from a specific destination, so instead, I just typed in Gig Harbor to serve until I got near enough to use the full address. I'd try again when I was much closer, but for now it was still going to be the 101 for a while and then a cut east across Washington, under the Olympic Mountains, to Gig Harbor and Ron's place. Once I was just outside of Gig Harbor, I'd reset the GPS to the exact address.

By the time the breakfast break and a couple calls home were finished, the fog had lifted, and it was not far to the bridge over the Columbia River at Astoria and my entry into Washington state.

Crossing the massive bridge over the expansive river was breathtaking, but I still could not find a place to stop and get a good photo of the enormous river I had passed over and the towering bridge on which I had crossed it. I had to settle for a shot from a north side lay-by with the high section of the bridge a dim, blue blur in the distance, belying its actual massive size and height above the water, very similar to Mackinac Bridge, not as long but high enough at 200 feet for ocean-going ships to easily pass beneath it into the Columbia River Gorge with plenty of room overhead to spare.

Finally, I was in Washington, my turn-around state. I followed the 101 only a short distance north before turning east and cutting across the state south of the Olympic Peninsula. I'd have loved to have ridden the circuit up the coast, over the top, and back down on the west side of Puget Sound, but with only thirty days, this was another instance of not being able to see and do everything. I had to be satisfied with a vision of the huge Olympic Mountains far off in the north on my left side. Despite being now in the temperate rainforest of the Olympic Peninsula, I had nothing but bright sunshine all day.

The cut east did not take long, and I managed it without getting on an Interstate. Mostly, it was on two-lane roads winding up and then back down from the north into Gig Harbor, on Puget Sound. I'd been a little intimidated to go there, as it was close to the big sprawl of the Seattle area, but I managed to navigate my way there with little traffic and on pleasant roads.

Now closing in on Gig Harbor, I reprogrammed the Garmin to find the address, and it led me to it flawlessly. Even when I missed a turn or two, it always adjusted and put me back on course.

Ron and Debbie's apartment was perfect, with a covered place to park the Tiger and restaurants within easy walking distance, virtually around the corner. I first unloaded the stuff I would need inside, then while I started a load of laundry, I contacted Brent, another author I'd worked with since the very beginning of Road Dog Publications and one of the few

I'd met face to face, who I was going to see in Boise. I hoped he would have a source for getting a rear tire for the Tiger and getting it changed and that I could use his garage for doing an oil change while the tire work was being done. The 705 Shinko on the rear was not too bad yet, with seven thousand miles on it and perhaps another thousand miles of life still in it, but Boise would be the last convenient spot to find a tire, get it mounted, and to also perform the oil change that was a few hundred miles past due before striking out across the country.

The initial arrangements made, I left the apartment and walked down to the Blazing Onion, where I had a great turkey burger with avocado, salad, and a huge beer. For once, I did not have to climb back onto my bike and ride back to wherever I was staying, so I indulged myself with the king-sized beer. The walk to the restaurant felt good and was exactly the right distance to help me unwind after the long day on the road.

Back at Ron's, I finished the laundry while catching up with the "Itchy Boots" YouTube channel. Noraly, the famous solo rider in the series, had hurt her leg in a bike fall and had gone to Moab to recover. Someone had told me about it and thought she and I had been in Moab about the same time, but as I watched her videos, it become obvious there was perhaps a month lag between her being somewhere and the time the video about the place was released. In the ones I watched there was way too much snow on the mountains compared to when I had been in the same areas, the snow almost being gone except on the highest peaks when I was there. By the time I had gotten to Moab, Noraly had probably been in Wyoming and working her way north into Montana or Idaho.

After the videos, I took a quick shower, then organized the maps for the upcoming ride to Idaho, tearing the appropriate pages out of the atlas, folding them, and placing them in order under the clear map cover of the tank bag. It would be two days to the Boise area, as it was around six-hundred miles from Gig Harbor. I wasn't going to force a fast one-day ride that long on myself. There was no need, and I was getting to like the three-hundred-mile range kind of days.

## THE GOLDEN GRASS DESERT

The phone woke me at 6:30. It was my son, who'd forgotten about the four-hour time difference between Florida and Washington. Still, it was good to talk with him. I had tried to call him a couple times as I'd traveled, the last time in Joshua Tree, only for the calls to go to voicemail to a voicemailbox that was too full to take any more messages. I'd sent texts as well, but he had not responded to those. I crawled back into bed after the call to try to get another half-hour of sleep, but as I was dozing off once more, the phone rang again. That time it was a friend of mine in Michigan checking up on me and my ride so far. After hanging up, I figured I might as well get up and make some breakfast while trying to complete arrangements to get my tire replaced.

I brewed some coffee and made some oatmeal, which I could barely get down. It tasted like gasoline. I needed to find another place to stow the stove, away from the food, or find a container for the food that would be impermeable to the gas odor of the stove. I'd found it impossible to get rid of the gas smell from the stove pump even when I left it to air in the sun for hours. I made a mental note to address that issue when I was home.

While drinking the coffee and gagging on the oatmeal, Brent sent me the contact information for Tom, a fellow Brent knew in Boise who could change my tire for me. I texted him. He said he didn't have a tire on hand, so I'd need to find one, but he could install whatever I could find. I called up Rocky Mountain ATV and ordered another 705 to be shipped directly to Tom. Rocky Mountain ATV had always been fast and had good prices. It had been my go-to place for tires for quite a while. At home, I've ordered a tire one day to have it arrive on my front porch the very next morning. This time they couldn't quite pull that off, but they could have it there Wednesday, the day after I'd arrive at Brent's. Good enough.

Today I'd ride halfway to Boise, then the following day I'd arrive there in the afternoon, on Tuesday. I'd stay two days with Brent and his wife, Julie. The extra time with them would be a bonus, and the tire could be taken care of the day after I arrived. While Tom installed the tire on Wednesday, I'd do the oil change in Brent's garage. I'd leave Boise on Thursday.

All the arrangements took a while. It was after ten by the time I left Gig Harbor. I defied my GPS's orders, because I knew the big highway I was very near would take me across Puget Sound and to Tacoma, on the east side of the sound. I could then hop on Interstate 5 for a dozen miles south, then catch a major route east and eventually away from the city to the highway I wanted to take into Washington. It would wrap around the north and east sides of Mount Rainier, before heading east into the interior of the state. The Garmin would not take me that way, even though I reset it to not Avoid Highways. But what I found out while on my way out was that the highway across the sound was a toll bridge, and I'd not un-checked that avoidance box, which explained the Garmin's desire to send me hundreds of miles out of my way just to get across the Puget Sound and on to Mount Rainier.

There was a lot of traffic. It was fast but manageable, and in a couple hours I was back in the countryside. I finally caught a glimpse of Mount Rainier in the distance. Its snow-capped peaks were magnificent, even from a great distance. I could see that the road would be getting closer all the time and that it would be the closest after it turned south on the eastern side of the great volcano. Rainier was massive, and I hoped when it came fully into view it would not be so close that I could not get it all in one photo. I rode and rode, but an abundance of evergreens along with a smaller mountain that sat to the north of Rainier blocked the view. I hoped I'd not chosen the wrong route and be cheated out of a good view of Rainier, but as I followed the route on the mountain's east face, the road bent right and an opening and pull-off appeared. There it was, clear above the surrounding forest and lesser mountains, its snow-covered peak gleaming white in the bright sunlight. It was truly spectacular, and I imagined that I must have felt like they do in Japan about Mount Fuji. I took several good shots with my phone but decided to get out the DSLR to really get some top-notch images.

Mount Rainier

Not long after that stop, the road veered east, away from Rainier, and followed a river coursing between jagged peaks and forested hillsides wherever it was not too steep for the trees to have a chance to hold on. I was getting a little hungry and was craving some pie, when I spotted a little café in a tiny little village and stopped for a break and to make calls home. The answer to my query about pie was a disappointment, I got a milkshake and some French fries instead.

After a couple hours, the route took me between smaller and smaller mountains, then hills with valleys filled with hop vines arranged so that, from the end of a row, they looked like half an

X chromosome. Hops, beer's little helper, were everywhere, the famous Cascade Hops being much sought after by both large beer makers and micro-breweries worldwide.

Hops fields

Eventually, the hops disappeared, and grape vines took their place, only to disappear again as the rounded hills went on for miles, treeless and covered with a short-nap, golden carpet of grasses. It was surreal, like someone had laid a sheet of gold velvet fabric floating on waves. It grew hot, up into the high-nineties. The landscape went on for hours, becoming a desert of nothing but golden grasses.

The road turned north, then east, then south again, mimicking the turns of the Columbia River and irrigation canals above the "Federal Nuclear Reserve," which I found out much later was the vast home of the Hanford Nuclear Reactor, the first reactor to produce plutonium as part of the Manhattan Project. The area could be looked at as a place of innovation and technological advances, even possibly bringing World War II to an end, but it could also be viewed as the site where man first perfected the art of death, bringing the world into the age of mutually assured destruction and someday, perhaps, the end of man itself. The entire area, once Native American land, is now a vast area of nuclear waste and is undergoing containment and mitigation, so hopefully, one day, the Native Americans can return to their ancestral homeland without fear of death by cancer. Although the track record of our government in the treatment of those First People does not bode well.

The golden hillsides continued until east of the reserve, where agriculture returned on the banks of the Snake River, with crops of all kinds—grapes, apples, peaches, hay, straw, wheat, and at one point there must have been rye, as the air was filled with the smell of fresh rye bread, as if a loaf had just emerged from an oven.

I had contacted a host from the ADV Tent Space List, a resource I had used many times before with great success, and for which I was also a host. Unfortunately, ADVRider had changed the list, and the listings no longer contained contact information in the original messages, so you now had to message any hosts within the ADVRider Forums, using their messaging system and hoping the host would see your message there. It was quite cumbersome and created a delay in getting information back and forth while on the road. I asked via messaging about stopping for the night in Pasco, at one of the hosts' place. I left my phone number and checked the phone often throughout the day but did not see any response from them. All the while, I kept heading their direction and hoping for the best. When I arrived in Pasco, I stopped again to check— no call. Then I checked ADVRider's messaging service and saw they had answered there, but that they couldn't host that day, as they were away. I checked GoogleMaps and found a spot, Sand Station Recreation Area, in the Columbia River Gorge and just twenty-two miles away. I reset the GPS for there and took off again.

I crossed the Snake River, close to where it emptied into the Columbia, and veered onto a highway that followed the gorge and railroad along the Columbia River toward Umatilla and crossed back into Oregon. I found the place. It looked like a great spot, right on the river, with even a swimming area roped off in it. I got off the bike to check it out when I saw a sign: "Camping Prohibited." Just my luck, and by then it was getting late. I got back on the highway and caught a road just a couple miles further along the river that intersected the river road and headed southeast, generally the direction I wanted to go.

The landscape turned barren again as I left the Columbia and was filled with gold hills like earlier, except here and there were fresh-cut fields. As I rode on, the shadows lengthened, and I tried desperately to find a stealth place to set up camp, but everything was wide open, with no place to hide my tent and bike, not even behind a shrub. At one point, I saw I'd be in Pendleton, Oregon, in about twelve miles, so I kept going, thinking I could check with someone there.

When I got into town, I pulled over and could see on the Garmin that an Interstate passed by Pendleton, so there was a chance there might be an option there. I searched on GoogleMaps and, to my relief, there was a KOA campground just off an Interstate exit and not far from where I'd stopped. I knew it would be more expensive than the National Forest Service campgrounds or State Parks that I preferred, but it would still be much less than a motel room.

My wagon for the night

When I found the KOA, I was glad to see there were a couple places to eat nearby as well. I checked with the woman at the desk in the campground office. She had a tent site or a site where I could stay in a restored Conestoga wagon.

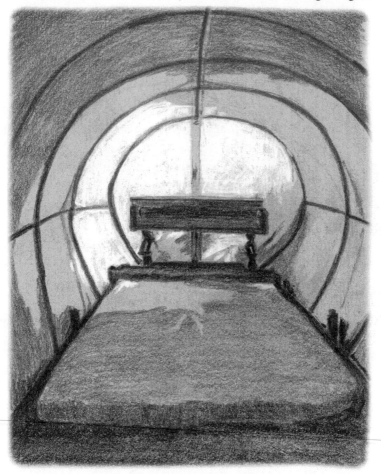

My Camp for the Night

Who wouldn't want to do that? It would mean I'd not even have to open the dry bag with all my camping stuff in it. And best of all, there would be no repacking it in the morning. It was seventy-five dollars for the wagon, but I felt sure a tent space would be at least fifty, so it was easy to decide on the wagon and get a unique experience in the deal. I made the arrangements, then went for a quick bite nearby at a restaurant at the same Interstate exit. It was almost dark by the time I got back and still very hot, but as I worked on my journal, the air slowly cooled enough to make sleep pleasant.

### ACROSS THE SNAKE AGAIN AND INTO IDAHO

I was up at seven-thirty and was packed and on the bike by eight. I grabbed breakfast at the place I'd eaten at the night before. Brent lived near Boise, but in a suburb called Kuna, so I set the Garmin for that town, as it would not accept the specific address yet, being so far away.

I headed south on US 395 and followed it all the way to John Day, where I caught another highway northeast initially, then turning southeast toward Vale. Along the way, I spotted two deer in the morning, one in the road that I had to almost stop for and another below the steep right shoulder in the ditch, with only its head level with the road surface. I was crossing more of that empty high prairie land I'd come to call the grass desert. I came across a tiny, abandoned cabin set among the golden hillsides and stopped to take a photo of the "little house on the prairie."

Little House on the Prairie

Somewhere along that stretch, I noticed my left turn signal was dangling by its wire. Luckily, I could see the screw was still in the base. I slowed down and began looking for a place to pull over to fix it when I spotted a small churchyard with a little apple tree to provide shade. I pulled in and parked on the gravel in the shade of the tree, dismounted, and got my jacket off and my tools out.

Stopping to reattach the turn signals

I made quick work of reattaching the signal and made sure it was tight, then checked the other and tightened it for good measure. A quick drink of water, and I was back moving amongst the prairie hills.

When close the Idaho state line, the GPS sent me south, along the west shore of the Snake River until at the same latitude as Boise, where it sent me east across the river and into Idaho, where fragrant onions were almost ready for harvest, with the top white part of the bulb just poking above the earth, potato fields were green and growing, and acres of mint permeated the air with a wonderful smell.

Now close, I reset the Garmin for Brent's street address, and it finally recognized it and led the way the remaining thirty miles to his garage.

It was great to see Brent and Julie again. I'd not seen them since 2011, eleven years ago, when we'd set up a booth for his new book, the first one published by Road Dog, and to promote the infant publishing imprint at the International Motorcycle Show in Daytona during the famous Bike Week.

We spent time catching up and talking about where I might head next, then ordered some Mexican food for delivery, followed by watching SpaceX's new launch of the Starlink satellites from Cape Canaveral. I called Andrea and told her that, if it was clear in Florida, she should try to watch it from our veranda, which we could usually do easily if the skies between us and the Cape cooperated. Brent and I talked until the long day caught up with us and we said goodnight. I headed upstairs to bed. The tire would be there the next day, and while it was being changed, I'd do the oil change after picking up the required oil, filter, and crush washer in the morning.

## New Shoe for the Tiger

At eight o'clock I was up and out of bed. I walked downstairs, where Julie and Brent were already. Julie made some French roast in her press while filling me in on the finer aspects of using one and gave me a granola bar, which is my typical breakfast back home. We talked about the day's plans. It was Wednesday, and my tire should arrive at Tom's soon. Brent and I went out to the garage, where I pulled out my tools, while he lent me others to make the job easier. I pulled the back wheel off the Tiger, sticking tape on the rim with an arrow indicating the direction of rotation, then we all piled into Julie's Toyota FJ to drop the wheel off at Tom's. He wasn't there but had left instructions for us to simply drop it on the trailer parked outside his garage, and he would retrieve it when my new tire had arrived, and he would start work on the change-over.

While Tom was changing the tire, we headed to the Triumph dealer to pick up a filter and crush washer, then made one more stop at an auto parts store to get oil and a cheap drain pan.

Back at the house, I got to work on the oil change. It was a quick and easy task, and I'd finished it in a half-hour, after which Brent and I retired to the kitchen for a "lunch" of homemade ice cream, caramel, and fudge.

After our sweet repast, we all drove over to pick up the wheel, to meet Tom, and pay him the meagre twenty dollars he had requested. He really only wanted to help a fellow motorcycle traveler, rather than make a business out of the work. He and his wife were very cordial. Brent and Julie had known them both for a while. Brent had their child in his class when he had been a teacher, so this gave them a chance to catch up a bit. Tom also had a Tiger, but it was the older generation 1050, which he was selling. It would be a nice find for someone. Within a half an hour, we drove off again with the retreaded wheel in the back.

Brent had an appointment that afternoon, so I was dropped off at the house so I could install the wheel while they could attend to that business. I also gave the chain a good shot of lube. The work didn't take long, installation of the rear wheel on the Tiger being quite a bit easier than it had been on the Bonneville, so I caught up on phone calls to home and to my brother who lived in Virginia while I waited for them to return.

Not long after five, Brent and Julie arrived, and we all went out to a nearby restaurant called Holy Cow for a dinner I had promised them as a thank you for all their help and hospitality. The burgers were huge and delicious, and I guessed I would not be hungry again until the next evening, if even then.

A quick stop at a Walmart to grab another freeze-dried meal, and then we were home, where we relaxed and talked while watching YouTube videos of four-by-fours crawling across the incredible Black Bear Pass between the Million Dollar Highway and Telluride and catching up on Itchy Boot's escapades. Before we had realized it, it was past eleven, so I headed up to bed. Julie had washed a load of laundry for me, and it was still in the dryer, but considering the late hour, I would just grab it and pack in the morning. The next day would be a long ride to West Yellowstone.

## Passing the Moon and Moose

It was an early morning wake-up, and I immediately got started packing. By eight, the Tiger was loaded and waiting while I had coffee and a breakfast bar and chatted with Julie and Brent.

By 8:30, I was rolling out of the driveway and heading in the direction of West Yellowstone, Montana. I'd pass through Little Caribou Targhee National Forest just before arriving there, and it looked like there were plenty of National Forest Service Campground options in that area. I wanted to get as close to Yellowstone National Park as I could, so I could ride through it the next day in the early morning and be through and on my way through Wyoming and onward toward the Badlands in South Dakota to possibly camp by late afternoon.

The first leg was fifty miles or so riding on an Interstate, not exciting, but really the only practical way for me to connect with Highway 20 that would shoot northeast and run along the southern edge of the Sawtooth and Bitterroot Ranges. The highway ran through the high plains, with the vast Snake River Prairie on my right to the south.

In the afternoon, the landscape quickly turned other-worldly, with jumbles of blackened rocks and outcroppings stretching away from the highway. I'd met the edge of Craters of the Moon National Monument. The landscape was the result of ancient volcanic activity. Craters and cinder cones were scattered throughout it. The road ran through the middle of the charred, ancient landscape, and there were many good viewpoints along the way. I stopped at the Visitor Center and again bought a sticker for the windscreen. There was a short route through the park, but it cost thirteen dollars to ride it, and because it was a National Monument and not a National Park, my lifetime pass would not benefit me there. I turned around and, instead, got back on the highway, along which were plenty more vistas that would not be a lot different than I'd have seen on the paid route, although I would not get quite such a close look at some of the volcanic cones. Besides, the day was getting on, and I wanted to find a campground early enough that I'd not arrived only to find them all full.

Craters of the Moon

I turned onto another road that would bypass Idaho Falls and would put me back on Highway 20 again past the city and after 20 had made its turn to the northeast, which I would take into West Yellowstone. Once again back on 20, I was soon again in the Caribou Targhee National Forest and started looking for campgrounds. There were many, so I waited until close to West

Yellowstone before I picked one, Big Spring Campground, four and a half miles east of the highway.

Upon arrival, I checked out the notice board. The water at the campground was not working, so the Park Service was charging only ten dollars, instead of the usual twenty, and my pass would give me fifty percent off that, so I did well to find a spot for the night for only five dollars. I looked for registration and payment envelopes, but the bin was empty. The host's trailer was nearby, so I went there and knocked, but no one answered.

I rolled through the campground and found a suitable, semi-shaded spot and set up camp. The sites were nice, with tables, fire rings, and platforms to use for cooking. There were also bear-proof boxes for storing food and fragrant stuff scattered about but located a little distant from each site. Perfect; even if a bear came around sniffing out a meal, it would not be drawn close to the tent or bike.

With camp established, I took a short walk. Nearby there was a historic wood and stone cabin, built in the nineteen-thirties and filled with original furniture and items from the time-period. I walked down a wooded path to get a look in Johnny Sack's Cabin, but it was closed when I arrived. It was set in a beautiful spot, on the edge of a large spring that fed a nearby river and was surrounded by woods. On the far side of the spring was the road I had come in on that continued past the cabin and eventually would hook up with a series of roads, some going east toward the Tetons and some leading back to the main highway. There was a parking area on the other side. A few tourists were enjoying the view over the spring on a short boardwalk with a white safety fence on the water side, but I was alone on my side of the stream. Then I noticed what all those tourists were looking at. A mother moose was feeding in the strong current with two young calves tagging along with her. It was a beautiful sight, and the moose did not seem perturbed by the gawkers. I took a few photos of them before they meandered around a bend and out of sight.

Moose at Big Spring

I wandered back to camp, but before I got there, I once again stopped at the host's trailer but received the same response to my knock—nothing. Registration and payment would have to wait until the next morning.

Back at my picnic table, I assembled my Dragonfly stove and prepared a pouch of freeze-dried chicken and dumplings. It was another hit and surprisingly quite good.

Once I'd cleaned up, I walked back to the cabin to see if I could spot any other creatures in or around the spring. Sure enough, a garter snake was lying across the path taking advantage of the sun-induced warmth. It made haste off the path when it sensed me and was gone instantly. Approaching the cabin, I didn't see anything in or near the stream. I started walking past the side of the cabin, when I almost walked into the mother moose that I had seen feeding earlier. I must have walked within a dozen feet of her when we noticed each other. Both she and I were startled, so I started slowly backing away. Once far enough from her, I turned around and went back to camp. Luckily, the mother left our encounter as just that, an encounter, and did not resort to an attack, as I had heard often happens, especially when they have their young nearby, as this one had.

At camp, I gathered up the trash from dinner and walked it to the bear-proof dumpster. Then I gathered all my food and toiletries and stashed them in a nearby bear box for the night. I dropped by the host's campsite, but again, no one was there. I decided to take one more hike to the spring before it got too late, but I would follow the road so I could get a look from the other side. It was a short walk, and most of the people had left, but I did talk to a family that was still lingering there, who bemoaned the fact that they had missed the moose.

I walked down onto the little boardwalk and could see both brook and rainbow trout as long as my forearm directly under my feet. There were at least a dozen floating with their heads facing into the flow of the water under the boardwalk as the stream crossed under the road to join the river. I was soaking in the beauty and tranquility of the spot, standing at the end of the boardwalk behind the two and a half-foot high, three-board fence, when suddenly there was a stir and a whooshing sound from the far side of the spring. I looked up to see what it was. The mother moose was charging across the spring followed by her two babies at full bore and heading almost straight for me. I wasn't sure what to do: should I run or should I stay perfectly still and so not seem threatening? I chose staying still. The whole contingent went flying past me, just a couple feet on the other side of the fence, up the bank, across the road, and disappeared into the woods on the other side of the road. That had been exciting and terrifying at the same time. That had been enough wildlife for me for the day, so I headed back to camp the way I'd come.

As the sun dipped behind the pines and the air started to cool, I worked on the journal before I lost all light and then crawled into the tent for the night. I was treated to the sounds of the forest creatures calling to each other as the day retired and the night took over.

## Yellowstone to Shell Creek

At dawn I got up immediately and started packing. I checked one more time at the notice board, and in the freshly filled bin were new envelopes. I grabbed one and, back at camp, filled it out. I wrote my pass number on the envelope and inserted the five dollars that was half of the reduced ten-dollar fee—a very good bargain.

By half-past eight I was gone and on my way to Yellowstone National Park. It was not far, perhaps twenty miles, and at the gate all I did was show my license and pass, and I was told, "Enjoy the park!"

In Yellowstone along the Madison River

The last time I'd been in Yellowstone, I didn't think it had lived up to its hype. But that time, I think the traffic and crowds had clouded my perspective. On this day, traffic and visitors were light, and I enjoyed passing through much more.

It was incredible to pass holes gushing steam from the bowels of the earth and crystal pools where formerly subterranean waters now found their way to the surface. The smell of sulfur was distinct in the air, reminding me of the smell of lit fireworks.

Beryl Spring

The route I took, cutting across the park from west to east, was spectacular. It followed the Madison River up its canyon, with rapids churning below the road and mountains and rock formations on each side and above me. It also ran through alpine meadows at over seven-thousand feet where a herd of bison were grazing, oblivious to all the people stopped on the road and lay-bys to watch them. Another herd was close to the roadside on both sides, and as I rode by, I passed by one only ten feet away from me. The RV ahead of me almost stopped completely, likely to get a photo of the beasts, but I was praying they'd keep moving. I was in the open and vulnerable if the big bull had decided it had enough, and I was not protected by a couple tons of steel surrounding me like those in the RV. Unfortunately, with having to be ready to move quickly, I could not take time to reach into my pocket and grab a photo for myself.

Gibbon Falls

Other than those bunch-ups where the road passed bison, traffic was quite light, and at times it felt like I had the road and park to myself. Eventually, the route skirted Yellowstone Lake, then followed the various creeks feeding the lake from the east, eventually following the North Fork of the Shoshone River as it exited the park.

Leaving Yellowstone, I was on US Highway 14, which I'd be on for the reminder of that day. With the park behind me, I soon found myself on the wide Bighorn Basin, a relatively flat area lying between the Rockies at Yellowstone and the Bighorn Range in the east. I passed through Cody, of Wild Bill fame. The town was capitalizing on its heritage, with Wild Bill placards pasted everywhere and every establishment trying to look like they were built in the 1800s, even if they were only built a few years before.

After Cody, it was the high plains again, with the blue shadow of the Bighorns up ahead and growing closer and more distinct all the time.

I'd set the GPS for Shell, Wyoming. I'd had a conversation with a fellow camper the night before who had mentioned a great campground near there called Shell Creek. Along the way, I stopped at a grocery store in Greybull, a bigger village before I got to the tiny settlement of Shell, to get a pre-made sandwich and trail mix. I thought I'd treat myself to a beer that night as well. So, I picked up a big twenty-four ounce can of Coors. After all, I was in the Rockies.

When I got to Shell, I spotted a campground, but it looked commercial and obviously was not the Forest Service Campground that the man had described. It was still early enough, and I knew there were a couple other Forest Service Campgrounds further along the same highway, so I continued east, keeping a sharp eye out for a sign to any campground, but hoping I'd find the elusive Shell Creek Campground.

Bighorn Mountains

Shell was at the base of the Bighorns, and as soon as I left it headed east, the road started to climb, with Shell Creek always at my side. The grade was steep, and there was an unending series of curves and switchbacks as I climbed.

I must have ridden twenty miles when I saw a brown campground sign up ahead, and as it got closer, I could read that it said, "Shell Creek Campground." I turned right onto the gravel road, where another sign announced it was two miles to the campground. The problem was that the area had thunderstorms hanging overhead all day. The road had been inundated ahead of my arrival, and it showed it. My anxiety of riding off pavement increased, but hey, it's only two miles, right? I rolled down the path, trying not to grip the handlebars too tightly and telling myself to expect the Tiger to do some wandering. Most of the road was benign, but a few wet places had my heart in my throat. In the end, however, I made it through unscathed, and my confidence level crept up . . . a little.

Shell Creek

I filled out an envelope and deposited the ten-dollar fee. Most of the sites were flooded from the previous rain and located next to Shell Creek, which flowed along beside them, swollen and close to the top of its banks. I found a site for tents only, but the gravel pad that had been intended for a place to pitch a tent was, instead, a small pool of dirty water. Nearby, in the tall grass next to the site, were a couple places where tall grasses had obviously been trampled and a couple tents must have stood. I chose one, then erected my tent on the spot. Before loading the tent with all my stuff, it was quite easy to move the whole assembly, so I moved it to another spot that seemed flatter and was less weedy, closer to the picnic table, and dry.

Once in place, I filled the tent with all the gear I'd need for the night and then sat on a wind-dried corner of the picnic table and started my feast of ham and cheese, trail mix, and beer. The wind was up and seemed to be very slowly drying the ground and grasses. I could see the pond in the gravel tent site gradually becoming a puddle.

While eating, I started on my journal. When I had finished my dinner, except for the beer, the rain started again. I grabbed everything that needed to stay dry and threw it into the tent and quickly disposed of my meal trash in a nearby bear-proof dumpster and put all my foodstuff from the bike into a bear-proof storage box.

My beer and I went back to the tent, inside of which I finished working on my journal while emptying my beer can. It would be an early night, but I hoped the rain would stop and wind continue to blow, so perhaps by morning camp and especially the road would be drier than when I had come in. Only time would tell.

## WHERE THE BUFFALO ROAM AND PRAIRIE DOGS PLAY

The rain had continued after my escape into the tent, well before it had become dark, but stopped later in the evening.

In the night in my little shelter, I'd had a terrible dream. I'd returned home to find my wife unhappy. There was a bill I'd taped up on my monitor where I'd see it that I had meant to pay before I'd left—the mortgage—and it was still there hanging there, unpaid, when I got home. I fussed about it, even though it had been my fault it had gone unpaid. My wife sarcastically said that all I had spent on the trip must have been worth it, because so many people would be so impressed by my feat. She seemed so dissatisfied with me that I asked her if she "wanted out," and her simple reply was, "Yes." At that moment our daughter had walked in, only catching the last few words of our conversation, and looked at me with a puzzled expression on her face. Then the dream ended.

I guess the costs of the trip were weighing heavier on my mind than I'd consciously thought. I did often find myself calculating in my head as I rode what the total of all the receipts that I'd been stuffing into my pocket would be. The dream disturbed me. Maybe what I was spending on this selfish trip— for what? my ego?—was a bad idea; what of the needs back home? I found it hard to go back to sleep.

I was up at 6:30, but it seemed that no matter what time I woke up, it was always took an hour and a half before I was ready to leave. The tent and fly were wet that morning. I just packed them, anyway, hoping I'd get a place for the night early enough that they'd have a chance to dry out before it was time to go to sleep.

I managed the couple miles out to the pavement on the gravel, the road having dried substantially from the wind after the rain had stopped in the night. The slippery parts from the day before were gone, and the ride out was quite easily accomplished.

I turned eastward at the pavement and continued out of the Bighorn Mountains, each mile being slightly lower in altitude. I followed the route until it merged with an Interstate for a while. I didn't mind several miles of high-speed, non-twisty riding for a change. It was not very long, however, before I turned off the freeway again and veered to the northeast onto a small US Highway, following it through rolling high prairie. There was a bicycle road race of some sort being held on the route. I think the event was to benefit MS research and treatment, because I saw several little shacks along the way marked "Break Stop" and emblazoned with Multiple Sclerosis Society logos. I whizzed by a dozen bicyclists, giving them full use of the right lane as I passed.

I should have filled up the Tiger at Sheridan, before taking this less-traveled route that would meet the Interstate again at Gillette. Passing through the first marked "town," I found nothing but a dozen houses and no gas station. My range had dropped considerably by then, as the speed limit was seventy and the wind was not working in my favor. I started calculating how far I'd get on what was left in my tank, how far it was to Gillette, and whether I'd have to break out my spare gallon to get there.

Luckily, the next village had gas and breakfast. I'd been looking for a place to eat ever since I'd left Shell Creek Campground. There was a solitary, older fellow in charge of the place, and he made me a delicious breakfast burrito in response to my query about food. The burrito was stuffed with eggs and Italian sausage, which I washed down with a couple cups of coffee he had brewed. The man was very amiable and sat down with me while we talked about hunting, the differences between Wyoming and Florida, and discussed whether Wyoming would stay the great place it was, or would people crowd in, as seemed to be happening everywhere, and turn tilled fields and untouched prairie into subdivisions. I thought they had some time, as he was bemoaning that Sheridan might get as big as 32,000, which didn't sound too massive to me. In the West, when you see big lettering on a map for a city, don't assume that signifies that it's a metropolis; it's only because they have more room for larger type. Wyoming is the least populated state, and on my map, Sheridan looked like a large city, but it appeared as barely a blip as I had passed by the Interstate. Meanwhile, a local man had come in, sat down with us, and joined the conversation. He asked if my bike was an "enduro" and commented how it looked like it was "ready for anything."

I paid my bill, said goodbye, and thanked my host for breakfast. It was so nice to connect with people I met on the road, and the proprietor had been kind, intelligent, and the salt of the earth. There, in the middle of the wind-swept prairie, I felt I had made a friend, which is something that usually doesn't come easy for me.

With the bike full, I had no worries about getting to Gillette, so my attention turned to getting a glimpse of antelope along the way, as I was told was likely before I would get to Gillette. I did see a herd of some sort of animal in the distance at one point, but they were too far for me to confidently determine if they were antelope or the ubiquitous deer. I had, at least, gotten to see a wild turkey just before I had found the gas station, so the afternoon ride was not void of wildlife.

At Gillette, I switched to another minor road that would go south, then turn east, before crossing the border between Wyoming and South Dakota and entering the southern part of the Black Hills.

Once in Custer, South Dakota, I turned north and followed a route I'd been on before, past the Crazy Horse sculpture, which could be seen clearly from the highway, jutting from the south end of a massive butte. I didn't stop for a photo this time, as I had taken plenty on my previous trip through the area a few years before.

When asking Julie, back in Kuna, for souvenir ideas for Andrea, she had suggested Black Hills gold. Passing through a very busy and motorcycle-filled Hill City, I stopped and found a pair of earrings made of the local gold in the form of leaves and grapes. Wine being Andrea's favorite beverage, it seemed fitting. Apparently, I had arrived in the Black Hills, south of Sturgis, a day after the big Bike Week had ended, and many bikers were still prowling the area, which explained so many bikes lining both sides of the street.

Still looking like Bike Week in Hill City

The task of picking up a souvenir accomplished before leaving civilization, I headed around the south side of Rapid City, leaving the Black Hills in my mirrors. I headed east, away from the city. Before I had gotten completely clear of it, however, I'd stopped to pick up a sandwich and beer to bring to camp. I was bound for a campground I'd stayed at and had really enjoyed in the Badlands years ago. It was situated below a ring of hills that formed a bowl, at the bottom of which were the campsites, with the road above them on the north and a small creek meandering nearby, a few hundred yards to the east. Bison had grazed close by the last time I'd camped there.

The campground was accessed from the west end of the park by the twenty-mile-long, gravel Sage Creek Road. I found the road, just past the quiet little village of Scenic. The road was as I remembered it, well graded and packed gravel, with a solid bed. It was easy to do forty-five without my usual uneasiness off-pavement. I found the camp and put up the tent with some difficulty because of a stiff, blustery wind. Somehow, I managed it by putting various heavy parts of my baggage on the corners while I set it up. Staking was mandatory.

Finally, all was set. I carefully walked across the mine field of prairie dog holes in the middle of the camping ring road, trying to avoid twisting an ankle by stepping in any of them, to the prairie on the far side of the campground. There, I watched a herd of bison grazing on the opposite bank of the creek. After a observing the big animals wandering toward the northeast for a little while, I headed back to the tent and picnic table and sat down to eat the ham and cheese sandwich I'd bought and down a can of Dale's Pale Ale.

Bison at Sage Creek Campground

As the day cooled down with the sun's descent, a BMW 1150GS pulled up. The rider, Carl, and I got to talking. I invited him to share my table and tent space. We had a lot in common, knowing many of the same adventure travel writers. He was on a ride to various destinations in the Pacific Northwest and had come in from Raleigh, North Carolina. As the afternoon waned and conversation flowed, he brought out some fine Laphroaic Scotch, which had a marvelous peaty and smoky flavor. We poured ourselves one, then two, as we talked and watched the day come to a close as the red sky darkened in the west above the surrounding hills.

With the sun's disappearance behind the horizon, the temperature dropped quickly to a comfortable level, and my new friend set up his tent while I worked on my journal and second cup of whisky.

The bison herd had moved out of sight by then. Hopes of a clear night sky were diminished as high clouds were moving overhead, nothing that would portend rain but only an obscured sky. The Badlands are one of the lowest, ambient-light polluted regions in North America, and we had looked forward to a clear and spectacular view of the Milky Way, which by nightfall didn't look likely.

The next day I planned a long day of riding, trying to get as many miles behind me as possible, as time was running out for me on this journey. I hoped only two days would be sufficient to get to South Bend, Indiana, but only the next day would tell if that would be enough.

## THE MIDDLE OF THE MIDWEST

In the wee hours of the morning darkness, I awoke to the clear voices of groups of coyotes near the camp talking to each other in coyote speak of all the things they were planning for the new day and where they'd found new prairie dog holes, while courting the particular coyote they had a keen eye for. Which one that was I wasn't sure; my coyote-speak translation skills were pretty rusty.

I did manage to go back to sleep despite their howling, but the group of young people in multiple tents next to us woke me up before six o'clock by talking in loud voices and laughing as if no one else was in the campground. It was annoying, but I vaguely remembered being that young myself and not thinking about the impact of anything I did on others, so I mentally gave them a pass.

So, not being able to go back asleep with all the ruckus, I got out up and out of the tent. Carsten had been woken up as well. He and I were discussing their rudeness, but I mentioned that at least they were young people enjoying themselves out in nature and not sitting home with eyes and thumbs glued to their smartphones. Carsten nodded in agreement. On this trip, I had been quite surprised at how many young people were camping and hiking, dispelling the popular idea that the new generation is composed of homebodies who are lazy and stuck on social media all the time.

I packed up the tent and its contents. Carsten provided water, which I'd run out of and which was not available at the campground, and I provided the ground coffee and a French press. I prepared a pot of coffee for both of us. I nibbled on a couple handfuls of trail mix while downing some coffee, and that was it for breakfast.

Carsten was staying on another day before moving west. We exchanged contact information, and both promised we'd get together in the future, either in Raleigh or Florida, for some riding. I finished loading the Tiger, shook hands with Carsten, and took off out of the campground, rattling along the corrugated road surface.

The Badlands

Back on Sage Creek Road, I bumped along toward the east, stopping once every so often for photos. I spotted a bighorn sheep below the road on a ridge between a couple gulches, but it was too far away for me to capture a good image, even if I had pulled out the DSLR with its long lens. It was still nice to see some bigger wildlife. Of course, prairie dogs abounded everywhere I looked. Further along, a herd of bison were on both sides of the road, with some crossing. Several vehicles had stopped, like me, to take in the up-close spectacle.

Other than spots of corrugations, the road had a pretty good surface, graded and well-packed, and at times I could get into fourth gear. After a dozen miles, the gravel met tarmac, and I turned south into the interior of the Badlands. I exited at the Interior Entrance Station, just past Cedar Pass at the southeastern end of Badlands National Park, but not before stopping at the Visitors' Center to pick up a Badlands sticker for the Tiger's windscreen.

Wall art in Pine Ridge Reservation

Once out of the park, I took South Dakota Highway 44, per Carsten's recommendation, through the Pine Ridge Reservation, occupied by the Lakota people. Passing through Wanblee, I spotted some beautiful wall art and had to stop to photograph it so I could post it on Facebook, tagging my friend Sam, because I knew he loved wall art and graffiti and often posted photos of any he found.

For most of the day, almost all the way to Iowa, the highway had very little traffic and a high speed limit. As I rode, the pinnacles and buttes disappeared and were gradually replaced by green fields of tall corn. When 44 ended at an Interstate, I took that to the next exit south to Highway 18, which I rode for the rest of the day. Not long after getting on it, I was in Iowa and heading east, just a little south of the latitude the previous highway had been running along.

I looked at the distance to South Bend when I got into Iowa and realized the almost six-hundred miles was much too far for me to cover the next day. I'd have to call Joe and give him an update. Meanwhile, I decided to ride for an hour or two more, getting well into Iowa before stopping for the day. More miles that day would mean fewer miles on the two following days. I hoped to find a city park campground that many of the small Midwestern towns often provided for travelers.

I was back on Central Time and had lost an hour. It was later than half-past-five when I got to the town of Spencer. I thought I'd get dinner there and ask about camping, but as I was riding through town, I spied a campground sign. I followed its lead and rolled into an almost empty and beautiful grassy and tree-filled campground. I made it to a suitable spot and then saw someone waving to me from a large building's patio. I walked up to find out that it was the host and that I'd missed the sign denoting the host's spot on the way in. She gave me the lowdown on the campground, and I handed her the fifteen-dollar fee for one-night's tent space. I mentioned I was going to ride into town for some dinner, then return to set up camp. She and her husband were at a picnic table operating a nearby grill. Byron, her husband, when he'd heard that I was going into town for food, came over and asked if I liked "tri-top," which was apparently something like brisket. He showed me the meat on the grill, and I eagerly accepted his offer as he handed me a cold Corona beer. We all got to talking and hit it off well. While digging into the tri-top and salad that they also had prepared, we had some great conversation, discussing all manner of topics, one of which was Iowa, which seemed to have the opposite problem that many of the states I had visited had. People were leaving the state. Houses and acreage could be bought for bargain prices. With not much to do other than farming in Iowa, many, especially young people, were looking for work and options in other states and in the cities. It made sense that as some state populations grew, there must a vacuum created somewhere else.

The host and her family were very gracious. I enjoyed making new friends yet again, but it was forecast to rain soon. So, after dinner I thanked them all for their hospitality and excused myself, so I could get camp set up in the remaining light and before any rain arrived. I just had finished up as the last of the day was turning to dusk. After walking up to the bath house to brush my teeth before retiring, I sat down at the picnic table and broke out my popup lantern and wrote in my journal until bedtime, while darkness grew overhead.

## GO EAST, YOUNG MAN

My Alarm Clock

Despite being roused by the sound of trumpeting geese leaving the nearby Little Sioux River, I disappointed myself by waking up late, and even more so when I remembered I was now in the Central Time Zone, and it was not eight, but nine o'clock. When that had sunk in, I quickly got up and got busy packing away all my gear. It was ten by the time I'd pulled out and was back on the highway.

Only five minutes out and still in Spencer, I stopped at a local diner and had coffee, breakfast, and a good time kidding around with the amazingly pretty and good-natured girls working there.

Back on the bike, the goal was to burn miles so the final push to South Bend the following day would be easy riding, allowing me to arrive early at my friend's place. It was almost six-hundred miles, so I wanted to get in at least four hundred this day, if possible. I stuck to the same highway I'd been following the day before, almost to the Mississippi River, approaching it from northwest of Dubuque, where I worked my way south on a variety of roads around the city until I got on the Interstate-like US Highway 20 that took me across the Mississippi River, still very wide, even that far north.

I followed the same route into Illinois and passed a KOA in Lena, where I was tempted to stop for the night, but there were hours of daylight left. I wanted to get more than halfway to South Bend so kept going. I had seen camping signs so far in Illinois, so I hoped that would continue to be the case, making finding a spot easy as I rode further east.

As the day grew from early to late afternoon, clouds thickened overhead, with spots here and there ahead of me obviously dropping rain. By five o'clock, I was ready to stop, so I started dutifully watching for signs. Around Freeport the GPS sent me south and off the bigger and more traveled highway. I followed a highway south through a land covered with corn in every direction as far as one could see. As I rode on, ahead I spied a huge sign saying, "No Through Traffic,

Road Closed," placed across the road down which the GPS wanted to send me. That was impossible, so I turned left and let the Garmin recalculate a way around.

Soon, the pavement was replaced by gravel, well graded, but looser than Sage Creek Road had been. It made me a bit nervous, but I continued for miles, turning after ten more onto another gravel road suggested by the GPS, and then another until, after what had to have been thirty miles of gravel, the unit finally told me to turn right back onto pavement.

While riding the gravel roads, the sky had gotten very dark overhead, and occasionally I received a spritz of rain on my visor. I hoped it wouldn't start raining in earnest, because I was concerned about how it might have affected the road conditions. I escaped that test, however, when I got back on paved roads before the rain decided to pick up. Luckily, it didn't last long, and within an hour the skies, while still overcast, quit sending down rain.

All the time since I'd turned south at Freeport and left Highway 20, I'd been watching for camping opportunities that never materialized. I wasted some time in a couple towns trying to find their parks and asking anyone I could find if it was allowed to camp in them, but with no success. One person did tell me that the next town had a campground, which was good news, because by that time it was getting close to sunset. But when I found the place the person had indicated and rode through it on its gravel paths, I could find no one there, not a soul. But everywhere were crosses, altars, and all sorts of religious items and symbols, making me sure it was not a public campground. I found an area with campers parked up, but again, no one was around. However, there was a sign with a phone number on it saying, "No Camping Without Registration," so I called the number but got no response. By then it was late enough that deer were beginning to move. I'd just seen one in the campground in an open sports field.

I hurried back out and back to the highway, hoping for a bigger town that might have a public campground or even a motel. In this remote farm area, I figured a room couldn't be as much as I'd had to pay back on the West Coast.

I asked another person in a little town about motels and was told there would be some in Sycamore, only six miles away, and barring finding one there, DeKalb was just a little further and would certainly have some.

When I got to Sycamore, I went back and forth, between each end of town, looking for a motel but without luck. Another person I asked there was not sure about there being any motels in Sycamore but was sure in DeKalb there would be plenty of choices. So, I headed toward DeKalb, where finally, as I approached its outskirts in the dusk, I found a motel.

The motel was reasonably priced, and I was out of time. The sun had already set. So, I took a room and grabbed my gear from the bike, dragging it inside.

The bike was parked directly outside my room's window, which eased my mind, and the motel also offered a complimentary breakfast, saving me both time and money the next day. It was not a bad deal for a third of what I'd paid for my last room at a rundown hotel with no air conditioning and no breakfast at all.

The next day it would be less than two-hundred miles to South Bend, so all that afternoon's riding at least had paid me back in one way.

## BACK HOME AGAIN IN INDIANA

I got up early and packed quickly, then rode around the corner to the porte cochère of the motel and parked under it. I went into reception and dropped off the "keys" and went into the adjacent dining room, where a very decent spread was laid out, with scrambled eggs, sausage, coffee, cereals, breads, and fruit, and even a self-serve waffle maker. I opted for eggs. sausage, a bagel with cream cheese, and coffee before riding out. It had been a nice stay at a fair price and a good breakfast as well.

I now headed south. DeKalb was just a little west of Chicago. To stay away from any part of the great megalopolis, I had to get south before I could turn east toward Indiana. I kept defying the Garmin's instructions to go east and instead kept south for thirty or so miles to ensure any route east from where I'd turn would clear the snarl of Chicago traffic and suburban sprawl. When I felt I'd traveled sufficiently south, I started to obey the Garmin again and turned to the east.

The route was pleasant enough, through field after field of tall corn, ready for harvest, and roadside ditches filled with blooming purple lavender, a beautiful contrast to the green of the crops. The only substantially large city I had to pass through was Kankakee, but it didn't take long to pass through and get back into the countryside on the other side.

When I finally crossed into Indiana, I took a series of northern and eastern stairsteps trending northeastward toward South Bend. Once again, I passed fragrant fields of mint and passed through North Judson, a tiny village with signs advertising their Mint Festival. I rode through little towns like Walkerton, where I recalled going to horse sales with my father and grandfather so many years ago, and North Liberty, planted in the flat and fertile American farmland of northern Indiana.

After those little towns, I was soon back on city streets in South Bend that I was familiar with from driving on them as a youth. I turned north onto Ironwood Drive toward Joe's neighborhood, in Twyckenham Hills.

I pulled into the driveway a little after two o'clock and parked up beside the garage. Joe hadn't heard me arrive. I took my time dismounting, and rounding the corner I ran into Joe, who gave me a huge bear hug. He had me roll the Tiger into the garage, where I pulled everything off that I'd need while staying there.

Joe was a bachelor for the time I'd be there, hence the free space inside the garage. Jan, his wife, had gone off to Indianapolis to house-sit for their daughter and son-in-law while they were at a conference in Denver.

I dragged everything in and deposited it all in the room Joe had set aside for me. The rest of the day was spent in conversation together, lubricated by good beer, reminiscing about old friends we'd shared in high school. He already had sausages on the grill behind the house, and we continued our catching up over dinner, and later, while watching some YouTube videos we had mentioned to each other that we thought were interesting.

We had a mutual friend, Cindy, from high school, who we called to set up a time the next day to meet with over lunch, then finished our day over sips of Maker's Mark bourbon.

With all the stair-stepping around Chicago that day, it had been an almost hundred-mile longer ride than it would have been going straight, but I suspect missing the big city actually saved time and, certainly, frustration. Nevertheless, the day had been exhausting, and now it was good to be stopped in familiar territory and in the comfortable company of an old friend.

## Old Friends and Laying Plans

I slept late—almost to nine o'clock. I guess the time changes had finally caught up with my biological clock. I heard a rap on the door and Joe asking if I was hungry, because breakfast was on the stove. That finally got me out of bed and into the kitchen.

Joe had made scrambled eggs with salami and coffee, even though he was a tea drinker himself. We sat over breakfast making plans for the day, with priority one being our noon meeting with Cindy at O'Rourke's on the Notre Dame University campus.

Joe walked the dog while I got a shower. Then he went for his daily run, which he'd been doing since high school, while I worked on the bike's left handguard that had been loosened in the second of my bike drops many days previously. It was just a matter of a bent bracket that, once bent back, restored the proper orientation and rigidity of the guard. I also took the opportunity to lube the chain.

About the time I was wrapping up the repair in the garage, Joe returned and noted we only had fifteen minutes before we needed to leave for O'Rourke's. He jumped in the shower while I packed up my tools, got dressed, and got my shoes on.

We left about half-past-eleven and got to O'Rourke's right on time, but there was no sign of Cindy. I realized I had said "Rohrs" to her on the phone, not "O'Rourke's," as the two places were close to each other and I had misunderstood Joe when he had suggested the place. I called Cindy, who was indeed at Rohr's, and she soon joined us at O'Rourke's, where we'd already picked a prime table by an open window.

Beer, conversation, and more beer flowed after hugs all around. Lunch was served, eaten, and removed from the table, with us all yacking until four hours had passed since we'd first sat down. Finally, we said our goodbyes. We'd invited Cindy to come down to Joe's to continue our conversation, but she had relatives she'd promise to go see, so Joe and I returned to the house alone, making a grocery stop on the way back.

With steaks on the grill after a few more hours of conversation and beer, Joe and I plotted our next get-together, but the next time we wanted to also invite other close high school friends like Cindy: our friend Bill, his wife, and Julie Bowland. We hatched a scheme for the next year to rent a cabin or two in eastern Kentucky at Lago Linda, where I'd camped with the Super Happy Fun Group back in late spring. We'd have a weekend of reuniting with friends we'd not, for the most part, seen in ages. When I called Cindy about the plan, she instantly said, "Count me in!" Joe could contact other friends while I was on the road.

After the call to Cindy, I touched base with a friend, Brent, outside of Cincinnati, who'd rented a cabin at Lago Linda the past spring and who had invited me to stay overnight the next evening. I could get more information on our options while visiting him. Meanwhile, I'd also contacted another friend, John, in Dahlonega, Georgia, two nights away, and had procured a place to stay there on my way home. After that stop in Dahlonega, a day later I'd be seeing Julie, giving me a chance to lay out the plans to her personally while staying with her on the last night of the trip. So, all my nights for the rest of the trip were planned, and I would not need to get out my camping gear again.

Joe and I wrapped up the day in front of the television talking and watching a survival show called Alone, until we both got so tired and bleary-eyed, we had to call it a night.

The next day would be a relatively short, easy day of riding to Brent's, which was only a little over a couple hundred miles from South Bend. Then I'd have a long, four hundred-mile ride the following day to Dahlonega. Then the ride to Valdosta, Georgia, to Julie's would only be another couple hundred. I went to sleep feeling pleased with my advance planning.

## A JAUNT THROUGH AMISH COUNTRY

I didn't let myself sleep in past seven o'clock. One lazy morning was all I could afford, so I climbed out of bed and joined Joe, already in the kitchen. While I prepared some coffee, Joe whipped up another round of scrambled eggs and toasted English muffins. After the second cup of coffee, I was ready to load the Tiger.

When completely reloaded, I checked the oil level and then the tires' air pressure, which I had neglected until then. Both were down slightly, but only by a few pounds. I used Joe's bicycle pump to bring them back up to specification.

I gave Joe a hug from both me and Julie, as I had been instructed to do by her on the phone that morning. Joe and

I both agreed we would not let such a long time pass before seeing each other again.

I climbed back onto the Tiger and backed it onto the driveway, punched the starter, and rode away toward the next state, Ohio, and my next destination, Brent's home in South Lebanon, northeast of Cincinnati.

It would be just an easy couple hundred miles that day, so it should be a relaxing ride. I set the GPS for Cincinnati, since as usual, it would not recognize the exact address until I was closer then rolled south and east away from South Bend and across the rich fertile fields of Indiana.

The entire day was spent rolling between high green cornfields and occasional fields of soybeans as I made my way southeast through Amish country. Everywhere I went, I passed signs to watch out for horse and buggies. Buggies were certainly around, as evidenced by the horses', well, evidence left behind on the country roads, and just after noon, I passed a horse-drawn carriage on a minor bridge, with me waving and getting waves back in return.

Ohio was a repeat of the farmland I had passed through in Indiana, but I had crossed into the state near Dayton, and so traffic had picked up. Soon I was in heavy traffic on city roads between Dayton and Cincinnati. Road construction and single-lane roads further complicated travel. There were short country sections between suburban sprawl, but eventually I was past the Cincinnati/Dayton corridor and on the east side, near South Lebanon. I entered the exact address once near town. The Garmin led me faithfully, and I soon found myself pulling into Brent's garage.

Brent greeted me cordially and showed me my room for the night, then he and I hung out in the kitchen drinking wine and talking about possible routes for the next day and discussing the state of current affairs in our country.

Brent ordered pizza for dinner and ran out to get it while his wife, Lin, showed me her quilting operation in the basement. She was a very accomplished quilter and had all the equipment necessary to do it on a grand scale. Soon, Brent was heard in the kitchen above us, so we climbed the stairs to meet him and get our plates filled with pizza.

Over dinner, the conversation flowed easily. We discussed travel magazines, possible advertising opportunities in them, books, and writing. Before long, we were both yawning. I said good night, because I knew I'd need to be up very early the next day, so the four-hundred-mile ride to Dahlonega could be completed early enough to have some quality time with John.

Brent agreed to lead me in the morning to the entrance onto the bypass I'd need to find to get me across the Ohio River and to US Highway 27 and off the Interstate in Kentucky.

I took a quick shower then retired to my room to jot down the day's events in my journal. The next day of riding was going to be long and hard, but from there to Valdosta, the following day, would be relatively easy, and from there to home would be even shorter, only a little over two hundred miles wrapping up the trip.

## RETURN TO THE APPALACHIANS

When morning came, I gathered all my things from the room and got to work packing it all on the bike. Then Brent, Lin, and I chatted over a couple cups of coffee, discussing good route options out of Cincinnati, across the Ohio River, and into Kentucky. The plan was to take I-275 around the city and across the river and then get off in Kentucky on the much smaller US Highway 27, the same route that eventually would pass through Lake Wales, and ride through the countryside on it for a while.

Brent saddled up on his Moto Guzzi and led me to the exit where I would get onto the Interstate, waving goodbye as I peeled away onto the busy freeway and toward Kentucky while he returned home.

The Interstate traffic was fast but not terribly dense. I chose a spot in the middle lane, set the cruise control a couple over the speed limit to avoid being run down by the mostly faster traffic whizzing by on both sides, and did my best to keep a space between cars in front and behind me. It was less than a half-hour riding the bypass before I'd crossed the Ohio River and was exiting onto Highway 27.

On the south side of the big coffee-with-cream-colored river there was an almost overwhelming sweet odor in the air, so intense it was almost like inhaling candy. I could not identify where it was coming from. I hadn't noticed any trees or plants that were obviously in bloom that might have produced the mango-like sweet smell. It persisted for miles into Kentucky as I left the river and rolled along on a roller coaster of small hills through an area thick with horse farms.

By the time I'd passed though half the state, north to south, I noticed the kudzu was back in full Southern force, thickly blanketing everything along the roadside that didn't move.

By Lexington, the Garmin was giving me an arrival time in Dahlonega well after six o'clock. I wanted to arrive earlier than that, so I decided to take nearby Interstate 75 for a while, hoping to cut back the ride time. I continued on the freeway, where most of the time I could keep up a speed of about seventy miles per hour, barreling south into Tennessee and almost to Georgia.

When I had arrived in Tennessee, the hills had transformed into the Appalachian Mountain chain and had doubled in height. Further south, I caught a minor highway off the Interstate that would eventually take me into Tellico Plains. Once away from the I-75 hustle, I found myself in a lush, green, mountainous landscape. I passed the western end of the Cherohala Skyway in Tellico Plains and continued toward the Georgia state line on one of my favorite mountain roads Tennessee Highway 68.

Once in the little twin villages that straddled the Georgia/Tennessee border, Copperhill and McCaysville, I caught Georgia State Road 60, which would take me past Suches and directly into Dahlonega. At least I thought I had, but just as I'd gotten onto it, I'd unknowingly turned back off. I'd made the mistake of trusting the Garmin, which resulted in me riding west on the Appalachian Highway instead. I could keep up steady Interstate speeds on that highway but would go far west of the direct route the other road would have taken to my destination. Admittedly, the Garmin knew that the "direct" route might look straight on a map, but that it was anything but and was filled with curve after curve as it twisted through the mountains, but that was one reason I had wanted to take it. I'd ridden 60 several times before and knew how fun negotiating its curves had been. The GPS had probably calculated that its route would save time, but its route certainly would not have given me reason to smile, like the other highway would have. And the route I had hoped to take would just have been simpler, as there would be no turning off it onto connecting roads until I had finally arrived in Dahlonega and was very close to John's house.

Once far enough south on the Appalachian Highway, I had to turn east for thirty to thirty-five miles to finally reach Dahlonega, where I stopped and entered the precise address in the GPS, so I could finish the ride to John's front door.

In less than a half-hour, I was parked in his garage, and soon after I had a bourbon in my hand and roast beef with rice and salad on a plate in front of me, prepared by my friend.

After eating, we went downstairs into John's "Temple of Speed," where he showed me all the motorcycles he'd collected and ones he was busy working on or restoring. He had a dozen or so in the Temple downstairs garage, but a dozen more were stored outside in a shed. John leaned heavily toward Yamahas and Ducatis, but there were other brands sprinkled around.

After the tour and bike talk, we headed back upstairs, where we watched a little television while we talked and grew sleepy. When our eyes could not stay open much longer, John retired to bed, as he had to leave early the next morning on a business trip, and I took a quick shower. What luxury that was now, having showers daily, after going for weeks without any on my ride while out west. Back in my room, I worked on my journal before I finally fell asleep.

That day had been a long endurance run of over four hundred miles, but I was looking forward to the next day being much less taxing, being only three hundred miles or so. I wouldn't have to rush out in the morning just to get there at a reasonable time.

## THE FAMILIAR RUN THROUGH GEORGIA

We were both up early. John had to leave for his business trip, and I wanted to be out of his way as he got ready to go. There was time for a quick cup of coffee, then we said our goodbyes, and I headed to the garage, rolling the Tiger out into the drive and turning it around so I could take off uphill to the street once I climbed onboard. I hit the starter, reached over to shake hands with John, promising I'd stop by again on a future trip and that next time we would go riding together, and rolled up onto the street and back toward the highway.

Now that I was in north Georgia, I could practically ride to Valdosta blindfolded, but well, I made the mistake of trusting that the Gramin would choose the logical route over to US Highway 129, famous for the Tail of the Dragon just a wee bit further north, and south on it to Athens, around on the bypass, then out the south side and into the countryside. Instead, it put me on GA 60, apparently wanting me to pass between Atlanta and Athens. That sounded good, but I'd tried it before, and it had turned out to be a maze of turns onto and off little roads and through tiny towns for miles. It just made more sense to jump over to 129 and head south. It being a bigger highway, it would not get mired down in so many places. But I failed to look closely at the GPS and just turned when it told me to. I realized after about fifty miles I was not going where I wanted.

After crossing Interstate 85, I looked for a way to jump back over. I was not too far to the west of my intended track, so a little past Belmot, I started weaving my way back over to 129. I got on it before Athens and was then able to continue on my preferred route around that big city, a reasonably easy affair, especially after I had ridden it so many times before. I was spit out on the south side and shot south, with my next goal Macon. My route passed mostly through empty forest and open land, with little traffic until almost in Macon.

The further south I rode, the pervasive kudzu diminished, while Spanish moss took on the role of covering everything with long, wind-whipped, gray beards. The smell in the air took on the aroma of freshly cut pine, evidenced by the many logging trucks hauling boles to the mills or chippers for processing, lodged between the half-dozen steel uprights of the trailer, with the spindly ends springing up and down yards behind the trailer and waving a red rag in warning. Soon I would be in the land of pecan groves and among fields of peanuts.

I was heading to see my dear friend Julie, who had recently retired from teaching art at Valdosta State University. We'd grown up together, along with Joe and Cindy, going to the same high school. Joe, Julie, and I were fast friends back then and all of us into art, in one way or another. And in one way or another, we all used our training in art in some form in future careers, but Julie had stuck to doing fine art and painting plein-air oils, largely most recently of the many springs and rivers in South Georgia and North Florida. She'd also traveled and had many beautiful works of art from other great areas, such as Utah, California, Hawaii, and the Blue Ridge. I'd always admired her for not compromising and creating work that was truly hers.

Now that Julie had retired from teaching painting, she was doing even more artwork, and people were really starting to notice. That afternoon, a group called WWALS Watershed Coalition, also known as Suwannee Riverkeepers, was having a music contest in a city park, where musicians could vie for having created the "Best Song" about southern rivers. As part of the event, one of Julie's paintings was being raffled off, along with one by another artist, to benefit the group and, therefore, the Suwannee River, a place that was dear to her heart and where she'd painted so many times. I was hoping to make it down early enough to be able to join her at the that event and another she'd mentioned would be going on earlier in the day at a different location nearby to have some beers together and enjoy some live music.

I thought my best bet for getting down to Julie's ahead of the festivities was to get on Interstate 75 at Macon for the run down to her place, which was just a few miles west of Exit 18. Living on the Florida Peninsula, virtually every trip I made to the Blue Ridge Mountains or further northeast into Appalachia, or even New England, first had to pass through central Georgia. I usually much preferred taking backroads and minor highways when making the trek, but I'd ridden through so many times that I'd not see much I hadn't seen before. Hitting the "slab" and heading directly south avoided all the little villages, which the backroads would inevitably take me through, along with allowing a higher speed, getting me to Julie's plenty early enough for me to join her for the fun afternoon and evening.

So, at Macon, I did just that and tore south at seventy to seventy-five miles per hour on I-75, stopping only once for fuel and for some iced tea, while I clued Julie in by text on my estimated time of arrival. Along the way, I got to witness the battle of the billboards. The evangelical right threw punches with "I'm still in control . . . Jesus," with images of tanks, solders, and helicopters surrounding Jesus; and "Join the living . . . Jesus" and "You decide . . . Jesus," both complete with a zombie apocalypse behind a loving Jesus. But the salvos were returned by the opposing team with "$TRIPPER$ . . . Need we say more?" and "Lion's Den Adult Super Store." Of course, political groups had their own row going on with "Making the Taliban Great Again" with Joe Biden pictured with turban and grenade launcher; and "Unfit and Unhinged . . . Vote Him Out," featuring a screaming Trump. Of course, pro-choice and pro-life billboards were fighting it out tooth and nail as well.

I was at Exit 18 at about two o'clock and rode west looking for the diminutive sign for Pinedale Circle, on the south side of the highway. It was perfect timing. By the time I'd parked the Tiger in the garage and rid myself of my heavy riding suit, Julie's brother, Dan, showed up with Thai food for lunch as Julie offered me a beer. It was just what I needed after that jarring 160-mile run down the Interstate in the blazing sun among the multitudes of trucks, trailers, and cars seeming to think there was no speed limit at all. To sit still in the quiet and cool of the air conditioning sipping a cold Two Hearted Ale was a little bit of heaven.

The other activity being planned preceding Julie's art raffle and musical event was a gathering in another Valdosta park with more music, but thunderstorms were moving in. Julie thought it wise to pass on that one and wait until the weather looked more promising before heading out to her event, which was not until early evening. That just gave us time for more beer and more conversation.

Late afternoon rolled around, and Julie and I climbed in her truck and Dan in his car, and we headed downtown ahead of the benefit to meet up with Emily, a friend of Julie, to have a few beers at a micro-brewery with a great atmosphere, being run in a collection of old brick waterworks buildings and complete with a food truck, if one was so inclined. When we all got there, the weather still looked threatening, so we opted for seats inside, where we could watch the dark, lowering clouds and the tree limbs blowing about in the gathering wind in safety, instead of out on their lovely rustic patio. Julie and I ordered a flight of a mixture of some unusual and some more-common-type beers to share in taste-testing, all having been brewed on the spot. We had plenty of time to enjoy our test flight, and then, once all were tasted and judged, we ordered a pint for ourselves of our favorites.

While we drank and talked, the weather moved on to the southeast, and the sky was looking benign for the charity event, so we all emerged from our storm-refuge brewery and crossed a rain-free parking lot to our vehicles and moved the party to the new location as the sun was sinking low.

The music had started before we'd arrived, and it was outstanding, the competitors predominantly playing in a style I'd call mellow folk, which seemed perfectly fitting, considering what the theme of the event was. After weaving our way through the crowd, halting from spot to spot as Julie was accosted by every other person as the celebrity of the hour, we set up our chairs and cooler, cracked open some cool ones, and sat back to enjoy the music.

The night set in, and the lights went on. Following the competitors and the award presentation, another band took the stage, made up in part by some of the competitors but with a completely different sound. It was a very surprising but enjoyable fusion of funk and jazz, with a young fellow singing who had a voice that was torn around the edges and sounding much older than his age. They were all very good musicians, but my eyes and ears were drawn to the drummer, who was simply amazing as he kept up with everything his fellow musicians were laying down.

Before it got too late, we bowed out and headed home, knowing Julie's painting would find a good home. We did not stay up long back at Julie's. I guess we were feeling our age a bit, because neither of us had anything pressing to get up early for the next morning. My ride then would be an easy couple hundred miles, and Julie, now retired, could take her time greeting a new day and do it as late as she liked.

## The Run Comes to an End

I drug myself out of bed not long after Julie was up. I poured myself some coffee and found her in the backyard, where I joined her, watching the squirrels scampering around and birds diving in for seeds. After a couple cups and morning conversation in the still cool yard, I headed back in to pack up. Backing out of the garage, I watched nervously for any signs of nails, because Julie's roof had been replaced recently, and I did not want a repeat of the morning I had spent last time repairing my rear tire in her drive. Fortunately, I escaped unscathed and hit the highway with tires still full of air.

I rode east toward the Interstate and stopped for a fuel-up at the exit. I'd decided, however, to not take the freeway but to take my time and wander south into Florida by back roads. It would take longer and be further than it would have been taking the Interstate, but it would be a much more relaxing ride, mainly through the countryside of North Florida and through small villages. There was no hurry, and yesterday's frantic ride on I-75 had been enough. Sure, I'd miss the billboards declaring, "We Bare All," and "After 18 days in the womb our hearts are beating," and of course, "Psychiatry ruins lives," with all their cunning subtlety, but I'd have to settle for views of horse farms, oak forests, and slow-flowing rivers.

In Valdosta, I turned south and had almost left the city when I was stopped by a motionless train parked across the road, with seemingly no intention of moving. I backtracked to the main road and headed east again into downtown, where I could catch my route south where it climbed high over the same tracks. Passing through a couple little settlements along the highway, within a half-hour I was back in Florida and in open country, running along a railroad track that mirrored the path of the road beside it.

After passing through White Springs, Florida, I crossed the Suwannee River and made my way into Lake City. I was detoured a few blocks out of the way there, due to road work, but eventually rejoined my route south. On the far side of the city, I was back in farmland and soon passed under I-75. I'd not had anything for breakfast, other than coffee, so I started looking for a place to get a bite as I passed through each small village. My search hadn't offered any options, and I was getting quite hungry by the time I got to High Springs. I stopped downtown to see if there were any dining options and stopped a young couple strolling on the sidewalk and asked them where I could get a good lunch. We were directly in front of a restaurant, The Great Outdoors, but it looked a little pricy, being housed in an old opera house and sporting cloth napkins on the tables, but the couple said it was good. I walked in, finding an elegant eatery with exposed brick walls and pecky cypress woodwork everywhere. I took a gamble and asked for a seat and was soon ensconced in a cozy booth with a huge and fabulous salad in front of me. It was delicious and covered in bleu cheese. To my surprise, the prices were quite reasonable, and I left with a bill not exceeding fifteen dollars. The lunch was just what I needed for the final push home.

From High Springs south until Inverness, other than passing through some small quiet villages, I was in the countryside and on empty country roads. At Inverness, I was back on a larger highway and amongst traffic, but only a few miles further on, I turned off the road again and rode down a tunnel of Spanish moss-draped trees in Floral City and out into the woods and fields again. I was then in very familiar territory.

The route had been my escape path many times before as I'd wound my way out of Florida and toward either Alabama or Georgia. I rolled east and south toward Bushnell, where I would have gotten off the Interstate if I had taken it instead. I rolled under I-75, through Bushnell, and further east through little Center Hill and toward the twin towns of Mascotte and Groveland, at the north end of the Green Swamp. Once past Center Hill, I turned left off the main county road and onto a small shortcut I had discovered that ran through Tuscanooga, a tiny settlement not big enough to warrant the name of even a village.

At the end of Tuscanooga Road, I was spat out onto the main east-west highway in Mascotte. I continued through Groveland, turning south to make my way through the west edge of the swamp for a twenty-mile run on an arrow-straight road almost to Polk City. I turned off before arriving in the little town and headed east then south again on minor county backroads that eventually took me south over Interstate 4. From there it was a turn on an old connecting road all the way to Haines City and US Highway 27, which I had left hundreds of miles before. Crossing the highway, I made my way through downtown Haines City to Scenic Highway. I rode it all the way south until I could see the pink marble tower at Bok Tower Gardens ahead on a ridge, just above our house.

After passing the turn to Bok Tower Gardens and turning off the highway, I was just a couple blocks from the house. I rolled around the last curve and up into the driveway, doing my usual U-turn in front of the garage door, so I could back my Tiger in. No one was outside and I had almost completely unloaded and was about to back the bike into the garage before anyone knew I was there. Andrea popped out of the house and took some of the luggage, followed by my daughter Tess, who gathered up the rest.

I quickly checked the odometer. It had been almost ten thousand miles since I had rolled out of that driveway thirty-four days earlier. I had passed through twenty-five states, six of which I'd never visited before, on this little ride around the block.

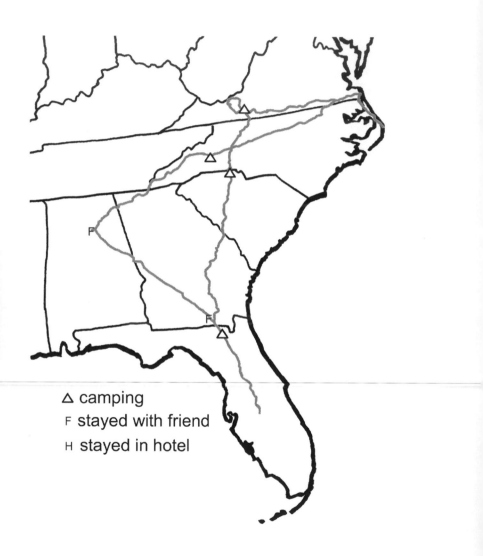

△ camping
F stayed with friend
H stayed in hotel

# A COMPLICATION

## EDITOR'S CAMPING WEEKEND

Once back home, I never quite know what to do with myself. Everything seems foreign, and it's hard to kickstart myself back into domestic action. But I had ridden a couple days past my work-start deadline for the next issue of the magazine, so I knew what I had to do and set to work catching up. Someway, we managed to get the next issue put together and to the printer before the mid-September deadline. That left until late September to get everything else done before I was to leave on another ride.

I had organized a new VJMC event called Editor's Ride-In Camping Weekend that I had been trying to make an annual event. I started it a couple years before, in September of 2019, held at Two Wheels of Suches, a motorcycle-only campground located in one of the best mountain riding areas in the country in the Blue Ridge Mountains of North Georgia. Although we had a small group of riders that first year, I was expecting it to grow, but by the time it rolled around again the next year, Covid had arrived and forced cancellation. Finally in 2021, on the third year, I was planning to resurrect the event, when I'd had my run-in with the deer in Virginia. By the time that September had rolled around again, the doctor still had not given me permission to ride, which put the brakes on the event a second time. But in 2022, I was once more fit to ride, and plans were set for the event to recommence, this time at Willville Motorcycle Campground in Meadows of Dan, Virginia, where the deer and I had collided the year before. I'd need to leave by Wednesday, September 21, to get to Willville for the weekend of the event.

With the time left, I worked feverishly on two books I had in production. The print version of one of them was done, except for the cover. Before I had left for the West Coast, I had painted an image from a place that had impressed the author and he'd mentioned in the book, and I was hoping to use the painted image in some way for the cover. I'd made up various layouts with the painting as the background but was not happy with the results. The author made some suggestions for adding a couple images that might work in the foreground combined with the painting, so I worked on drawing and painting those and then processing the images for use in different combinations with the painting, but I was still not satisfied. So, I started from the ground up, putting together several other designs that were completely different and abandoning the painting idea. I thought I finally had some good options days before I would leave. I sent the author the ideas, hoping by the time I returned we would have a final design and I could complete the book and get it to press. The other book's interior I'd completed a few days after signing off on the next magazine issue, giving final approval for printing. I'd completed the book's cover by then as well.

Besides the book work, I had hundreds of emails to catch up on that had gathered in my inbox while I'd been traveling. Also, both business and household bills had to be organized and paid that were coming due before I was to leave, along with those that would come due while I'd be gone.

Finally, because this was a vintage event, I wanted to ride my vintage 1978 Suzuki GS550e to the event. It had sat in the garage for a while and needed an oil change, so that task would have to be completed in the short time I had left. I ordered a new oil filter and bought oil in advance of doing the change the week before the event. When I went to the garage and prepared to do the work on the Suzuki, I was surprised when I saw the inline fuel filter crumbling and in pieces dangling from a stiff fuel line. That would add to the work, I thought, but as I took a closer look at the filter, I saw it was filled with rust—even more work. The tank would have to come off and be de-rusted with acid before I could restore the fuel line and filter and do the oil change.

I had the tank finished and ready to go back on, along with new line and filter, by the middle of the week. I'd also pulled the bank of four carburetors and cleaned them thoroughly by Friday. On Saturday, I began the work of reinstalling the carburetor bank on the bike. That was usually a difficult job. Often when the carburetor bank would finally get attached to the intake boots on the engine side, they would not fit inside the boots on the airbox side. I started early in a hot garage, and after hours of getting the bank in one side and having it pop out the other, then repeating the process over and over with the same results, I was defeated. I could not spend another day struggling with that; there were still so many loose ends to tie up before I left. I would be riding a modern British bike to a vintage Japanese motorcycle rally again, but it could not be helped. When I got back, I'd tackle it again, so I could ride the Suzuki to the other, last big event of the year, the Barber Vintage Festival. I turned my attention to other things in preparation for leaving on Wednesday.

## TO THE SUWANNEE

I wanted to arrive at Willville early on Friday afternoon, which meant a departure on Wednesday, allowing myself three days for the ride north of 750 miles. As usual, the night before I'd checked the bike over, adjusted the tire pressures, checked the oil level, packed everything, and loaded it all on the waiting Tiger in the garage. The only things for me to do in the morning before leaving would be to put on my riding jacket, pants, and boots.

My first day's goal was White Springs, Florida, less than thirty miles from the Georgia state line. I left the drive and pointed the front wheel north. Instead of threading the many backroads of Florida, I decided this time to ride north to catch the Turnpike to I-75 to save time and to ensure an early arrival at camp.

I only took the scenic route as far as Haines City, where I jumped west a couple miles to get on the main north-south US Highway that ran up the spine of the state. That highway would get busy with all the commuters storming into Orlando, as it ran north and connected to the main Interstate running through the busy city. So, I made sure to leave our place early enough to get ahead of that mayhem. Once past the Interstate, traffic would diminish, and before it could build up as the day grew, I would hop onto the turnpike, which was not usually very crowded, and take the expressway north-northwest to I-75. I'd take 75 all the way to the White Springs exit, avoiding all the bigger towns, like Ocala and Gainesville, as the freeway passed beside but not through them.

I settled into my Interstate groove, riding about five under to conserve fuel and trying to stay out of everyone else's way. It was still September in Florida, so it was going to be hot. After I had gotten off the turnpike, it was already growing warm, so I removed my sweatshirt I'd donned under my jacket to ward of the coolness of the early morning. The heat increased as the day went on. I stopped at Micanopy for gas and to open all my jacket vents and to unzip my sleeves so air could rush up into the jacket as I moved along at sixty-five miles per hour. Across the side road was the Café Risqué, so famously touted along the highway on huge billboards announcing "We Bare All!"

I skipped the strip club, which was also, strangely, a restaurant and caught up with the traffic heading north back on the freeway. Soon, I was dropping down a slope and speeding across the wide, low, green, and wet Paine's Prairie Preserve, with the wetlands lapping up on both sides of the raised roadbed. The highway rose again on the north side, and almost as soon as it did, I was passing to the west of Gainesville, the big college town that was home to the University of Florida. The traffic increased as I approached and then decreased again as I passed, but never got too heavy, because the Interstate ran well away from the city center through outlying country. I was two-thirds of the way to my day's destination, and the day had become stifling hot.

I'd left early and taken the Interstate to not only avoid morning traffic around Orlando, but also so I could arrive at Suwanee River Resort early enough in the afternoon to not have to arrange an after-hours arrival, which would involve calling from the gate and having someone come out to open it for me. I also wanted to be there early enough that I could set up my tent mid-afternoon and enjoy some of the amenities of the resort, especially the pool, after such a hot ride up.

I crossed I-10, the east-west freeway running from Jacksonville on the East Coast and eventually ending, or starting, depending on your point of view and direction of travel, in Los Angeles on the West Coast. In just a few more miles I was at my exit to White Springs.

Suwannee Valley Resort had a restaurant and bar, but they were usually only open during the weekends, so to make things simple and quick, I grabbed a bite to eat at a McDonalds at the exit before heading toward White Springs and the resort. That out of the way, I still wanted to have a snack and some beer for my stay at camp, so I passed my turn and crossed the Suwannee River into the tiny town of White Springs and grabbed what I needed at a convenience store before heading back across the river.

Turning left on the other side of the Suwannee River, I wound my way back to the campground that sat on the west bank of the river. I checked in at the office and then was led to my tent space, where I quickly got out of my hot riding gear and the little clothing I had under it and got busy setting up my tent.

The sun was still blazing, so the pool was my first destination. Taking one of my beers with me, I walked down the steps into the relief of the cool, clean, blue water and took a seat, neck deep to absorb as much of the relief as I could. It was a quiet weekday and only a couple others were in the pool at the other end, so I sat in silence, sipping and relaxing as the heat of the day melted away.

As the day drew to a close, I headed back to my site and got ready for the night. It was the night each week that my friends from the Supper Happy Fun Group gathered for a Zoom meeting to catch up with each other. I sat down at my picnic table, set up my phone, making sure it only showed me above the waist, and joined the conversation. Of course, I got some good-natured ribbing for being clothes-less for the meeting, even though, as far as they knew, I was only shirt-less. Still, we all had our usual good time, and no one forbade me from joining again, so I guess my offense was not serious.

My phone's battery had not been up to the task, and by mid-meeting, I bid goodnight to my friends, and turned in.

## Into the Carolinas

In the morning, I disassembled camp and loaded it all onto the bike, then reluctantly threw my riding clothes on for the day's ride north. I was aiming for another resort like Suwannee River that I had visited before that was located a couple miles south of the North Carolina state line.

Before leaving White Springs, I stopped at the quaint Fat Belly's diner for a substantial breakfast, having decided I'd skip lunch that day. After eggs, bacon, and grits, washed down with black coffee, I rolled out of the gravel parking lot and onto the highway I'd be following for almost half the day.

It was another sunny and hot day as I made my way toward South Carolina. I would be taking all back country roads for the entire day, riding out of White Springs on US 441 through the East Georgia woods and farmland. That route took me all the way to McRae-Helena, Georgia, where I fueled up before veering off to the northeast, bound for a crossing north of Augusta into South Carolina.

I left the land of pecan trees and entered the land of snowy cotton fields and fragrant pine woods as I approached Augusta. At Wrens, I once again diverted north, avoiding the city, and wound my way around the west side of town and to Strom Thurmond Dam. Riding on top of the dam, I crossed the Savannah River where it formed Clark's Hill Lake to the north and rolled into South Carolina at, where else, Clark's Hill.

Heading north, following the eastern shore of the lake, I soon turned back to the northeast and aimed for Greenwood and a few miles past that, Lake Greenwood, a widening of the Saluda River that lay across my path. Beyond the lake was Waterloo, where I stopped again for gas. I was a little blue as I passed through there, as it had been the home town of a dear friend I had worked with, who had passed away a few years before. He had hosted and fed me on the start of one of my first big solo motorcycle adventures, when I had been heading to Quebec and the Bay of Saint Lawrence. There would be no stopping at his place for conversation or rides on his pontoon boat on the lake anymore.

I shook off the melancholy, and continued north toward Graycourt, where I shifted more northeasterly and toward a crossing of the main northwest/southeast corridor through the center of South Carolina, Interstate 26.

I'd first intended to cross over the Interstate and continue winding my way on minor back roads toward my final

destination, but Carolina Foothills Resort lay directly north
of Spartanburg, a large city that was part of a two-city metro
area comprised of it and Greenville to the west. If I'd stuck to
my original plan, I'd have to do a lot of maneuvering off and
onto little roads to wrap around Spartanburg on the east away
from the city and then return west once past it. My brother
used to live only a mile or two west of I-26 on the north side
of the area. I had visited him many times, meeting up to ride
in the mountains in North Carolina or to deer hunt in the
woods behind his house and knew that 26 would cut quickly
and efficiently directly between the two big cities, and I could
easily exit it once past and be within miles of the campground.
So, I changed my plan and decided to take the freeway for
that run past the two cities. Just a mile past Moore, I hopped
onto the freeway and set the cruise control. The traffic was
not heavy, and it was easy enough to negotiate, as I would
not have any turns to make until my exit once past the metro
area, where traffic would have thinned out. I passed Exit 15,
where I used to turn off for my brother's place near Inman
and continued for only two exits until I was on the route that
would take me toward Chesnee and the campground.

    After exiting the freeway, I was only ten miles away from
my turnoff to Carolina Foothills Resort, so I stopped to pick
up something to eat and a couple cans of beer to bring with
me to camp. I got back aboard the Tiger for the final stretch
and found Mahaffey Cooley Road, the miniscule side road
that led north to another, tinier connector, which brought me
to the aptly-named Carolina Foothills Drive that led into the
resort.

    I'd ridden almost four hundred miles that day, which
resulted in me arriving at my destination after-hours, so I
stopped at the call box and rang up the attendant, who rode up
to open the gate for me. I had been there a couple times before,
so I knew where to go; checking in and out would have to wait
for the morning. I knew I'd be arriving late, so I had called
ahead. I remembered that there were small, screened cabins of

a sort, really just small screen enclosures that could be rented for not much more than a tent site, so I had arranged to take one of those so I would not have to set up the tent but only drag my sleeping pad and bag off the bike. That would make packing up the next morning simpler and quicker.

In just a few minutes, I had my pad and bag laying on the floor inside the shelter, had stripped off my riding gear and clothes, and was walking up to the pool area, where I could sit at a table and enjoy my sandwich and beer.

The place was eerily quiet, and I did not bump into anyone. I ate my meal in silence as the afternoon waned and the air cooled. The first time I had visited there, there was a lot of activity, and friendly people had even invited me to join them for a potluck dinner. It had been a very friendly place, which had prompted my desire to return, but this time all I heard was crickets. Finished with my meal, I took a quick shower and hopped into the empty pool to cool down and relax for a few moments.

The place was still as nice as I had remembered it, but as I walked back to my cabin as the sun was slowly disappearing among the trees, I was a little let down. I sat in my camp chair on the little porch in front of my shelter while watching the day quietly come to an end. I was deep in thought, or perhaps dozing, when a bearded, younger fellow, Nick, walked up and began asking about my bike.

I was glad for the company. We had a nice conversation about the Tiger and bikes in general and about where I was going to and coming from. I mentioned that the times I'd been there before I'd found it a very friendly spot, being invited the first time to a dinner and the second time for steak, when I'd met someone who lived there in a nearby trailer and we'd struck up a conversation, but I was surprised how quiet it had been this time. He replied that it was the end of the season and mid-week, so things were winding down for the year, and activities would probably mostly be just on weekends from then until the season started up again in the spring.

Nick mentioned he had just moved to the park, into a mobile home near the gate. He said that there were quite a few who lived there most of the year and that he had made some great friends who had helped him get his home established after a divorce. Some of his friends were there that night. He offered to take me around and introduce me. I had nothing planned, so I tagged along as we walked around the grounds and he showed me where this or that friend lived. We found a group of his friends on a porch outside their trailer, sitting around a table, having some beers, and watching a game on TV. Nick introduced me around to the four, a beer was produced for me, and I was invited to sit down and join them. While we drank and watched the game, conversation flowed, and I was made to feel welcome—quite a contrast to what my earlier solitary experience had been.

After a while, Nick and I walked to his trailer, so he could show me his new place, which he was very proud of and for which he was quite grateful because of the kindness of his friends who had made it possible. It was situated on the edge of the resort, so that if you came in the front door, you'd be coming in from outside the park and if you exited the back door, you'd be exiting the house into the park. We chatted a while longer before I felt the need to get some sleep and to conserve some energy for tomorrow's ride, so I told him I needed to head back to my shelter and thanked him for his company. He said that if I ever was in the area, I was more than welcome to stay with him and save my money by not having to pay for a tent space or shelter. He accompanied me back to the cabin, as I had been a little turned around as we had meandered around the grounds in the night, and he got me back without me having gotten lost or stumbling over something in the dark that he knew to avoid.

By then it was much later than I had planned to go to bed, close to eleven, but the time spent with nice people was worth a little sleepiness. Because I had ridden so far that day, the final stretch up to Willville would be easy going, so the next day's ride would not be too taxing anyway. I was out almost as soon as I was in my bag and my head hit the rolled-up towel that I used for a pillow.

## Passing the Scene of the Accident

Despite the late night before, I awoke refreshed. I took the time to head up the hill, still unclothed in the chilly morning air, to the clubhouse to make some coffee in the community kitchen. The walk was bracing and the coffee good and strong. I sat inside and had a few cups, then went to take another shower before loading the bike and climbing into my road gear. There was no need to hurry, with less than two hundred miles to go that day. The office would not open until nine, anyway, and I still needed to settle my bill there.

The office opened on time, and by quarter-past-nine I was rolling out of the gate and out onto the main road. Turning left onto the road, it soon turned to gravel as I passed into North Carolina before eventually finding pavement again.

I followed a series of small country roads heading north until Rutherfordton, where I got onto a small US Highway that trended more to the north-northeast, slowly merging with the Appalachian range as it trended northeasterly to eventually meet up with my route. Before it could, however, the road took a more parallel track and I rolled along with the main part of the range to my left while I stayed in the foothills between them and the Piedmont.

By Morganton, I needed gas again, so I stopped to get off the bike for a bit and to fill up. After that brief rest I continued, passing into Virginia around Mount Airy. By Fancy Gap I had joined the Appalachians' main range and exited the highway to join the Blue Ridge Parkway for the rest of the ride to Willville.

As I approached Meadows of Dan, I had my eyes peeled for the telltale marks of motorcycle pegs having dug into the pavement. I knew I had hit the deer very close to the exit to Meadows of Dan, because when I had finally gotten a message out to my friend who was camping at Willville, it was only a few minutes before he'd shown up on his Bonneville, parked on the road with his headlight facing the oncoming lane, and was helping me up. I searched for miles before that exit but never did spot the place I had gone down. Perhaps they had already patched the parkway there. I tried to recognize any signs of the area as I remembered it, but by the time I finally turned off the Blue Ridge Parkway, I'd not seen any signs of my debacle.

I rolled into Meadows of Dan but turned the wrong way onto Jeb Stuart Highway and found myself where it joined the bypass on the other side of the little village before I'd realized my mistake. I turned around and proceeded the way I had come and passed under the parkway and toward where the same bypass joined the highway on the west end. There stood the big Willville Motorcycle Campground sign. I turned left and rolled down the gravel track and into the tent camping area below the hill.

The last time I'd been at Willville I didn't get much of a chance to check it out, having arrived in the dark with road rash up my arms where my sleeves had ridden up, a twisted ankle, and a wrist broken in two places. Most of my time there was spent near the bathrooms cleaning and dressing wounds and getting my wrist wrapped up. I only got as far as the campfire ring that night, where a shot or two of medicinal whiskey eased my pain. This time, I rode down the hill, past the bath house, and found a shady, grassy campground with a small creek burbling beside it. At the uphill end of the camping area was the communal campfire area, perfect for sharing lies with other campers after the sun went down. It was a great spot to use as our headquarters for the weekend of riding we were planning.

I spotted a very nice old Honda DOHC 750 near a tent, and I knew I had found one of my fellow members. I pulled in beside Kent and set up my tent near the creek next to his, so we could share the picnic table. He had assured me by email before

I'd left that if I could not get the Suzuki done in time, he would not make fun of me if I had to be on the Tiger. He was true to his word . . . mostly. His bike was impeccable and such a dark purple that, if you didn't look closely, you'd think it was black. He had owned it since new. We conversed while walking over to where Mark and Keith, a couple other members, had set up on the other side of the creek in a shady alcove on the far side of a footbridge just wide enough for a motorcycle. We all made plans for a meet-up at Jane's Country Café in town, where we could rough out some plans for riding the next day.

After a quick dinner at Jane's, at camp we met up with Christopher, a new VJMC member with a beautiful CB400F, with those wonderfully sculpted four-into-ones sweeping across the front of the motor to join each other and the muffler on the right side of the bike, and his dad, Dan. So, we had a group of six club members.

Laughing around the campfire

Friday evening was spent around the campfire getting to know each other along with the other campers who were spending the night there, while enjoying laughter, the warmth

of the fire, and a few good IPAs. It was an eclectic group, full
of fun and life. To me that is the best part of camping—the
camaraderie that develops with the simple act of sitting
together around a warm fire.

Saturday morning found the club members and me once
again at Jane's for breakfast. We ran into Randy, a fellow camper
who had been developing a riding route over the last few years.
He was supposed to ride it with pals over the weekend, but
they were a no-show, so our riding plans changed, and four of
us decided to follow Randy, while Mark and Keith decided
to chart their own course and do some riding on their own in
the area.

This part of western Virginia was full of established, named
routes for motorcycling, some famous some less so, but all fun.
Randy's would eventually be added to the list of routes with
names like "Claw of the Dragon" and "Back of the Dragon."

At Big Walker Lookout

Randy took the lead, of course, followed by the father
and son duo, Kent behind them, and me following up so I
could try to get some GoPro footage, from which I'd hoped
to pull some good stills for the magazine coverage of the

event. We headed west on US 58, also known as Jeb Stuart Highway, toward Galax, then followed other small roads turning north, eventually ending up at Big Walker Lookout on a high ridge overlooking a long valley to the north and the West Virginia state line. There was a hundred-foot-high fire tower-like structure you could climb for a more elevated view, but I declined paying the eight dollars to climb hundreds of steps to the top. We were already at over 3,400 feet, high above the valley below, so the view from just another hundred feet higher would not counterbalance the pain my legs would have later suffered resulting from the climb.

Looking north from Big Walker Lookout toward West Virginia

After a break and a snack at the lookout, we turned east and soon found ourselves on twisting county roads heading east toward Pulaski. The road soon turned to gravel. We all stopped to discuss the situation, and all agreed to give it a go and continue. We had already hit a short section of gravel earlier in the day, but it did not last more than a couple miles before it hit pavement again, so we all felt confident, sure this section would be the same.

We twisted up and down, negotiating multiple hairpins on the gravel, but instead of a short off-pavement jaunt, we ended up riding ten miles. The surface turned out not to be too bad. It was hard packed with only a thin layer of loose stones on top and occasionally a looser ridge between the tire tracks. The Tiger took it all in stride, being the kind of road it was built to travel. The only concern was hitting one of the many deep potholes, which were difficult to see in the dappled sunlight and shade we were passing through in the deep woods. Some were deep enough that they might even challenge the nine and a half inches of suspension travel the Tiger had, not to mention the strength of its rims.

I think Randy still had some kinks to work out on his route planning, as he was on a Harley-Davidson Ultra Classic, not exactly made for offroad riding. Everyone else was on street tires, except me, but we all fared well, and not a scratch was put on any of the bikes, other than when we stopped to take a break and a misplaced kickstand on uneven ground ended in a dropped stationary bike. Luckily, it was not one of the vintage ones, and the damage was only very light scratches to a fairing and a sore leg for the rider, who had tried to catch it as it started on its inevitable trip toward the ground. And, no, it was not me . . . for once. Ironically, the drop happened when we went at the end of the gravel section, with the pavement only twenty feet ahead.

Back on tarmac again, we scooted south toward Hillsville, then east, back to Meadows of Dan. We'd ridden from about 10AM until 5PM and arrived back in town hungry. Someone suggested a food truck a little east of "downtown" Meadows of Dan. Cockram Mill was an interesting place. The food truck was positioned directly in front and served up some very good seafood and other fare. I had a shrimp po' boy that was out of this world. We all picked up our meals, walked through the mill building, out the back door, and dined on a porch above the creek behind the mill. It was a marvelous place to relax after the long day and get some energy back while watching the creek and listening to the water make its way downhill below us.

Gathering at Cocknam Mill

The day had been a blast, dinner was perfect, and the capper was the time we spent around the campfire that night talking routes, bikes, and whatever else flowed from the conversations looping around the fire. Eventually, Randy found a guitar, and songs rose with the flames into the cool night air. Then Christopher took over from Larry and played some he knew. They were quite talented and played the way I wished I could, having only mastered a rudimentary knowledge of "cowboy chords." A deer wandered by trying to figure out what was going on at the circle of humans, but of course, they were soon chased off by Will's dogs. We all probably stayed up a little later than we should have, but that was a sign of how much fun we'd had.

## BRO' BOUND

Everyone dispersed in the morning. I had decided to visit my brother in Virginia Beach before riding home, so after a quick breakfast at Jane's, I headed east for a five-hour ride to the coast. There was not really a good route to take, other than staying on the highway Meadows of Dan was on and keeping on it until the Norfolk/Virginia Beach metro area, where I'd have to rely on the Garmin to keep me off the Interstates. I might avoid the freeways, but there was no way to avoid the heavy traffic in that busy city.

What I didn't realize was that, meanwhile, Hurricane Ian had decided to take a run at Florida When I'd first heard of the storm, its track took it more northward and into Tampa, which would mean most of it would skip Lake Wales, with only its milder, outlying downwind arms brushing home as it headed northeast through the state. When I finally pulled into my brother's driveway and checked the weather, it had changed course, with its center now aimed squarely for southwest Florida and into the state on almost the identical path Hurricane Charly had taken back in 2004, which had deroofed our veranda, dropped a tree on our garage, flattened our fence, and hit the limits of our homeowners' insurance policy.

There was no way to return to Florida without riding through the heart of the Category 4 storm, so I waited it out at Tim's. That, however, gave me the chance to spend more time with my younger brother, who I didn't get to see very often anymore, after he'd moved away from Florida. We spent the week cooking out, doing a few repairs around the house that he needed two people to accomplish, and generally just hanging out together.

I'd check in from time to time with Andrea, giving her the lowdown on what I had learned about the expected conditions she'd be experiencing and when, and what actions to take depending on what the storm did. In Florida we were prepared for hurricanes and had a generator on hand in case power was lost, which was the worst most likely situation to happen. I probably did little more than scare her, but I wanted to be sure she was prepared and knew what to do. She assured me she was ready and not too worried.

I had a friend from the VJMC who lived in Kitty Hawk, just an hour or two away from my brother's. Andy and I had met at several club events. When all the other members had gone back to their hotel rooms with their wives after our communal dinners, Andy and I would go off in search of some entertainment instead, hanging out at nearby biker bars or pool halls or whatever we could find in the area. I knew Tim would hit it off with Andy, just as I had, so one day I suggested that Tim take a little time off from his work-at-home job and we both hop in the pickup for a drive down to the seashore to meet up with Andy.

We met Andy at his canal-front house where he showed us his bachelor pad and his classic Penn Yan tunnel-drive boat sitting on a lift above the canal. Andy had been an airline pilot for years and told interesting stories about that life before we headed out for beers and a bite to eat. Along the way, he drove us to the Wright Brothers National Memorial, entering from a free access point at the back of the park adjacent to a small airport. We watched a small plane going through preparations for leaving and then its take off before walking across the huge meadow where history had been made a hundred and nineteen years before. We marveled at how quickly, after that 1903 flight, airplanes had become commonplace and so advanced that by 1914 they'd played an important role in fighting World War I. Leaving the park, we decided beers were in order before lunch, so Andy suggested Swells a Brewin', a nearby microbrewery between Kill Devil Hills and Nags Head. We took turns buying rounds as we had our own hurricane party on top of the micro-brewery's roof watching the great Atlantic Ocean over the rooftops of seaside homes across the street. Hunger caught up with us, and we moved the party to Hurricane Moe's, back in Kitty Hawk, for some delicious seafood, before heading back to Andy's, where we'd left Tim's truck. We'd all had a great time, and Tim had made a new friend, who I am sure he'll look up next time he heads down to the Outer Banks.

Back in Virginia Beach, I watched news and waited for Hurricane Ian to pass. The destruction was incredible in Fort Myers and, especially, Sanibel Island, which was cut off from the rest of Florida when the storm washed away the only causeway connecting it to the mainland. After Ian's eye had crawled across Florida and our house, trailing its destructive arms to the northwest and southeast and was headed back out to sea, temporarily, at Daytona Beach, I made some calls home and was assured that we had no damage, well, no serious damage anyway. We'd had some branches come down in the tree-line on the north side of our house that took out the little metal chimney that served our water heater, but that was all. It would be a fairly simple fix when I got home.

As Ian passed out of Florida, it reentered the US coast at Charleston and headed toward us in Virginia Beach, so if I'd ridden home then, it would still have been through heavy rain and wind the whole time, and by the time I would have gotten there, I'd have to turn around again and head to Birmingham for the Barber Vintage Festival, my next magazine assignment. So instead, I lingered a while longer at Tim's until after Ian had passed north of the Chesapeake, then I rode directly to Birmingham.

### DIVERTING DIRECTLY TO BIRMINGHAM

Barber Vintage Festival started on Thursday, October 6, and ran through the following Sunday. I needed to leave Virginia Beach on Tuesday to arrive in Birmingham by Wednesday evening, so I could register and get to work first thing on Thursday morning.

Tim promised he'd be in Florida for Thanksgiving as I rolled out of his drive on Wednesday. It would be two long days of riding over the nearly 800 miles to Birmingham and the festival. I found a campground a little past halfway and set it as my destination in the Garmin and began the long negotiation of the city's traffic-packed roads until I'd exit west of town back onto the highway that ran toward Willville. I did not stick to that highway long, however, and turned off at Franklin, Virginia, where I refueled then continued west-southwest into North Carolina.

Passing along the rolling hills of the Piedmont in fair weather, now that Ian was well away and causing mayhem in the Northeast, I took a series of minor highways. I grabbed a quick lunch in Louisburg before attempting to run the gauntlet past the bigger cities of Durham and Greensboro on my way toward Lake Lure, where my campground destination lay. At Durham there was nothing else to do but jump on I-85 and get as quickly as I could to the other side of the city and to Sailsbury. Upon emerging from Salisbury and getting back on less-trafficked country highways, I was entering the Appalachians again as I inched toward River Creek Campground.

Just a few miles before Lake Lure, I turned left off the highway, crossed a creek, and turned immediately again to my left onto a gravel drive into the campground. After a quick search around the grounds to find the person in charge, I was checking in. I was shown a spot directly next to the creek, down a steep hill from the main drive and below a row of large trailers above the bank, where a walnut tree had been dropping its big, green nuts, which were scattered about and covering the downhill drive to the campsite. It looked a little tricky but doable and was a very short drop, so I got back on the bike and rode down to my site. It was late in the season, and the campground was eerily silent. The site along the creek had makeshift rope swings hanging from branches extending out over the water. I imagined the place was a popular family spot in warm weather.

The tent was set up and filled with my gear quickly as the sun dropped lower in the sky and the shade beneath the many trees deepened. I took a short walk along the creek, finding that the campground was much bigger than I'd assumed, with other campsites peppered along the track that followed the stream. By the time it was dark, it was time for another Super Happy Fun Time Zoom call. I dialed in and, for as long as my battery lasted, sat in the dark, video-chatting with my friends, illuminated only by the meagre light my little pop up lantern and my phone screen provided. Before the phone got so low it would turn itself off, I said my goodnights and turned in.

As I started to drift off to sleep, I was startled by a loud BANG, then silence. Again, I began to fall asleep when BANG again. I started to put two and two together, remembering the walnut trees. The huge missiles were dropping from the branches high overhead and impacting the aluminum roofs of the carports attached to all the trailers on top of the bank above me. Mystery solved—no gun shots, just tree bombs. Once I had realized what I was hearing, I was able to finally sleep, and surprisingly, they did not wake me up the rest of the night.

## BACK TO ANOTHER BARBER VINTAGE FESTIVAL

Thursday morning, I quickly broke camp and reloaded the Tiger. The ground was soft, and after removing the kickstand puck I had placed under it the night before, I had to roll the heavy bike to a more solid place where I could mount quickly before the stand would sink in. That accomplished, I rolled easily up the steep grade to the driveway and back out onto the main road across the creek, bound for Birmingham and the Barber Vintage Festival.

I twisted my way toward Lake Lure, hoping to find something for breakfast, either there or in the little town of Chimney Rock a little further west, but passing though Lake Lure yielded no eateries open for breakfast. In Chimney Rock my hopes were raised when I spotted a little diner and pulled in, only to find that it was closed on Wednesdays. I figured surely something would show up soon on this main road from the touristy area around Lake Lure into Asheville. Stopping to ask someone at a little barbecue place I spotted, which did not serve breakfast and was not open yet, I was given directions to a place I could get fed just a little further "down the hill" at County Line. What I found was a gas station, but inside was a small restaurant and a place to sit and eat, so I ordered some eggs and potatoes, and washed it down with coffee. It was obviously a popular local joint, and everyone who came and went seemed to know everyone else. It was the perfect place for me to stop just before I had to negotiate Asheville's traffic. I hopped west on I-40 to whizz past the city, and as soon as I emerged on the far side, I rolled off onto a road that would cut through the mountains southwest toward Rome, Georgia, skipping Atlanta altogether in favor of enjoyable mountain roads.

At Rome, I veered west on a highway that approached to within a few miles of Interstate 59 where it paralleled the freeway for a while but kept mostly in the country, other than passing through a few small towns, then curving away from I-59 as it approached Leeds, Alabama.

As I usually do, I was going to stay with my friend, Ken, just inside the Birmingham city limits and only a couple miles from Barber Motorsports Park and Leeds. When I got to the main intersection for Barber, I curved right, passing under another Interstate then curving back west to run beside it just a mile or so, where I turned left onto a minor side street that crossed back over the freeway and into Ken's neighborhood.

I made my way down Ken's rustic and hickory nut-strewn driveway, but I had negotiated it so many times before, it did not present much of a challenge. I parked safe and sound in front of his cabin door, which I found locked. I gave Ken a ring, and he informed me he was on his way back and would be there soon. While I waited, I began the task of pulling the gear I'd need off the bike and piling it on the walk, in front of the cabin.

Ken was true to his word and arrived as soon as I had finished, and within a couple more minutes, my gear and

I were inside, and Ken and I had cold beers in our hands. Sitting beer in hand on the big couch, we picked up on what had happened since my last visit a year before, on my way to the UP for the shakedown cruise of the Tiger.

## Let the Festival Begin!

The next morning, after a couple cups of coffee, Ken hopped on his Husqvarna as I got onboard the Tiger, and we rolled back out the bumpy, uphill drive to the road and headed over to Laney's, a nearby, popular diner in Leeds, for some breakfast buffet, before we'd split up for the day. Ken was going to join friends in the swapmeet area, and I had to start work, getting the photos I'd need when it came time to put together the next magazine issue, with the article on the Vintage Festival as the cover story. First, before heading into the motorsports park, I had to check in at the will-call area at a hotel just outside the entrance drive to the park to pick up my credentials for entry. Surprisingly, it was not very busy when I arrived, and the process was over in just a few minutes, and I was back on my way to work.

Approaching the checkpoint, I flashed my wrist-banded arm and was waved through. I turned right and circuited the track until I spotted the club banners at the southwestern end of the loop. As I pulled off the main road into the club area, I was briefly stopped by security, but when I informed them that I was part of the VJMC I was let in. I idled my way onto the grass and wove past people meandering around, parking up near the club's tent pavilion, the lone British bike in a sea of vintage Japanese beauties.

In past years, the club had a three-acre area just to the right of the entrance onto the ring road that circled the track. For 2022, the venue had been moved to the far end of the circuit. The previous year Birmingham had received heavy rain before the event, and much of our area had been soaked, so much so that, even after a day of full sun and blazing heat on Friday, the main bike show on Saturday had to be held along the edge of the paved road. The grassy field where the show usually was held still felt much like a huge, green sponge. I assumed the new spot had been assigned to us to address the situation, should there be rain again. It was just as large as the old area but was at the high end of the park, up a small rise, so drainage would be much better. It turned out, at least that year, with a blazing sun and clear skies all weekend, that rain would not be a complication, but each year can vary, so we would be in a better situation for subsequent years. The club also benefited from being directly across from where one of the trams stopped to let people on and off.

The tram would be my preferred method of transportation for the entire weekend while I was in the park. There were several, train-like trams running the circuit all day long and any visitor could ride them for free. At any stop, even at the busiest of times, the wait would not be long for an opportunity to move to another section of the park. Taking the tram freed me up from having to negotiate the crowded rim road, finding a place to park at each stop, then digging into my tailbox to grab my camera equipment, and repeating the process each time I needed to go to the next area. It also, more importantly, meant I did not have to don my riding gear and helmet and swelter in the rising heat of the Alabama sun.

I went to work, grabbing all the shots I could of the bikes that so far had been lined up in the VJMC area. The big show featuring stock, restored Japanese motorcycles would not be until the following day, so I concentrated, instead, on the many custom bikes lining up for Friday's Misfits Bike Show, a show that had, until that year, been the Café Racer Bike Show, but had been renamed and modified to give all modified bikes a chance to compete, even if they did not fall into the "café" category. The change resulted in over thirty bikes instead of the dozen or so they'd typically had. I took a variety of shots of practically all the bikes, and then, when the winners were announced and handed their trophies, I made sure to get a group photo of all the winners with their bikes and trophies.

With the Misfits Show completed, the activity shifted to the tent, where a couple of presentations were being given that afternoon, one about restoration and the other about customization. Snapping away from various angles, I ensured I'd have what I'd need of the workshops.

As the VJMC activities were winding down and with not many of the Saturday bike show entries in the field yet, I turned my attention to getting shots of other activities to illustrate how much there was to do beside showing bikes during the festival. I grabbed a tram and headed out.

Trials at BVF

The first place I hit was the Trials racing in the woods on the north edge of the park. I wandered down the steep, dirt path through the trees, avoiding vintage scramblers and dirt bikes rolling up and down the trail to an active race. There I spent considerable time trying to capture the action and spirit of the unique kind of sport that Trials is. As one race would grind to a halt, another would start up somewhere else in the woods, and I would scramble up and down to get the best place to grab shots there, with the bikes braaaapping past me up rocky, dry stream beds or popping over logs placed in the way. I made sure to get good photos of one of the VJMC members who was competing as he blasted by me. I think Trials was my favorite event during the festival. I loved seeing all manner of bikes and riders, both young and old, delicately balancing their way through the course, popping wheelies over logs, or falling backwards down particularly tricky sections, all the time trying their best not to "dab" with a foot on the ground. It also was nice to be in the shade of the trees and out of the sun, which by the afternoon was relentlessly hot.

After Trials, I made my way through part of the swapmeet, grabbing photos as I walked, but primarily wandering through for the fun of seeing what I might find among the piles of rust, rubber, and oxidizing aluminum.

Satisfied with what I'd been able to capture that Friday, I went back to the VJMC area to sit in the shade and chat with friends before getting all my riding gear back on and heading back to Ken's for the night.

## THE MAIN EVENT

Saturday was going to be my busiest day and mainly taken up with the big bike show the club put on. They'd had the show since the inception of the Barber Vintage Festival, and it always drew many bikes and large crowds of spectators. 2022 would not be an exception.

Ken and I headed out early, but instead of Lancy's, we decided to make a stop at the new Buc-ee's, a gigantic gas station combined with an enormous, almost supermarket/restaurant-like convenience store. I'd never been to one so was curious about them after hearing from so many who had gone there the previous year, when it had first opened in Leeds. Inside, after topping up my fuel at one of the hundreds of pumps, the size of the place and activity within was almost overwhelming. There were rows of coffee machines spitting out whatever type or flavor you could possibly desire along one part of the back wall. Scattered across the center were areas where different food or candies were being made and sold. On the east end were rows and rows of all manner of snacks, both from national brands and Buc-ee's own label, including a wall section devoted just to jerky and another to trail mixes.

The Saturday VJMC bike show

Ken and I settled on huge breakfast burritos and coffee and went outside the set of sliding doors to eat, sitting on stacks of sixty-pound bags of feed corn, while we watched excited kids run up to see the bronze beaver statue of the company's mascot.

Ken was going to spend the day at the swapmeet again, so we once again parted ways, with me headed to the VJMC area to work. Already by the time I arrived and parked in the same grassy spot I had vacated the night before, the crowds had arrived, and hundreds of bikes were lined up or being put into their positions by the show handlers, with pre-1960s Hondas here, 1970s Yamahas there, and competition bikes in their own respective areas organized by classes.

It was already hot, so I tucked under the pop-ups in front of the big tent to talk with fellow board and club members while downing a cold bottle of water, before braving the sun and starting the long day of photography. Hundreds of perfectly-restored Japanese bikes glinted in the sunlight Most of my day was spent at the bike show venue, with short breaks taken in the shade of the pop-ups for rehydration before heading back out for more photography work.

*A rare "Dragon Tank" Honda in the museum*

After I'd captured images of most of the bikes and groups of bikes in the show and before the winners would be announced and the trophies handed out, I hopped on a tram bound for the museum. Having let my museum membership lag, I handed the counter person the nineteen-dollar admission and started my walk-through of the enormous collection. I needed some generic images for the article of what it was like in the museum but also knew an upcoming article would be written about police models, so I made sure I got images of all the ones in the museum display. As I strolled through the different levels and snapped photos, I made sure to not only get shots of the bikes, but also right afterward to get shots of the display placards so I could identify the particular details, if need be, for captions.

Wandering back out into the brilliant Saturday sunshine, my next tram stop was near the track, which had AHRMA (American Historic Racing Motorcycle Association) racing going on constantly throughout the weekend. I climbed up to my favorite viewing spot on the tree-covered hillside above the back straightaway, where I grabbed some photos of the racing, trying to get them over the top of the fence and waiting for the right moment when groups of racing bikes were bunched up in a turn to make a more dramatic composition.

The track and museum at BVF

Racing photos acquired, I made my way back to the VJMC area for the awards presentation. The Grand Marshal, AMA Hall of Famer Brian Slark, who had always been an ardent supporter of the VJMC and had personally been there whenever I had a question about old bikes, was on hand to give the trophies out as I took the individual winner photos and the final group photo of all trophy winners. Following the bike show would be a member barbecue, at which I'd be doing my last photo work of the day. Taking a break in the shade, I waited until the food was ready to be served and the serving line was started, then took the photos I needed before calling it a day.

I was glad to be done, with only getting pictures of the parade laps on the track the club members would be doing the next day as my last task for the entire event. I made my way up a steep, green, grassy hill to the RV camping area above the VJMC venue and found my old friends, Russ and Amy, and the group of people they were camping with. Instantly, I had a cold beer in my hand, the brand Russ had remembered I liked from when we had gotten together in Eureka Springs earlier in the year. He had picked it up just for me. As evening fell, we gathered under a pop-up around a campfire while enjoying drinks and the camaraderie you can only experience with fellow motorcyclists.

After a couple hours hanging out with my old and new friends, and after I had taken a sufficient break from drinking beer, I made my way back in the darkness to Ken's, making sure to slow and to be on the outlook for deer as I crossed the bridge into his neighborhood. I thumped back down the drive and parked up in front of the cabin and met Ken inside, where we were free to have a few more beers and catch up on motorcycle You Tube channels we had both been following.

### I Shirk My Duties, Accidentally

Sunday morning saw us both back at Barber's, Ken again heading to his friend's booth and me to the VJMC area, where I'd wanted to catch up with the VJMC riders who were going to do the parade laps on the track. This is a much-anticipated activity, granted as a thank you from George Barber for the club's support of and participation at the festival since its inaugural year. I have ridden the track twice and thoroughly enjoyed the thrill of negotiating the track that so many professional riders had raced on before. Although I would have preferred to have been able to open her up and really give the track a go (being parade laps meant no passing and that speeds were kept relatively low), to ride following the straights and curves through the sinuous track was great fun and allowed each rider a little Walter Mitty experience. But somehow, I had misread the schedule and arrived when I thought they would be registering for the laps, but they were actually already on the track. I guess I can't get it right every time, and I knew a friend would be there shooting as well and that he would be glad to share any photos with me for use in the magazine, so my bases were covered.

That put an end to my official duties for the Barber Vintage Festival, so I headed down to the swapmeet area to find Ken and his friends, who had a few contiguous spots. There were a series of pop-ups there, so I settled in for a beer and some of the fare they were cooking on their grill for lunch. We hung out in the shade as the afternoon grew old and it was time to start loading up and clearing out. Ken and I lent our hands to the task, and in a couple hours, we were finished and riding back out of the park.

Instead of heading back to the cabin, however, Ken had offered to buy us beer and dinner and knew the perfect small micro-brewery near his home that also served great food. True Story turned out to be tucked back into a small strip mall just a few miles west of Ken's place and served up some interesting beers. As we were sipping on our first pints, a group of three riders, riding adventure bikes like us, came in and sat down at the end of the bar, around the corner next to us. We all got to talking bikes and travel, and soon the group of two had become five. Soon, burgers were in front of us all, mine being a particularly delicious concoction of meat, bread, pimento, and jalapeño; which I hoped I would not regret later on. More beer followed the food, along with conversation. It was a homy little spot, and it felt so comfortable being with mates that were on the same wavelength. It was a thoroughly enjoyable capper to the night.

Back at the cabin, I plugged everything in that I would need charged for the next day's journey south and packed up the bike with all but what I would need for the last night at my friend's house. We wound up the night early and soon I was fast asleep, anticipating riding once again the next day.

Last Stop, Valdosta

A quick cup of coffee and a goodbye to my good friend in the morning, and I was off, heading for the last time up the hickory nut-carpeted driveway, back over the little bridge across the Interstate, and back onto the highway bound southeast for the Florida/Georgia line.

I had filled up at Buc-ee's the day before, so I passed it and Leeds and turned off to ride across Dunavant Mountain, passing Vandiver and Sterrett and emerging at Vincent, where I caught a short section of a connecting highway to the main southeast/northwest highway running toward the Georgia state line, roughly aiming at Columbus. Before I reached that city straddling the state line, I turned off the major highway and skirted south around Opelika to a crossing of the Chattahoocheee River at the aptly named Cottonton.

I continued southeast through Georgia's cotton and peanut fields, passing numerous pecan groves on my way to Albany. The earthy, subtly delicate smell of cotton ready to be picked was wafting through the air I was breathing, barely detectable but omnipresent. At Albany, I found the highway that would carry me directly to Julie's little neighborhood, just six miles short of the intersection with Interstate 75 in Valdosta.

The day's ride would be less than three hundred miles, so I was in no hurry and kept my speed down under the limit and conserved fuel. Before five o'clock, I was at my friend's house. As usual, the garage door was open so I could park inside. I idled in and parked to my left, wanting to leave adequate space on the right so we could pass through the garage easily without tripping over the Tiger.

After I'd dismounted, I realized I had miscalculated and parked too far to the left beside a stack of boxes, making it very difficult to get to or from the left side of the bike. I decided all I'd need to do was roll it forward a couple feet, where the boxes would not be in the way, so I grabbed the handlebars while standing on the right side of the bike, stood the bike up, and slowly rolled it forward the required distance. What I hadn't seen or heard was the kickstand popping back up, and when I released the bike, it crashed down on its left side. I could not easily get to the left side of the Tiger, so I attempted lifting it from the right but unsuccessfully. I climbed across the bike and found a small spot for my feet on the far side and began lifting, but as soon as the front wheel contacted the concrete floor of the garage, it tried to roll forward. About that time, Julie had come to the garage, not having heard me pull in earlier.

Luckily, the boxes had cushioned the Tiger's fall, and it was resting on them at not too extreme of an angle, so working together, with Julie holding the front brake, I thought I could lift it up again. I told Julie what I needed and where to stand, so as the bike came up, she would not be in an awkward position, and then I lifted with all my might. This time, it worked, and the bike was soon again stable on its sidestand, with no damage to it or to the boxes it had fallen on. That was an awkward arrival, but no harm had been done.

Soon, I was inside with a beer in my hand and Julie starting dinner, talking to my dear friend from high school days. Danny had lived with Julie the last few years, but the last time we'd talked, his wife and daughter were going to return from Romania to Valdosta, and he was going to rent a place for his family in town, so I thought he would not be around on this visit. It turned out I was wrong about the timing. His family had not arrived yet, so I had the chance to see him again too. Another brother, Steve, also lived only a couple houses over from Julie's place, so before the afternoon was over, we were walking Bruno, Julie's loveable black mouth cur, and visiting with Steve. The last time I had passed through, Steve had recently had an operation on his ankles, but he had, surprisingly, recovered quickly and was already walking when I'd shown up again. We walked the dog back to Julie's and Steve joined us there soon after. I'm very fortunate to still be in contact with some of my closest childhood friends and so have what I consider family situated right where I often pass on my way in or out of Florida, giving us a chance to keep the flames of friendship going after so many years.

## MY HURRICANE-DELAYED RETURN HOME

After being delayed weeks past my initial return time home, I decided I'd get on the Interstate for most of the ride home; fuel efficiency be damned. I gave my host a bear hug and eased out of the garage, down the driveway, and up the street to the main highway to Valdosta.

With the entrance ramp to I-75 a hundred feet ahead of me, I turned right into a gas station to top up the tank before committing myself to the vehicular mayhem of the freeway. Topped up and with a range of 240 miles, I rolled out of the station and turned right, accelerating up to seventy and merging with the traffic heading south. I was once more witness to the many pro-life and pro-choice signs blaring their messages to passing motorists. Traffic was not too heavy, so I got up to speed, got in the middle lane, set the cruise control, and tried to relax as I blasted toward home.

I stayed committed to the freeway all the way to Bushnell this time and rolled off the Interstate and onto quiet country roads again within a hundred miles of home. I knew the roads there like the back of my hand. I hadn't even tucked maps in my tank bag window for the ride home. I took my usual route winding south and east through Centerhill, then taking the Tuscanooga Road shortcut to the little town of Mascotte and its neighbor, Groveland. I turned south for the run through the Green Swamp on a highway unfettered by stop lights and endowed with a sixty mile per hour speed limit. I sped south along with the many trucks bound either for Lakeland or I-4 to connect with either Orlando to the east or Tampa to the west, while suicidal drivers unsatisfied with any speed limit at all zoomed passed us like we were parked.

I slowed as I got to the construction zone surrounding the I-4 exit and was soon south of the freeway and heading east toward Haines City, just ten miles away. Once there, I turned south on State Road 17, the same "Scenic Highway" that would take me to within a couple blocks of home.

Once past the diminutive village of Dundee, from the ridge top I could see the tower at Bok Tower Gardens, situated only a mile up the hill from our house. I was almost home.

I made the final run down the hill past the elementary school, turned right on our street, negotiated two curves, and pull into our driveway, ready for once to take a break from the highway and just be where I was for a while.

# END OF A WHIRLWIND YEAR

A year passed between my leaving for Michigan's Upper Peninsula in 2021 and returning home after the Barber Vintage Festival in 2022. When I'd left the odometer on the Tiger read under 3,500 miles, and a year later it read 27,306 miles. I rode the Tiger almost 24,000 miles. To put that in perspective, the circumference of the earth is about 24,902 miles. I covered those miles and saw many places while still working for the magazine, running the publishing business, and doing a few book designs.

Vast stretches of time are not a prerequisite for adventure. Perhaps *adventure riding* needs a new definition. It doesn't have to mean selling everything and circling the globe, as so many adventure books make it seem. While those rides around continents and the world are wonderful, adventure can also be found within shorter periods of time. Not everyone can sell everything and travel the world or has a partner willing and able to do it too. Not everyone is without children, who need to be raised and educated. All those responsibilities don't mean adventure is unreachable. With planning ahead and acting when opportunities appear, adventure can be had for almost anyone.

I got to challenge myself over that year. I love the idea of riding off pavement, but in practice, it fills me with anxiety, especially on a heavy bike like the Tiger, but the way to get better at something is to do the very thing that scares you. I got the opportunity during that time to ride off pavement many miles and was able to push my limits to a point beyond where my comfort level had been before. And pushing limits is largely what makes a ride an adventure.

The ride, particularly in the West and Southwest, gave me a chance to reflect on my dad and what he had loved. At times, I felt almost like he was there with me. If we humans go on in some way after death, the one sure way we do is in the minds and memories of those who follow us. Dad lived on in those moments when I stared at a butte painted in the light of a setting sun, took in a vista across a many-layered canyon, or rode across a cactus-strewn desert. I'd not trade that for anything.

Making the available time count is my goal. I don't know when that time will run out, but there's nothing like the prospect of going blind and a serious crash to wake you up. As I type this, it is difficult to see the words on screen as a recurring optical migraine shoots a dazzling circle of jagged light across my vision. It's intermittent, but another sign that time is limited. It reminds me to make the most of it. Edna Saint Vincent Millay said it beautifully:

*My candle burns at both ends;*
*It will not last the night;*
*But ah, my foes, and oh, my friends—*
*It gives a lovely light!*

I can at least look back at this year in motion and know I'd made the time count.

So for that year in motion I beat the odds. My dark scythe-toting neighbor may have inched closer (he always does) but has yet to move in next door. Maybe he'll stay put for a while, as I wring a little more out of what this world has to offer. All I can do is try.

# ACKNOWLEDGEMENTS

I'd like to thank the many helpful people I've met in the Vintage Japanese Motorcycle Club, who were always willing to lend a hand and share their knowledge with me as I learned the ins and outs of working on and riding motorcycles. They have made my riding career possible. I'd also like to thank my fellow authors at Road Dog Publications, who have given me inspiration and confidence to get out there on the road and see the world and for their understanding when I disappear on my own adventure rides. And to my proofreader, Randy Mayes, for her help with both books and magazine issues, for her generosity and keen eye to catch the stuff I've missed.

Finally, I'd like to thank my family for their patience through the years as I have tried to find my way in the world. It's not always been easy, but they've never discouraged me from pursuing my dreams.

# Appendix I

## Equipment

### Motorcycle

Motorcycle: 2018 Triumph Tiger 800 XCa
Tires: Shinko 720
Panniers: Nelson-Rigg Hurricane Dry
Pannier and Tail Racks: Homemade from ½" Steel Tubing
Tailbox: Harbor Freight Apache 3800
Roll Bag for Camping Gear: Turkana Duffalo 40 Liter
Tank Bag: Nelson-Rigg Hurricane Adventure
Tool Tube: Homemade from 2" PVC
Extra Fuel: Rotopax 1 Gallon
GPS: Garmin XT

### Riding Gear

Jacket: Aerostich Darien
Pants: Aerostich Darien Light
Boots: Forma Terra Evo Dry X
Gloves: Rev'it Fly 3 (warm weather)/Joe Rocket Ballistic
    Ultra (cold weather)
Helmet: Scorpion AT950

## Camping Gear

Tent: REI Groundbreaker II with Footprint
Sleeping Bag: Ascend Hoodoo 20° F
Sleeping Pad: Thermarest Trail Lite
Stove: MSR Dragonfly
Fuel Container: MSR 1 Liter
Camp Chair: Merutek

## Tools

RRR Tool Solutions Tool Roll
Homemade 12 Volt Compressor in Dry Box
Tire Tools in Tool Tube: Motion Pro Beadbreaker II
        (aluminum) and Motion Pro Small Tire Irons

# ROUTES

## TURN BY TURN ROUTES

*(Reconstructed using Google Timeline and my rusty memory, so routes are approximations. Directions following road/highway indicates general direction of travel. CR stands for County Road)*

### NORTHBOUND IN OCTOBER 2021

*Oct. 7*—North Wales D. N > Dr. J A Wiltshire Ave. W > FL 17 N > FL 544 W > US 27 N to Haines City > Old Polk City Rd. NW > Old Grade Rd. N > Deen Still Rd. W > FL 33 N to Groveland > (towed to Orlando) > FL 50 W to Mascotte > Tuscanooga Rd. NW > CR 469 N to Center Hill > FL 469 W > FL 48 W then NW to Floral City > US 41 N to Dunellon > Pennsylvania Ave. W > Cedar St. N then W > CR 336 NW > US 98 N to Perry > US 19 NW then N to Thomasville, GA

*Oct 8*—US 19 N to Albany > US 82 NW to Dawson > GA 520 NW to Richland > US 280 NW to Harpersville, AL > US 231 N > AL 25 NW to Leeds > US 78 W > Rex Lake Rd. S to Barber Motorsports Park > Rex Lake Rd. N > US 78 W > Riverview Dr. S to Ken's

*Oct 9*—Local in Birmingham/Leeds

*Octo 10*—US 78 W > I-20 W > I-65 N to Shell > AL 157 NW > AL 101 N to Loretto, TN > US 43 NE > US 64 NW then W to Clifton Junction > US 641 NW then N to Murray, KY > KY

80 W (becomes TN 121) to Mayfield > US 45 N to Paducah > I-24 N > KY 305 W > KY 358 NW to Fern Lake CG

*Oct. 11*—KY 358 SE > KY 305 E > I-24 N > IL 146 W to Anna, IL > US 51 N > IL 15 E > US 51 N to Pana > IL 16 E > US 51 N to Decatur > I-72 NE > US 51 N to Bloomington > I-74 NW then N to Hotel

*Oct. 12*—I-74 N > I-55 E > I-39 N > IL 17 W then N to Camp Grove > IL 40 N then NW too Mt. Carroll > US 52 W to Savanna > IL 84 N > US 20 NW > IL 84 (becomes WI 80) N to Cuba City, WI > "H" W > US 61 NW to Tennyson > WI 133 SW then W to Cassville and Sandy Bottoms Up CG

*Oct. 13*—"VV" N > Main Street to Glen Haven > Dugway Rd. N > "A" N to Bagley > "P" NE > "X" NW > "C" NE > US 18 N > WI 35 N > US 14 N > WI 35 N then W to Trempealeau > WI 35 N to Centerville > WI 93 N to Eau Claire > Golf Rd. W > Rudolph Rd. N > Jensen Rd. W > Anita Dr. N to Ron's place

*Oct. 14*—Anita Dr. S > Jensen Rd. E > US 53 N to Bloomer > Chippewa Rd. (becomes Main St.) NE > Main St. N > "F" N > "M" E > WI 40 NE then N to Radisson > WI 70 NE then E > "EE" NE then E to Park Falls > WI 13 N then NW > WI 77 N to then NE to Ironwood, MI > US 51 N > US 2 E to Wakefield > MI 28 NE to Bergland > MI 64 N then E to Ontonagon > MI 38 SE > MI 26 NE > Pike Lake Rd. SE. Beaver Rd. N to Pike Lake CG

*Oct. 15*—Beaver Rd. S > Pike Lake Rd. NW > MI 26 NE to Houghton > US 41 NE > MI 26 N to Eagle River > MI 26 NE to Copper Harbor > US 41 SW to Houghton > US 41 S then E to Harvey > MI 28 E to Christmas and Munising Tourist Park CG

*Oct. 16*—MI 28 E then S > MI 94 E > MI 117 S > US 2 E then SE to St. Ignace > I-75 S > US 31 SW then S then SW > US 131 S to Plainwell > MI 89 NW to Allegan and hotel

*Oct. 17*—MI 40 S > Red Arrow Hwy. W > Johnson Rd. (becomes Paw Paw Rd.) S > MI 51 S to Dowagiac > MI 62 SE then S then SW > Redfield St. W > Gumwood Rd. S > Adams Rd. W > Grape Rd. S > IN 23 SW > Ironwood Dr. S > Ridgedale Rd. W > Woodmont Dr. S to Joe's place

*Oct. 18*—Stayed in South Bend

*Oct. 19*—Woodmont Dr. S > Brookmede Dr. E > Ironwood Dr. S to South Bend, IN > Ireland Rd. E > IN 331 S > US 6 E > US

33 S then SE to Wolf Lake > IN 109 S to Columbia City > IN
9 S to Huntington > US 224 SE to Markle > IN 116 SE then E
> Skeets Rd. E > OH 49 S > OH 29 SE to Urbana, OH > US
68 S to Red Oak > US 62 SW to Ripley and Logan's Gap CG

*Oct. 20*—US 52 E > US 68 S to Lexington, KY > I-75 S > US 25 S
> KY 461 (becomes KY 80) SW > KY 192 S > KY 914 S > KY
1247 S > KY 90 SW to Albany > US 127 S to Static > TN 111
S > TN 84 SE then S to Monterey > Holly ST. SW > Stratton
Ave. SE > US 70N SE > I-40 SE > TN 101 NE > Tuttle Ln. NW
to Andy's place

*Oct. 21*—Tuttle Ln. SE > TN 101 SW > TN 392 SW > US 127
S then SW > TN 111 SE > US 27 SW > TN 153 S > I-75 SW
then S to Ringold, GA > GA 151 S > Mt. Pisgah Rd. SW >
Nickajack Rd. NW > Beaumont Rd. S > GA 95 S > GA 136
SE to Calhoun > River St. S > GA 53 SW to Rome > US 27 S >
GA 100 SW then S then SE to Ephesus and room of the night

*Oct. 22*—GA 100 NW then N then NE > US 27 N to Rome >
GA 53 NE > US 41 N > GA 225 NE > US 76 E > US 411 N
to Etowah, TN > TN 310 E > TN 39 SE to Tellico Plains and
Cherohala Mountain Trails CG

*Oct. 23*—Locally in Tellico Plains

*Oct. 24*—TN 39 E > TN 68 S to Copperhill, TN/McCaysville,
GA > GA 5 S > US 76 SW > GA 52 E to Dahlonega > US 19
S > GA 60 SE to Gainesville > US 129 SE to Athens > GA 10
SW then S > US 78 E > US 129 S to Macon > I-75 S > GA 133
NW to Julie's place

*Oct. 25*— GA 133 SE > I-75 S > CR 470 E to Sumterville, FL > US
301 N > CR 471 S > FL 48 E to Center Hill > CR 469 S > FL
50 E to Groveland > FL 33 S > Deen Still Rd. E > Old Grade Rd.
S > Old Polk City Rd. SE to Haines City > Main St. E > 10th St.
S > FL 17 S to Lake Wales > Dr. J A Wiltshire Ave. E > North
Wales Drive SE to home

## FLORIDA INTERLUDE

### Rally in Crystal River, 2021

*Nov. 12*—North Wales D. N > Dr. J A Wiltshire Ave. W > FK 17 N
> FL 544 W > US 27 N to Haines City > Old Polk City Rd. NW

> Old Grade Rd. N > Deen Still Rd. W > FL 33 N to Groveland > (towed to Orlando) > FL 50 W to Mascotte > Tuscanooga Rd. NW > CR 469 N to Center Hill > FL 469 W > FL 48 W then NW to Floral City > US 41 N to Inverness > FL 44 W then NW to Crystal River > FL 44 SE > CR 491 S > Oak Park Blvd. SE > Stage Coach Trail E then NE > US 41 N to Floral City > FL 48 SE > Trails End Rd. N then NE > Withlapopka Dr. N then NW > Gobbler Dr. SW then W > US 41 N to Inverness > FL 44 W then NW to Crystal River and hotel

*Nov. 13*—FL 44 SE > CR 491 S > US 98 SE > Cobb Rd. S > Cortez Blvd. E to Brooksville > Emerson Rd. S > Culbreath Rd. S > Bayhead Rd. E > Lake Iola Rd. SE > St. Joe Rd. E to Dade City > FL 579 S > Clinton Ave. E > Fort King Rd. S to Zephyrhills > Andre Rd. E > US 301 S to Coney Island Grill > US 301 N > Clinton Ave. W > Fort King Rd. N > Meridian Ave. W > 21st St. N > Lock St. W > Blanton Rd. N then W > Spring Lake Hwy. SW > Bayhead Rd. N > Powell Rd. NE > Emerson Rd. N > US 98 NW to Coney Island Grill > US 98 SE > Emerson Rd. S > LF 50 W > CR 48 (Cobb Rd.) N > US 98 NW > CR 491 N > FL 44 NW to Crystal River

*Nov. 14*—FL 44 E > CR 251 SE > CR 470 SE > US 301 N > CR 470 (becomes FL 48) E to Yalaha Bakery > FL 48 SE > FL 19 S then SW to Groveland > FL 50 E > FL 33 S > Deen Still Rd. E > Old Grade Rd. S > Old Polk City Rd. SE to Haines City > US 27 S > FL 544 E > FL 17 S to Lake Wales > Dr. J A Wiltshire Ave. E > North Wales Dr. SE to home

## The VJMC at Daytona Bike Week, 2022

*Mar. 4*—North Wales Dr. N > Dr. J A Wiltshire Ave. W > FK 17 N > FL 544 W > US 27 N to Haines City > Old Polk City Rd. NW > Old Grade Rd. N > Deen Still Rd. W > FL 33 N to Groveland > FL 50 W > FL 19 NE to Altoona > FL 42 NE to Deland > FL 44 E to Volusia County Fairgrounds > I-4 SW to Lake Monroe and hotel

*Mar. 5*—I-4 NE to Volusia County Fairgrounds > I-4 SW back to hotel

*Mar. 6*—I-4 SW > FL 46 W to Mt. Dora > US 441 S > CR 448 W > FL 19 SW to Groveland > FL 50 E > FL 33 S > Deen Still Rd. E

> Old Grade Rd. S > Old Polk City Rd. SE to Haines City > US 27 S > FL 544 E > FL 17 S to Lake Wales > Dr. J A Wiltshire Ave. E > North Wales Dr. SE to home

## Super Happy Fun Times, 2022

*Jun. 7*—North Wales Dr. N > Dr. J A Wiltshire Ave. W > FK 17 N > FL 544 W > US 27 N to Haines City > Old Polk City Rd. NW > Old Grade Rd. N > Deen Still Rd. W > FL 33 N to Groveland > FL 50 W > CR 471 N > CR 469 W to Center Hill > FL 48 W then NW to Floral City > US 41 N to White Springs > FL 136 W to Suwannee Valley CG

*June 8*—FL 136 E > US 41 N > US 129 N > US 221 N > US 441 N to Athens, GA > US 78 NE then W > US 129 N to Cleveland > GA 115 SE > Pless Rd. NE > Stoval Rd. NE to Serendipity Park CG

*Jun. 9*—Stovall Rd. SW > GA 384 S > Ga 115 E to Clarksville > GA 385 NE > US 23 N to Dillsboro, NC > US 74 NE to Waynesville > US 19 W > US 276 N > I-40 N then W to Knoxville > I-75 N to London, KY > KY 30 NE to Vincent > KY 399 N to Lago Linda CG

*June 10*—KY 399 N > KY 52 NW to Raveena > KY 89 N > Joseph Proctor Memorial Bypass SW > KY 52 SE > KY 89 S to McKee > US 421 SE > KY 587 E then N then E > KY 11 N to Beattyville > KY 52 No then W > KY 399 to Lago Linda CG

*Jun. 11*—KY 399 N > KY 52 SE to Beattyville > KY 11 N to Slade > KY 15 E > Tunnel Ridge Rd. N > Tunnel Ridge Rd. S > KY 15 SE to Compton > KY 746 NE > US 460 W > KY 77 S then SW then W to Nada > KY 11 SE to Zachariah > KY 1036 W then SW > KY 52 SE > KY 399 S to Lago Linda CG

*Jun. 12*—KY 399 S to Vincent > KY 30 SW to London > US 25 S to Williamsburg > KY 92 W to Pine Knot > US 27 S to Harriman > TN 29 SE > US 70 SE > TN 58 SW > TN 68 E to Turtletown > TN 294 E then SE > US 74 E > US 19 S > GA 180 (Wolf Pen Gap Rd.) SW to Suches, GA > GA 60 S to Two Wheels of Suches CG

*Jun. 13*—GA 60 SE > US 19 S > GA 60 SE to Gainesville > US Bus 129 S > US 129 S to Athens > Ga 10 SW then SE > US 129 S to

Ocilla > US 319 SW to Tifton > I-75 S to Valdosta > GA 133
NW to Julie's place

*Jun. 14*—At Julie's place

*Jun. 15*—GA 133 SE > I-75 S > US 41 S to Floral City > FL48 SE
to Bushnell > CR 476 E > CR 567 E then S > FL 48 E to Center
Hill > > CR 469 S > FL 50 E to Groveland > FL 33 S > Deen
Still Rd. E > Old Grade Rd. S > Old Polk City Rd. SE to Haines
City > Main St. E > 10th St. S > FL 17 S to Lake Wales > Dr. J A
Wiltshire Ave. E > North Wales Drive SE to home

## This Time Northwest, 2022

*Jun. 21*—North Wales D. N > Dr. J A Wiltshire Ave. W > FL 17 N
> FL 544 W > US 27 N to Haines City > Old Polk City Rd. NW
> Old Grade Rd. N > Deen Still Rd. W > FL 33 N to Groveland
> FL 50 W to Mascotte > Tuscanooga Rd. NW > CR 469 N to
Center Hill > FL 469 W > FL 48 W then NW to Floral City >
US 41 N to Dunellon > Pennsylvania Ave. W > Cedar St. N then
W > CR 336 NW > US 98 N to Old Town > FL 349 N > US 27
NW > CR 53 N > GA 333 NW to Quitman, GA > US 84 to
Thomasville and Josh's place

*Jun. 22*—US 319 SW > Meridian Rd SW > Fairbanks Ferry Rd.
W > CR 157 N > US 27 NW > US Bus 27 W to Altapulgus >
Altapulgus Rd W to Faceville > GA 97 (becomes FL 269 A) W
the SW > US 90 W to Marianna, FL > FL 73 NW > US 231 N
to Campbellton > FL 2 W > FL 81 N > AL 87 N to Samson, AL
>FL 52 W then NW to Opp > US 84 W to Laurel, MS > MS
15 NW then N to Philadelphia, MS > MS 16 W to Edinburg >
Mars Hill Rd. N > MS 19 W then N > MS 35 N then NW to
Grenada > MS 8 W > I-55 N to Batesville and hotel

*Jun. 23*—Us 278 W to Marks > MS 316 NW > US 49 N to Barton,
AR > AR 1 N to Colt > AR 306 W > AR 193 N > US 64 W
to Bald Knob > US 167 SW> AR 13 W then S > AR 36 W
to Quitman . AR 124 W > US 65 N then NW to Bear Creek
Springs > US 412 W to Alpena > US 62 W to Eureka Springs
and hotel

*Jun. 24*—US 62 E > AR 23 (Pig Trail) S to Ozark > I-40 W to Alma
> US 71 N to Fayetteville > AR 16 E > AR 265 N > Mission

Blvd. (becomes Bowen Dr.) E > Becomes CR 45 NE > Becomes AR 303 E > US Bus 412 SE > US 412 E > AR 23 (Pig Trail) N > US 62 W to hotel

*Jun. 25*—Locally in Eureka Springs

*Jun. 26*—US 62 W > AR 392 S then E > Creel Rd. S > AR 43 S> AR 206 S then E > AR 7 S to Jasper > AR 74 NE then SE to Piercetown > AR 123 N then NE to Western Grove > US 65 SE to Bee Branch > Gravesville Cutoff Rd. SE to Gravesville > AR 124 E to Rose Bud > AR 5 S > AR 31 E then SE > AR 267 (becomes AR 13) E then SE to Hickory Plains > AR 38 E > AR 11 S to Hazen > US 70 E to De Valls Bluff > AR 33 S then E > US 49 SE to Rich, MS > US 61 N to Evansville > MS 4 E > Arklabutla Rd. NE then E to Coldwater > US 51 N > MS 306 E to Marty's place

*Jun. 27*—MS 306 E > MS 305 S > MS 4 E to Chulahoma > Odell Rd. S to Laws Hill > MS 310 E > MS 7 S > MS 9W SE > MS 9 S to Calhoun > MS 8 E to Vardaman > MS 341 S > MS 340 E > CR 426 E > MS 15 S to Maben > Maben Bell Schoolhouse Rd. E > Douglastown Rd. SE > US 82 E > MS 182 SE then E > MS 25 S then SE > Columbus Ave. S to Louisville > MS 14 W > S. Church Ave. S > MS 15 S > MS 19 SE then S to Philadelphia > MS 16 E > MS 495 S to Bailey > Dogwood Lake Rd. E > Cook Rd. SE > Poplar Springs Rd. S > Old Country Club Rd. SE then E > MS 39 S to Meridian > MS 19 E then SE > Becomes AL 10 SE to Butler, AL > AL 17 S to Silas > US 84 E then SE > CR 23 SE to Frisco City > AL 21 S to Huxford > Huxford Rd. E > Butler St. S > Sardine Rd. E then SE > AL 113 S > US 31 SW then S > FL 4 E to Jay, FL > FL 89 S > CR 164 E to Cobbtown > Cobbtown Rd S to Hidden Lake CG

*Jun. 28*—Cobbtown Rd. N > Greenwood Rd. N > Country Mill Rd. E > FL 87 S > Coldwater Church Rd. E > Lews Rd. S > Springhill Rd. E then SE to Springhill > Red Rock Rd. NE > Bryant Bridge Rd. SE > US 90 E then NE to Crestview > FL 85 S to Niceville > FL 293 E then SE > FL 20 E > FL 267 SE to Newport > US 98 E then SE > CR 336 SE . FL 40 to Dunellon > Cedar St. S > Pennsylvania Ave. E > US 41 S to Floral City >CR 616 S > CR 476 E > FL 48 E > CR 471 S > FL 50 E to Groveland > FL 33 S > Deen Still Rd. E > Old Grade Rd. S > Old Polk City Rd. SE to Haines City > US 27 S > FL 544 E >

FL 17 S to Lake Wales > Dr. J A Wiltshire Ave. E > North Wales Drive SE to home

## A Ride Around the Block, 2022

*Jul. 19*—North Wales D. N > Dr. J A Wiltshire Ave. W > FL 17 N > FL 544 W > US 27 N to Haines City > Old Polk City Rd. NW > Old Grade Rd. N > Deen Still Rd. W > FL 33 N to Groveland > FL 50 W to Mascotte > Tuscanooga Rd. NW > CR 469 N to Center Hill > FL 469 W > FL 48 W then NW to Floral City > US 41 N to Dunellon > Pennsylvania Ave. W > Cedar St. N then W > CR 336 NW > US 98 N to Newport > FL 267 NW > FL 20 W to Blountstown > FL 71 N to Marianna > FL 73 NW to Campbellton > US 231 N then NW to Troy and CG

*Jul. 20*—US 29 W to Greenville, AL > AL 263 NW to Pleasant Hill > CR 12 W > CR 85 NW > AL 41 N > US 80 N to Selma > AL 28 NW to Livingston > US 11 N > AL 28 W > AL 17 N > AL/MS 16 W > US 45 N to West Point, MS > MS 50 W > MS 15 N to Woodland > MS 340 W > MS 341 N to Vardaman > MS 8 W to Calhoun City > MS 9 N > MS 9W NW > MS 7 N > MS 328 W > MS 315 NW > US 278 W to West Marks > MS 316 NW > US 49 N to Helena-West Helena, AR > AR 1 N to Marianna > US 79 W > AR 78 NW to Hunter > US 49 N to Fair Oaks > US 64 W to Bald Knob > US 167 SW to Searcy and hotel

*Jul. 21*—AR 385 N > AR 157 N to Pleasant Plains > US 167 N to Batesville > AR 69 NW to Melbourne > AR 9 N to Brockwell > AR 56 W > AR 223 N to Pineville > AR 177 NW > AR 5 NW to Mountain Home > US 412 N to Maurices > US 62 W > AR 28 NW > AR 201 > Becomes "J" in MO) > US 160 W to Gainesville, MO > MO 5 NW to Ava > MO 14 NW > "Z" NW > US 60 W to Cody > CR 125 N > "E" W > US 65 N to Lincoln > "C" N to Windsor > Hwy "WW" N then W > MO 23 N to Knob Knoster and Knob Knoster State Park CG

*Jul. 22*—US 50 W > MO 7 N > Bundschu Rd. W > Little Blue Pkwy. NW > MO 291 N then NW > Mt. Olivet Rd. NW > MO 92 W > US 169 N then NW to Saxton > Riverside Dr. N > Gene Field Rd. W > I-29 N > US 59 N to Savannah > US 71 N

> MO 148 N > Becomes IA 148 N to Bedford, IA > IA 2 W >
US 71 N to Atlantic and Sunnyside Park CG

*Jul. 23*—Local between Atlantic and Marne

*Jul. 24*—US 6 W to Omaha, NB > 13th St. S > Fort Crook Rd. S
> NB 370 W > US 6 SW to Hastings > US 34 W to McCook
and Karrer Park CG

*Jul. 25*—US 34 W to Brush, CO > CO 71 S to Last Chance > US
36 W to Watkins > Watkins Rd. S > Airline Rd. W > Gun Club
Rd. N > Hampden Ave. W > CO 83 NW > I-225 SW > Quincy
Ave. W > Monaco St. S > Belleview Ave. W > Santa Fe Dr. S >
Bowles Ave. SW > CO 75 S > Chatfield Ave. W > Deer Creek
Canyon Rd. W > Mica Mine Gulch Rd N to Mountain Air
Ranch CG

*Jul. 26*—At Mountain Air Ranch CG

*Jul. 27*—Deer Creek Canyon Rd. N > Turkey Creek Rd. W > US
285 SW to Fairplay > CO 9 S to Hartsel > US 24 SW to Antero
Junction > US 285 S to Poncha Springs > US 50 W to Montrose
> US 550 (Million Dollar Hwy.) S to Ouray and Ampitheater
CG

*Jul. 28*—US 550 S to Durango > US 160 W > CO 184 NW > US
491 NW > US 191 N to Moab, UT

*Jul. 29*—US 191 N > UT 313 to Canyonlands NP > US 191 N >
I-70 W > UT 24 S then W > UT 12 S to Calf Creek Canyon
CG

*Jul 30*—UT 12 S then W > UT 63 to Bryce Canyon NP > US 12
W > US 89 S to Kanab > US 89A S then SE > AZ 67 S to Grand
Canyon NP and North Rim CG

*Jul. 31*—US 89A E then S to Bitter Springs, AZ > US 89 S to
Flagstaff > US 89A to Sedona > AZ 179 S to Village of Oak
Creek > Castle Creek Rd. W then S > Verde Valley School Rd.
W > Vulte Rd. N to Tim's place

*Aug. 1*—Vulte Rd. S > Verde Valley School Rd. S then E > AZ 179
S > Beaverhead Flats Rd. SW > Cornville Rd. W to Clarkdale >
US 89A N then SW to Prescott Valley > Viewpoint Dr. S > AZ
69 SW > Montezuma St. N > Whipple St. W > CR 10 (Iron
Springs Rd.) NW then W then S > CR 15 (Kirkland Valley
Rd.) SE > AZ 89 SW to Congress > AZ 71 SW to Aguila > US
60 W to Hope > AZ 72 NW > AZ 95 N to Parker > CA 62 W
to Joshua Tree NP CG

*Aug. 2*—CA 62 W > CA 247 NW to Lucerne Valley, CA > CA 18 NW to Victorville > US 395 N to Convict Lake CG

*Aug. 3*—US 395 N to Minden, NV > NV 88 S > Watrerloo Ln. W > NV 207 NW > US 50 S > Pioneer Trail S > US 50 S > CA 89 SE to Picketts Junction > CA 88 SW > Mormon Emigrant Trail NW > Sky Park Rd. SW > Pleasant Valley Rd. W to Diamond Springs > CA 49 SW > Pleasant Valley Rd. W > Motherlode Dr. W to Shingle Springs > Ponderosa Rd. NW > Meder Rd. NW > Cambridge Rd. N to Skinners > Green Valley Rd. W > Natoma St. W > Folsom Lake Crossing NW > Folson-Auburn Rd. N > Douglas Blvd. W > Roseville Pkwy. NW > Pleasant Grove Rd. W > Ardley Dr. and Aaron's place

*Aug. 4*—Ardley Dr. NE > Mayhill Dr. SE > Village Green Dr. NE > Fiddyment Rd. N > Sunset Blvd. (becomes Oil Derrick Rd. then Howsely Rd.) W > Pacific Ave. N > Catlett Rd. W > CA 99 N > Powerline Rd. S > Lee Rd. W > Garden Hwy. S > CR 22 W > CR 102 S > Covell Blvd. W > Vic Fazio Hwy. S > Russell Blvd. W > Pedrick Rd. S > Sievers Rd. W > Currey Rd. (becomes 1st St. then Rio Dixon Rd.) S > Hawkins Rd. W > Lowes Rd. S > Fry Rd. W > Leisure Town Rd. S > Vanden Rd. SW > Peabody Rd. S > Air Base Pkwy. W > I-80 (Dwight D. Eisenhower Hwy.) SW to Cordelia > CA 12 NW > Sonoma Hwy. W > Napa Rd. W > Leveroni Rd. NW > Arnold Dr. N > Agua Caliente Rd. NE to Santa Rosa > Mission Blvd. N > Montecito Blvd. (becomes Fountaingrove Pkwy.) W > Chanate Rd. W > Mendocino Ave. S > Steele Ave. W > Marlow Rd. N > Marsh Rd. W > Marsh Rd. E > Marlow Rd. N > Piner Rd. W > Olivet Rd. N > River Rd. W to Guerneville > CA 116 W > CA 1 N > Point Cabrillo Dr. N to Caspar Beach CG

*Aug. 5*—Point Cabrillo Dr. E > CA 1 N to Leggett > US 101 N> Avenue of the Giants N > US 101 N to Gold Beach and Indian Creek CG

*Aug. 6*—US 101 N to Florence, OR

*Aug. 7*—US 101 N > WA 107 NE > WA 8 E > WA 108 NE to Shelton, WA > WA 3 NE > WA 302 SE then E to Purdy > Purdy Dr. S > Burnham Dr. SE > Soundview Dr. S > Harbor Country Dr. E to Ron's place

*Aug. 8*—Point Fosdick Dr. N > Olympic Dr. NE > WA 16 SE > I-5 S > WA 512 E > WA 167 E > WA 410 E > US 12 SE to Yakima

> WA 24 E > WA 240 SE > US 12 S then E > US 730 W > WA 37 SE to Pendleton and KOA CG

*Aug. 9*—US 395 S to Mt. Vernon, OR > US 26 E to Vale > Lytle Blvd. SE > Janeta Ave. E > Jefferson Dr. S > Owyhee Ave. E > OR 201 S > ID 19 E > US 95 S > ID 55 E to Marsing, ID > ID 55 E > Marsing Rd. S then E > ID 45 N > Locust Ln. E > Columbia Rd. E > Ten Mile Rd. S > Ardell Rd. E > Coral FLS Ave. S > Tiger Eye St. W > Klemmer Ave. N to Brent'splace

*Aug. 10*—Locally around Kuna

*Aug. 11*—Klemmer Ave. S > Tiger Eye St. E > Coral FLS Ave. N > Ardell Rd. W > Ten Mile Rd. N > Amity Ave. E > Meridian Rd. N > I-84 SE > US 20 E > US 26 NE > ID 33 NE > US 20 N > Big Springs Loop Rd. E to Big Springs CG

*Aug. 12*—Big Springs Loop Rd. W > US 20 N then E to West Yellowstone, MT > US 191 E then S > US 20 NE > US 14 E > CR 17 SE to Shell Creek CG

*Aug. 13*—CR 17 NW > US 14 NE > I-90 E then S > US 14 SE > I-90 E to Moorcraft > US 16 SE to Custer, SD > US 385 N to Three Forks > US 16 E then N > Byp. US 16 NE to Rapid Valley > SD 44 SE to Scenic > C590 (Sage Creek Rd.) N then E to Sage Creek CG

*Aug. 14*—C590 (Sage Creek Rd.) E > SD 240 SE to Ben Reifel Visitor Center > SD 377 SW to Interior > SD 44 S then E to White River > US 83 S > SD 44 (becomes IA 44) E > I-29 S > US 18 E to Spencer, IA, and East Leach Park CG

*Aug. 15*—US 18 E to Floyd > US 218 S > US 18 E > IA 188 E > US 63 S > IA 93 E to Fayette > IA 150 S > IA 187 E then S > IA 3 E to Luxemburg > US 52 S to Dyersville > US 20 E to Freeport, IL > IL 26 S > Montague Rd. E > Tower Rd. S to Byron > IL 72 E to Genoa > IL 23 S to DeKalb and hotel

*Aug. 16*—IL 23 S > US 34 SW > IL 23 S > US 53 S then W > 17th Rd. S to Ottawa > US 6 E to Morris > IL 47 S to Dwight > IL 17 E to Momence > IL 114 E > IN 10 E > IN 49 N to Wheatfield, IN > IN 10 E > US 421 N > IN 10 E > IN 39 N > 50th St. E to Knox > US 35 N to South Center > US 6 E to Walkerton > IN 23 to North Liberty > Ireland Rd. E > Ironwood Dr. N > Brookmede Dr. W > Woodmont Dr. N to Joe's place

*Aug. 17*—Locally around South Bend and Notre Dame University

*Aug. 18*—Ironwood Dr. S > New Rd. E to Woodland > IN 331 (Bremen Hwy.) S > US 6 E > IN 331 S > IN 25 E to Mentone > IN 19 S to Akron > IN 114 SE > IN 15 S to Gas City > US 35 E > CR S500E S > Wheeling Pike SE > IN 3 > US 35 SE to Muncie > IN 32 E to Farmland > IN 1 S to Modoc > US 36 E > IN 227 S to Richmond > US 27 S > US 40 E > Old National Rd. (becomes Eaton Pike) E > CR 335 SE > US 35 SE to Eaton, OH > OH 122 SE to Middletown > OH 4 S > OH 63 E > OH 741 S > Bethany Rd. E > Mason Morrow Millgrove Rd. E to South Lebanon > Main St. S > CR 153 E > Zoar Rd. S to Grant's Pass and Brent's place

*Aug. 19*—Zoar Rd. E > Emerald Dr. S then W > Cochran Rd. S > US 22 SW > OH 48 S to Murdock > Murdock-Goshen Rd. SE to Goshen > OH 132 SW > I 275 S then SW > US 27 S > Us 68 S > US 86B NE > KY 1678 SW > US 60 SE > KY 627 SW > I-75 S to Knoxville, TN > I-640 SW > I-75 S to Sweetwater > TN 68 to Copperhill, TN/McCaysville, GA > GA 5 S to Blue Ridge > US 76 SW to Ellijay > GA 52 SE then E > GA 52 (Dawsonville Hwy.) to Dahlonega > US 19 S > GA 115 NE > Gold Crest Dr. SE to John's place

*Aug. 20*—Gold Crest Dr. NW > GA 115 SW > GA 60 Walnut Rd. E > Ward Rd. E > GA 332 NE > Creek Nation Rd. SE > GA 124 E > GA 11 NE > US 129 SE to Athens > GA 10 W > US 78 E > US 129 S to Tifton > US 319 W > I-75 S to Valdosta > GA 133 NW to Julie's place

*Aug. 21*—GA 133 SE > US 84 NE > US Bus 41 SE > US 41 S to Floral City > CR 616 S > CR 476 E > FL 48 E > CR 471 S > Tuscanooga Rd. to Mascotte > FL 50 E to Groveland > FL 33 S > Deen Still Rd. E > Old Grade Rd. S > Old Polk City Rd. SE to Haines City > US 27 S > FL 544 E > FL 17 S to Lake Wales > Dr. J A Wiltshire Ave. E > North Wales Drive SE to home

## A COMPLICATION, 2022

### Editor's Camping Weekend

*Sep. 21*—North Wales Drive NW > Dr. J A Wiltshire Ave. W > FL 17 N > Ernie Caldwell Blvd. NW > Pinetree Trail N > Ronald Reagan Pkwy. W > US 27 N > Florida's Turnpike NW > I-75

N > FL 136 > White Springs Ave. S > Stephen Foster Dr. SE to Suwannee Valley CG

*Sep. 22*—Stephen Foster Dr. NW > White Springs Ave. N > FL 136 E to White Springs > CR 135 NE then N > GA 94 E to Fargo, GA > US 441 N to McCrae Helena > US 280 NE > US 221 N to Laurens, SC > SC 14 N to Graycourt > SC 101 N to Woodruff > US 221 N > I-26 N > SC 11 E > Bishop Rd. NE > Rabbit Moffitt Rd. N > Carolina Foothills Dr NW to Carolina Foothills CG

*Sep. 23*—Carolina Foothills Dr. SE > Rabbit Moffitt Rd. N > Lambs Grill Rd. NW > CR 1356 N > CR 1004 N > CR 1106 N > US 221 N to Rutherford, NC > US 64 NE to Lenoir > NC 18 NE to Moravian Falls > NC 16 N to Wilkesboro > Cherry St. N > Main St. NE > US Bus 421 NW > NC 18 N > NC 268 NE > US 601 N to Mt. Airy > US 52 NW to Fancy Gap, VA > Blue Ridge Pkwy. E then NE to Meadows of Dan and Willville CG

*Sep. 24*—US Bus 58 W > US 58 W to Galax > Larkspur Ln. NW > Glendale Rd. SW > VA 721 (Cliffview Rd.) NW > Fries Rd. W then SW > Ivanhoe Rd. N > VA 602 (Brush Creek Rd.) W then N > VA 690 (Cripple Creek Rd.) W then N then W > VA 653 N then NE > VA 654 N then NE > VA 667 W > VA 666 N > VA 665 W > VA 680 NE > US 52 NW then NE to Bland > VA 42 NE > VA 733 SE to Pulaski > VA 99 W > US 11 S > VA 100 S > CR 669 S > US 68 E > US Bus 58 E to Willville CG

*Sep. 25*—US Bus 58 E > US 58 E to Suffolk > US Bus 460 E > Military Hwy. E then NE > Indian River Rd. SE > Ferrell Pkwy. E > Princess Anne Rd. SE > Nimmo Pkwy. E > Upton Dr. N > Tennyson Rd. NW > Shubert Rd. W to Tim's place

*Sep. 26-Oct. 4*—Locally around Virginia Beach with a day drive to Kitty Hawk, NC

## BACK TO ANOTHER BARBER VINTAGE FESTIVAL

*Oct. 5*—Shubert Rd. E > Tennyson Rd. SE > Upton Dr. S > Nimmo Pkwy. W > Princess Anne Rd. NW > Ferrell Pkwy. W > Indian River Rd. NW > Military Hwy, SW then W > US Bus 460 W to Suffolk > US 58 W to Franklin > VA 671 W then SW to Boykins > VA 186 SW to Garysburg, NC > US 301 S to

Halifax > NC 561 SW to Louisburg > NC 56 W to Creedmoor > US 15 SW > I-85 SW then W to Salisbury > US 601 N > US 70 W to Morganton > US 64 S then W to Rutherford and River Creek CG

*Oct. 6*—US 64 W > I-40 W > US 23 SW then W > US 74 SW > US 23 S > US 64 SW then W to Hayesville > US 69 S > US 76 W then SW > GA 136 NW then SW > GA 53 W > Union Grove Rd. (becomes Calhoun Bypass) W > GA 53 SW to Rome, GA > GA 1 W > GA 20 (becomes AL 9) SW to Centre, AL > US 411 W then SW > Ashville Rd. SW to Leeds > US 78 W > Riverview Dr. to Ken's place

*Oct. 7-9*—Locally in Birmingham/Leeds area

*Oct. 10*—Riverview Dr. N > US 78 E > AL 25 SE > US 231 SW > US 280 SE to The Bottle > AL 147 S to Auburn > University Dr. E > Moores Mill Rd. E > AL 169 SE > US 431 S to Pittsview > Cottonton Rd. E then SE > AL 208 (becomes GA 39) E > US 27 S to Lumpkin, GA > Chestnut St. S > Main St. (becomes Holder Rd.) E > GA 520 SE to Dawson > US 82 SE to Albany > US Bus 82 S > GA 234 E > GA 133 SE to Julie's place

*Oct. 11*—GA 133 SE to Valdosta > I-75 S to Bushnell, FL > FL 48 E to Center Hill > Tuscanooga Rd. to Mascotte > FL 50 E to Groveland > FL 33 S > Deen Still Rd. E > Old Grade Rd. S > Old Polk City Rd. SE to Haines City > Main St. E > 10th St. > FL 17 S to Lake Wales > Dr. J A Wiltshire Ave. E > North Wales Drive SE to home

# Also from Road Dog Publications

*Those Two Idiots!*[1][2] *by A. P. Atkinson*
Mayhem, mirth, and adventure follow two riders across two continents. Setting off for Thailand thinking they were prepared, this story if full of mishaps and triumphs. An honest journey with all the highs and lows, wins and losses, wonderful people and low-lifes, and charms and pitfalls of the countries traveled through.

*Motorcycles, Life, and . . .*[1][2] *by Brent Allen*
Sit down at a table and talk motorcycles, life and . . . (fill in the blank) with award winning riding instructor and creator of the popular "Howzit Done?" video series, Brent "Capt. Crash" Allen. Here are his thoughts about riding and life and how they combine told in a lighthearted tone.

*The Elemental Motorcyclist*[1][2] *by Brent Allen*
Brent's second book offers more insights into life and riding and how they go together. This volume, while still told in the author's typical easy-going tone, gets down to more specifics about being a better rider.

*A Short Ride in the Jungle*[1][2] *by Antonia Bolingbroke-Kent*
A young woman tackles the famed Ho Chi Minh Trail alone on a diminutive pink Honda Cub armed only with her love of Southeast Asia, its people, and her wits.

*Mini Escapades around the British Isles*[1][2] *by Zoë Cano*
As a wonderful compilation of original short stories closer to home, Zoë Cano captures the very essence of Britain's natural beauty with eclectic travels she's taken over the years exploring England, Ireland, Scotland, and Wales.

*Bonneville Go or Bust*[1][2] *by Zoë Cano*
A true story with a difference. Zoë had no experience for such a mammoth adventure of a lifetime but goes all out to make her dream come true to travel solo across the lesser known roads of the American continent on a classic motorcycle.

*I loved reading this book. She has a way of putting you right into the scene. It was like riding on the back seat and experiencing this adventure along with Zoë.* —★★★★ Amazon Review

### Southern Escapades [1] [2] by Zoë Cano

As an encore to her cross country trip, Zoë rides along the tropical Gulf of México and Atlantic Coast in Florida, through the forgotten backroads of Alabama and Georgia. This adventure uncovers the many hidden gems of lesser known places in these beautiful Southern states.

*. . . Zoë has once again interested and entertained me with her American adventures. Her insightful prose is a delight to read and makes me want to visit the same places.*—★★★★★ Amazon Review

### Chilli, Skulls & Tequila [1] [2] by Zoë Cano

Zoe captures the spirit of beautiful Baja California, México, with a solo 3 000 mile adventure encountering a myriad of surprises along the way and unique, out-of-the-way places tucked into Baja's forgotten corners.

*Zoe adds hot chilli and spices to her stories, creating a truly mouth-watering reader's feast!*—★★★★ Amazon Review

### Hellbent for Paradise [1] [2] by Zoë Cano

The inspiring—and often nail-biting—tale of Zoë's exploits roaming the jaw-dropping natural wonders of New Zealand on a mission to find her own paradise.

### Mini Escapades around the British Isles [1] [2] by Zoë Cano

As a wonderful compilation of original short stories closer to home, Zoë Cano captures the very essence of Britain's natural beauty with eclectic travels she's taken over the years exploring England, Ireland, Scotland, and Wales.

### Shiny Side Up [1] [2] by Ron Davis

A delightful collection of essays and articles from Ron Davis, Associate Editor and columnist for *BMW Owners News*. This book is filled with tales of the road and recounts the joys and foibles of motorcycle ownership and maintenance. Read it and find out why Ron is a favorite of readers of the *Owners News*!

### Rubber Side Down[1][2] by Ron Davis
More great stuff from Ron Davis.

*[Ron] shares his experiences with modesty and humor, as one who is learning as he goes along. Which is what we all do in real life. And he does what all the best motorcycle writing does: he makes you wonder why you aren't out there riding your own bike, right now . . . his work simply helps you stay sane until spring."* –Peter Egan, Cycle World *Columnist and author of* Leanings 1, 2, and 3, and The Best of Peter Egan.

### Beads in the Headlight [1] by Isabel Dyson
A British couple tackle riding from Alaska to Tierra del Fuego two-up on a 31 year-old BMW "airhead." Join them on this epic journey across two continents.

*A great blend of travel, motorcycling, determination, and humor.* —★★★★★ Amazon Review

### Chasing America [1][2] by Tracy Farr
Tracy Farr sets off on multiple legs of a motorcycle ride to the four corners of America in search of the essence of the land and its people.

### In Search of Greener Grass [1] by Graham Field
With game show winnings and his KLR 650, Graham sets out solo for Mongolia & beyond. Foreword by Ted Simon

### Eureka [1] by Graham Field
Graham sets out on a journey to Kazahkstan only to realize his contrived goal is not making him happy. He has a "Eureka!" moment, turns around, and begins to enjoy the ride as the ride itself becomes the destination.

### Different Natures [1] by Graham Field
The story of two early journeys Graham made while living in the US, one north to Alaska and the other south through México. Follow along as Graham tells the stories in his own unique way.

### Thoughts on the Road[1][2] by Michael Fitterling
The Editor of *Vintage Japanese Motorcycle Magazine* ponders his experiences with motorcycles and riding and how they've intersected and influenced his life.

### Northeast by Northwest [1] [2] by Michael Fitterling

The author finds two motorcycle journeys of immense help staving off depression and the other effects of stress. Along the way, he discovers the beauty of North America and the kindness of its people.

> *. . . one of the most captivating stories I have read in a long time. Truly a MUST read!!*—★★★★★ Amazon Review

### Hit the Road, Jac! [1] [2] by Jacqui Furneaux

At 50, Jacqui leaves her home and family, buys a motorcycle in India, and begins a seven-year world-wide journey with no particular plan. Along the way she comes to terms with herself and her family.

### Asphalt & Dirt [1] [2] by Aaron Heinrich

A compilation of profiles of both famous figures in the motorcycle industry and relatively unknown people who ride, dispelling the myth of the stereotypical "biker" image.

### The Dog, The Hog, & the Iron Horse [1] [2] by Alex Kendall

An Englishman seeks out the "real" America and Americans on three trips across the US; one by bus, east to west; another by train west to east; and finally on an iconic Harley-Davidson motorcycle from north to south. Inspired by "beat" writers, join Alex on his exploration of this land of Kerouac and Thompson.

### Chasing Northern Lights [1] [2] by Miguel Oldenberg

A Venezuelan immigrant sets out to get to know his new country on the motorcycle ride of a lifetime.

### The Tom Report [1] [2] by Tom Reuter

Two young men set out from Washinton state on Suzuki DR650 dual sport motorcycles. Join them and a colorful cast of fellow travelers as they wind their way south to the end of the world. Their journey is filled with fun, danger, and even enlightenment.

### Minotaurs, Motorcycles, & Banjos [1] [2] by Steven Sherrill

A ride through Appalachia visiting the graves of the author's old time folk music banjo heroes, accompanied by his alter-ego and a banjo aboard a Royal Enfield motorcycle.

*A Tale of Two Dusters & Other Stories*[1][2] *by Kirk Swanick*
In this collection of tales, Kirk Swanick tells of growing up a gear-head behind both the wheels of muscle cars and the handlebars of motorcycles and describes the joys and trials of riding.

*Man in the Saddle*[1][2] *by Paul van Hoof*
Aboard a 1975 Moto Guzzi V7, Paul starts out from Alaska for Ushuaia. Along the way there are many twists and turns, some which change his life forever. English translation from the original Dutch.

Distributed by:
NBN
national book network
Road Dog PUBLICATIONS
www.roaddogpub.com
Also available for [1] Kindle from amazon.com & [2] Nook from bn.com